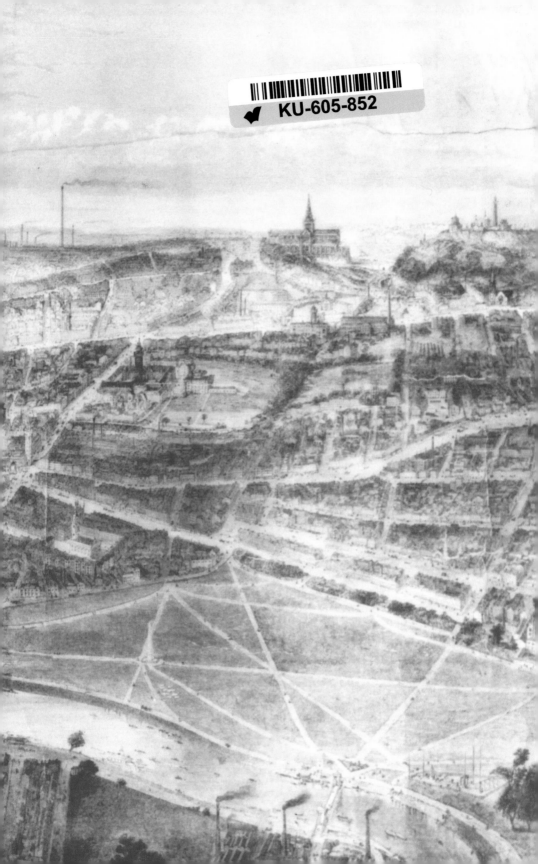

William Motherwell's
Cultural Politics
1797–1835

William Motherwell's
Cultural Politics
1797–1835

MARY ELLEN BROWN

THE UNIVERSITY PRESS OF KENTUCKY

Publication of this volume was made possible in part
by a grant from the National Endowment for the Humanities.

Scholarly publisher for the Commonwealth,
serving Bellarmine University, Berea College, Centre
College of Kentucky, Eastern Kentucky University,
The Filson Club Historical Society, Georgetown College,
Kentucky Historical Society, Kentucky State University,
Morehead State University, Murray State University,
Northern Kentucky University, Transylvania University,
University of Kentucky, University of Louisville,
and Western Kentucky University.

Editorial and Sales Offices: The University Press of Kentucky
663 South Limestone Street, Lexington, Kentucky 40508-4008

05 04 03 02 01   5 4 3 2 1

Library of Congress Cataloging-in-Publication Data

Brown, Mary Ellen, 1939-
   William Motherwell's cultural politics / Mary Ellen Brown.
      p. cm.
Includes bibliographical references (p.   ) and index.
   ISBN 0-8131-2188-4 (alk. paper)
   1. Motherwell, William, 1797-1835—Criticism and interpretation.
   2. Politics and literature—Scotland—History—19th century.
   3. Scotland—Intellectual life—19th century. 4. Scotland—
In literature. I. Title.
   PR5101.M3 Z59 2001
   821'.7—dc21   00-012270

This book is printed on acid-free recycled paper
meeting the requirements of the American National Standard
for Permanence of Paper for Printed Library Materials.

Manufactured in the United States of America

As always

for

Perrin and Torrence

According to the esteemed fashion of real
bony-feedy book manufacturers, I ay like to stick
a wee bit morsel of verse or prose at the head
of ilka chapter, just to let the reader get an inkling
of the nature and speerit of its contents.
—William Motherwell,
Memoirs of a Paisley Baillie

Contents

Illustrations

Acknowledgments

Last things are really first things: this study could clearly not have been undertaken without an array of help and support—both institutional and individual. I write this at the end to chart the beginnings.

Indiana University and various offices—Research and the University Graduate School and the Dean of the Faculties—have over the years provided considerable research support. The concluding work was generously facilitated by the Fulbright Commission. I gratefully recognized their enabling role in making this research possible.

I could not have done this work without a variety of libraries, most particularly the University of Glasgow Library's Department of Special Collections, where most of the relevant holograph materials are housed. In addition, I have used with good results the Paisley Central Library; Glasgow's Mitchell Library; the materials housed in Pollok House, Glasgow; the National Library of Scotland, Edinburgh; the Houghton Library of Harvard University; and the collections at Indiana University. To the staffs of these various institutions, I say a special thank you.

I am grateful to the Scottish National Portrait Gallery, Edinburgh, for permission to reproduce the Andrew Henderson portrait and the Augustin Edouart silhouette; to the Glasgow City Archives for use of the Sulman print of Glasgow; to the University of Glasgow Library, Department of Special Collections, for photographs from *Glasgow Illustrated in a Series of Picturesque Views* (1834); to The Trustees of the National Library of Scotland for permission to print a page from George Thomson's *Select Melodies of Scotland* (1823); and to the Keeper of the Records of Scotland, The National Archives of Scotland, for allowing me to reproduce the first page of SC58/79/1.

On a more individual note, I must begin by mentioning the debt I owe to Pierre Bourdieu, who generously welcomed me to his seminar at the École des Hautes Études en Sciences Sociales during 1991–92. For a number of years I have benefited from the discussions and presentations given by the Cultural Theory Seminar, now affiliated with Indiana University's Institute for Advanced Study, and by the annual gatherings of the Ballad Commission of the Société Internationale d'Ethnologie et de Folklore. During the final research on this project, I was associated with the Department of Scottish Literature at the University of Glasgow, whose members of the faculty and staff were unfailingly supportive.

John MacQueen, Bridget Fowler, and John Morris all read an earlier draft of this work; their comments and suggestions have pointed me in productive directions and saved me from unwitting errors. I realize full well the time and energy expended on their parts in reading and responding to my work in the midst of their own busy and productive activities. During final revisions, Torrence Lewis cast his keen editorial eyes over the manuscript and made helpful suggestions.

William Motherwell's Cultural Politics has been long in the making, at least in part because the doing of it has afforded me so much pleasure: here at last I have been able to take the time to pursue the little highways and byways; and I have done it in my own sweet time. If my own interest and enthusiasm have run away with me, perhaps this can be excused when I say that I have simply had fun in the learning that has been a part of the doing of this study: remembering the chance discovery of Glasgow's Saracen's Head—in the 1830s an inn Motherwell frequented; the recognition of Motherwell's 1598 folio black-letter edition of Chaucer in the library of James Barclay Murdock, a late-nineteenth-century Glasgow bibliophile; not to mention my excitement in finding records, housed now in Register House, Edinburgh, that Motherwell actually wrote and signed when he was sheriff clerk depute. Recognizing the impossibility—even with all the help and support I have received and here gratefully acknowledge—of fully revealing the life of any individual, past or present, I yet hope that you will begin to acquire a sense of what life might have been like for William Motherwell and the fascinating times in which he lived.

Glasgow and Bloomington

Toward a Biographical Social History

The Antiquary "lamented, very much, the spirit of improvement
that was going on here [Paisley], as well as in Glasgow,
Edinburgh and other towns, that he had passed through, and
which, in its reckless course, was removing these great landmarks
by which historians were enabled to trace, with precision, the
progress of society and civilization."
—William Motherwell, *Memoirs of a Paisley Baillie*

I MET WILLIAM MOTHERWELL, or at least his name, many years ago
when I first became interested in ballads. I found his *Minstrelsy: Ancient
and Modern,* published in 1827, amazingly perspicacious, especially the
lengthy introduction describing the ballad's characteristics and outlining the
history of the appearance of Scottish ballad texts in published collections. I
have continued to consider that essay an ideal summary statement about the
ballad, as a way to begin thinking about theories such as oral formulaic
composition for Motherwell's *avant la lettre* position on that and other questions. When I was asked to write a chapter some years ago on "The Study
of Folk Tradition" in nineteenth-century Scotland (see Gifford, *History of
Scottish Literature*), I thought immediately of Motherwell and devoted a
portion of the chapter to him, analyzing in detail the introduction to his
Minstrelsy.

I pointed out Motherwell's involvement in a loose-knit movement (perhaps concern) in support of a kind of cultural nationalism: the interest in
preserving relics of the past that suggest a distinctly Scottish culture/na-
tion—a kind of national pride despite political amalgamation with England.
I spoke then of Motherwell as an early collector of ballads at a time when
many other enthusiasts were drawing a large portion of their compilations
from manuscripts and earlier printed collections; I pointed out his articulation of "modern" editorial principles, which I have come to see latterly as an
early discussion of "authenticity"; I was intrigued by his awareness that

ballads exist in multiple versions, all equal—though, admittedly, he preferred the "oldest," "earliest" ones. And I liked his delineation of some of
the stylistic characteristics of ballads: their use of commonplaces—perhaps
as aid to memory, perhaps as structure for creation; the spare, elliptical quality of the narratives which bespoke an audience familiar with the stories; the
irregularity of the meter, hidden by the music, which he saw as a vital aspect
of the ballad. Perhaps even more, I was taken with his reference to the performance of ballads—they were often prefaced by the singers with historical and circumstantial information that served to fill out or complete the
spare narrative—and with his conviction that because ballads are tied in
some way to larger cultural currents, their presumed decline was a result of
the rapid changes in life then underway (thus the importance of his kind of
antiquarian rescue operation). My admiration for William Motherwell was
increased by this close rereading of his work, and I decided I should certainly know something more about him, how he came to ballad study, just
who he was. I had come to feel a kind of historical friendship with him: we
seemed to share many interests.

I learned almost immediately that to focus only on his ballad work,
and particularly his *Minstrelsy,* was to truncate his activities and interests,
for he was poet, sheriff clerk depute, editor and contributor to the periodical
press, journalist, a lover of fun and jokes, an outspoken conservative politically and culturally, good friend, and boon companion. What's more, he was
clearly in "the thick of things," so to speak, in the West of Scotland in the
first third of the nineteenth century. I began to think an examination of his
life might allow me to say something about Scottish history in addition to
revealing the details of his life and perhaps uncovering more about his ballad enthusiasms.

And so this study began with summer research trips to Scotland and
visits to libraries for published and manuscript records. I felt very much at
home in this process, running into names and personages with whom I've
been familiar for much of my scholarly life. There was Robert Burns, for
instance, whose life and absorption into traditional culture dominated my
early academic endeavors. Motherwell had, in fact, been a member of a
Burns club, served at one point as secretary of the Paisley Burns Club, and
written an ode to Burns's birth for the sixteenth annual celebration:

Oh then no paltry bliss 'towould [*sic*] be
Nor bootless spent festivity
To hail once more his natal day. . . .

At the time of Motherwell's death he had been collaborating with James Hogg on a new edition of the works of Burns. I encountered more old friends through his correspondence: he wrote frequently and with familiarity to Peter Buchan, who shared his fascination with balladry but with less certitude of its value and from a less secure economic position—implicit and recurring topics throughout their correspondence. Motherwell often exchanged letters with R.A. Smith, lover of Scottish melodies and his companion in literary "highjinks." He admired Walter Scott, telling Buchan that he loved Scott and looked forward to every morsel of gossip about him, and they too corresponded briefly. He contributed to the collections of George Thomson; he shared texts with C.K. Sharpe and David Laing.

I read Motherwell's poetry and lengthy biographical sketches about him. I pored over his notebooks and the commonplace books in which he "committed to paper all those loose ideas which float across the brain with the hope that by doing so he might get better acquainted with himself." I read his contributions to the periodical press, examining with particular interest the *Glasgow Courier,* the Tory newspaper he edited for the last five years of his life. If I began to feel less personal affinity with him—his all-male society, his political views, which were distinctly out of step with the Enlightenment, with progress, with change—I began to sense the complexity of his life and to surmise that I ought really be able to use his experiences to say something about the times. The materials were at hand.

Then I took another trip, both physically and intellectually: I went to Paris, not trying to recapture the Auld Alliance but somehow forging one. I had been very interested in the work of ethnologist-turned-sociologist Pierre Bourdieu, now professor at the Collège de France, in particular his analysis of French society, *Distinction: A Social Critique of the Judgement of Taste.* I felt intellectually challenged by his ideas, hoping to appropriate some of them for a projected study of ballad taste. Motherwell would figure in that project so I took along my collection of materials, intending to examine them if I had time, preparatory to writing up my findings, perhaps in a long essay of biographical reassessment. I did find time to begin looking again at the materials, simultaneously reading some Scottish social history, principally the first volume of T.M. Devine and Rosalind Mitchison's *Social History of Modern Scotland,* and attending Bourdieu's seminar at the École des Hautes Études en Sciences Sociales on *champs,* or "fields."

Fields are the networks of different areas of value, concern, and influence within a social world, each having their own implicit focuses, rules, and logic; each privileging certain positions, certain kinds of accumulated capital; and within which people are located differently and occupy different social spaces in the hierarchy. At a lecture at the Bibliothèque Nationale early in 1992, Bourdieu, in summarizing positions articulated in his then–recently published book *An Invitation to Reflexive Sociology,* coauthored by Loic J.D. Wacquant, likened the social world, the *champs,* to a Calder mobile, with different spaces but interconnected. He offered a cogent recapitulation of the concept:

> In analytic terms, a field may be defined as a network, or a configuration, of objective relations between positions. These positions are objectively defined, in their existence and in the determinations they impose upon their occupants, agents or institutions, by their present and potential situation (situs) in the structure of the distribution of spaces of power (or capital) whose possession commands access to the specific profits that are at stake in the field, as well as by their objective relation to other positions (domination, subordination, homology, etc.).
>
> In highly differentiated societies, the social cosmos is made up of a number of such relatively autonomous social microcosms, i.e., spaces of objective relations that are the site of a logic and a necessity that are *specific and irreducible* to those that regulate other fields. (97)

My examination of published and manuscript records over a period of time provided the raw materials; specific studies of Scottish social history helped me to see how Motherwell was very much a part of the cultural currents, how he was situated in a number of activities that showed his participation in the life of the times. The concept of field helped me see and identify the areas of Scottish society in which Motherwell participated as distinct yet interrelated fields. While Bourdieu says he vacillates between thinking of fields as real and/or as an academic construct useful for analysis, I am clearly using the concept as a construct that has given me a way of getting into the complexity of the social world and Motherwell's position within it. For the concept and the visual metaphor of the Calder mobile together suggested that Motherwell, the man, might be likened to the central structure, with all the connecting parts referencing his different activities and interests, the fields. The concept implies, of course, that lives are unities and that I might be able to uncover the values and concerns that suggest coherence.

Without my realizing it, the study of Motherwell had become something other than I had originally anticipated through the fortuitous convergence of my prior research, social history, and the concept of field, illustrating beautifully how implicated I/we as individuals are in what we do, where we happen to be, what we happen to read—that what we do is indeed individually subjective, that our studies may tell as much about ourselves as they do about those we study. In the course of thinking about and writing this book, I have had further occasion to both read and reflect on the methodology I have employed. In addition, then, to the Scottish scholars—past and present—whose work has been essential to my own study, and to Bourdieu, whose concepts really made this work seem possible, I have been influenced by scholars occupying a number of different disciplinary positions whose scholarship nevertheless seems in some ways to have certain things in common: a recognition that many of our studies have been neither broad nor deep enough, that they have sometimes been biased/limited by that narrow focus, and that our attempts to get inside any cultural/societal context are never fully successful or even possible. This polyvocal, transdisciplinary dialogue emboldened me to pursue the course I had chosen and to begin to refer to what I do as historical ethnography. While I have not exactly taken any specific models or approaches from these works, I have always been encouraged by the congruence of their goals and stated caveats because they are similar to my own: to get as deeply into this subject, from as many angles, as possible in order to come as close as possible to what may have been the case. The "depth research" of Juha Pentikainen, the "thick description" of Clifford Geertz, the more nuanced literary history of the "New Historicists," and the sociocultural/intellectual history, with roots in the Annales School, of Roger Chartier—all have served as exemplars of the kind of work I have hoped to achieve. Both synchronic and diachronic studies, then, have been asking ever-expanding questions. And I have often thought of what I have tried to do as structurally similar to the childhood, elaborated address:

Jane Smith
Main Street
Everytown
USA
Western Hemisphere
World
Universe

Which is to say that this book seeks to give a fuller picture of one Scot—William Motherwell–to expand our understanding of his ballad studies in the context of his other professional and avocational involvements, to explore those other areas as available choices in his day and time, and to look at both the man and his activities within the milieu in which he lived. In other words, this study places Motherwell at the center and seeks to use wider events not as isolated moments but as a means of opening up aspects of his social world. In the process I hope to identify some of the literary and political interests and pressures (with echoes reverberating from the French Revolution and the Napoleonic Wars) current in Paisley and Glasgow early in the nineteenth century by examining the way these ideas and thoughts played on one man, a moderately public figure. In doing so, I hope to unravel, following Geertz, the webs of significance, the meaning of Motherwell's interests to himself, to his friends and correspondents, and to see how these proclivities interact and interface with the larger culture.

The "times" might be characterized as transitional, a period of largely peaceful revolution, toward selective assimilation with England, toward "capitalism" and more "democratic" principles. This is, of course, much too simply articulated: "we" can see looking back that those developments were apace at the turn of the century. Yet the alternative to assimilation, that is, nationalism, was very much a force in contemporary thought. Nicholas Phillipson describes accurately one existential paradox for concerned Scots: "The basic ideological problem which confronted Scotsmen was to define and secure some sort of national identity for Scotland, while at the same time accepting the fact that the Union would grow closer and threaten the very identity they sought to preserve" ("Nationalism and Ideology," 185). One response was "literary nationalism," something Phillipson refers to as "an ideology of noisy inaction" for its seemingly overt political paralysis and acceptance of assimilation even while affirming a Scottish way of life as in the novels of Walter Scott, the earlier works of Robert Burns, and the proliferation of collections of ballads and folksongs justified on the basis of their Scottishness. Peter Buchan's preface to *Gleanings of Scotch, English, and Irish Scarce Old Ballads* provides a typical expression of this literary or cultural nationalism: "The ancient Ballads of Caledonia are venerated by those lovers of their country who delight in the native imagery of their homes, and in hearing the martial and warlike deeds of their forefathers said or sung in the enchanting voice of their fair countrywomen." I am inclined to see this literary or cultural nationalism as a complex choice—if not active, at least conscious, affirming a preference for cultural over political manifestations of nationalism, for Scotland, the expression of a *mentalité* rather than a physical practice or overt activity, as in the bearing of arms or the participation in political demonstrations.

All, then, was not moving smoothly toward assimilation: there was a flair-up of overt nationalism in 1826 around a reform bill that had the potential to change the Scottish banking system and alter the jury system—changes that would have affected "Scottish" life, that would have touched everyday life in a way that the long-ago union of the crowns (1603) and union of the Parliaments (1707) had not. And throughout this period, persons such as William Motherwell were focusing on supposed "Scottish" artifacts, like the ballads, as a form of nationalism. In fact, the texts chosen for publication—sometimes garnered from earlier printed collections, from manuscript materials, and, increasingly, from the mouths of people—became in some circles a selected/selective sign of Scottishness, one proof of Scotland's right to be.

The politics of this activity deserve attention. When using folkloric materials, traditional verbal artistry, to bolster claims for national identity, collectors and compilers of material have often looked for help from persons the least implicated in the times—holdovers of an earlier way of life, often the least educated, residents of rural, isolated areas. What those people know and have is more important and certainly easier to deal with than the people themselves—complex human beings all; so the materials have been taken out of their mouths, out of their normal context, often edited and prettified for genteel consumption, commodified and fetishized to serve another purpose. In the Scottish context, then, ballads were one such commodity abstracted by antiquarians and cultural nationalists for their presumed "national" qualities. This kind of appropriation can be analyzed from a number of perspectives. Certainly without it, we would lack important historical records/artistic documents and know far less about certain kinds of activities. On the other hand, this appropriation might be seen as wrenching significant cultural capital from a people in the absence of reciprocity, as an implicit form of dismissal of those people by the "knowledgeable" outsider who had other agendas, perhaps personal, aesthetic, or political. Dave Harker, in a 1985 study, *Fakesong,* provides an overly polemic survey of the appropriation and commodification of folksong materials in the British context, stressing the classism implicit in the activity of collecting and abstracting materials by one class of people from another—the bourgeois from the working class. In doing so, he suggests they exploited the people, obscured the international similarity of materials and lived conditions, and selectively used and obscured their materials. I am indeed in sympathy with the general outlines of his argument: it is important to analyze the motivations of the collectors/compilers of material and to understand the complex set of circumstances that brought such a man as William Motherwell to the topic, neither to praise nor to condemn, but to understand. Unfortunately, Harker's work is too doctrinaire to recognize the subtlety of individual and particular situations.

Recent work offers more specific and considered analyses of the processes and motivations for interest in a particular group of people and their culture: Ian McKay reveals the process in the Nova Scotian context; David Whisnant interrogates the Appalachian situation; Eric Hobsbawm and Terrence Ranger have called attention to the "invention of tradition." Motherwell's life and activities speak to an early moment in the conscious valorization of the past and a selective—for it is always already selective—showcasing of old literary and cultural practices. Unlike some later and continuing approaches, his was not a clearly articulated antimodernity; nor did he identify a segment of the population as "the" folk. He was, finally, adamantly against restoration, stressing and valuing the variability and multiformity of the ballad. His interests and concerns derive, of course, from his own particular cultural and historical environment and offer a detailed instance of a proclivity that has led elsewhere to invention and fabrication, subalternization and commodification, celebration and criticism.

In Scotland, early in the nineteenth century, there was an expanding market for collections of ballads and songs—a taste for things "Scottish"—and a corresponding expansion of activity; in part this was probably fueled by nationalistic sentiments. The interest in ballads and songs was one response to a *coupure,* a rupture with the past, that was occurring simultaneously with the larger political questions of assimilation or nationalism, and the development of classes was but one of the aspects of the change. Throughout this period, the Industrial Revolution was a potent force and had far greater daily impact on people's lives than the issue of nationalism: the artisanal/agrarian world of the past was being replaced by a capitalist economy that radically shifted the relationships of people, broke down what has often been romanticized as a relatively homogeneous society into a classed society—an unequal distribution of economic capital and an unequal valuation of cultural capital—and introduced juridical rule for the familial or quasi-familial rule of the past. The Reform Bill of 1832 and its call for male suffrage might be said to mark the rise and public recognition of the concept of "citizen" and a concomitant awareness of divisions—local, regional, county, nation—to which one might belong and in which one might participate as citizen. Traditional relationships and connections between people were radically changed by the dominance of a money economy, and subsequent reform bills sought to redefine, in permanent, legal form those rights and responsibilities, to cancel and/or affirm through legal maneuvers the changes that had taken place. If, looking back, all this seems like progress, it was clearly not always so designated by those who lived through it: the Reform Bill of 1832 and its call for suffrage—clearly a legislative response just in the nick of time to the Radical Wars or uprisings against the "new" or changed world—responded to the need to incorporate more people into the decision-making process and marks a legislative attempt to open the system to a broader, more formalized constituency. Motherwell was against the 1832 bill, not, I suspect, so much because he liked the status quo, but because he felt an "emotional" loss for what he felt/wished had been—the good old days, the always elusive better times in the past, and an innate conservative preference for the known over the unknown. This ideological penchant was worked out in a number of ways: overtly in his role as editor of the *Glasgow Courier* and in more muted fashion through the writing of poetry and ballad editing and collecting—all of which make more sense and are far more interesting when seen against his life and times, his *habitus.* Another concept following Bourdieu, *habitus* refers to "semi-learned grammars of practice" (*Outline of a Theory of Practice,* 20), systems of how to be that derive from social origin, education, and economic position and that constrain an individual within a particular social location or class. A *habitus* comprises a range of ideas/beliefs—that is, aptitudes, attitudes, tendencies—held by a group of people occupying similar social space and inclines agents to act and react in certain ways; the *habitus* structures perception and serves as a generative principle; it reflects and reinforces itself.

As will become clear, William Motherwell's *habitus* gave him possibilities and potentialities, a perceptual framework that informed his involvements in the various fields of which he was a part. He had acquired more cultural capital—through education and association—than might have been expected; and he took that capital and strategically deployed it to enter a kind of politico/literary Tory world, thereby consolidating his middle-class position, which may well have distanced him from aspects of his natal and early lived experiences. He did not like the chaos of the transitional world in which he found himself, becoming late in life a spokesperson for conservative positions; he both consumed and produced antiquities, surviving artifacts of an almost forgotten or largely fabricated or imagined past. Both reflect a freely chosen conservative ideology and one current in the life of the times in which he is so richly embedded and implicated—a perspective and position often invisible in historical accounts that focus, with hindsight, on the hegemonic/winning position. Accepting "the task of restoring to men the meaning of their actions" (Robbins, *Work of Pierre Bourdieu,* 37), I hope to make sense of Motherwell's life and activities within his particular social world: Motherwell was a minor cultural actor, with modest power and influence, but very much an active participant in some of the ideological struggles of the early nineteenth century.

Gulielmus Motherwell, Willyan Moderwell, William Motherwell

> ... his humanity, his benevolence, and his urbanity—the inherent
> attributes of his high and chivalrous nature.
> —*Glasgow Courier,* 3 November 1835

WILLIAM MOTHERWELL'S OWN LIFE interestingly reflects some of the radical changes and shifts taking place in early nineteenth century Scotland. He came from a propertied agricultural/artisanal background of the sort that all but disappeared during his lifetime: he made his name and place as a member of the rising middle class, as a city dweller. In fact, his life and involvements provide a grass-roots avenue into the social history of Scotland during the first third of the nineteenth century. His experiences open up a number of arenas—political, cultural, social, literary, and regional: his lived environment was the West of Scotland, but his actions and beliefs are at once Scottish and British. A chronological account of his life offers the necessary structure, a prelude, as it were, to examining ways his experiences move beyond the ordinary and mundane and reveal his insertion into the times.

Born 1 October 1797 in Glasgow, where he died on 1 November 1835, he was the third son of six children (David, John, Margaret, Amelia, Elizabeth) of another William, an ironmonger originally from Stirlingshire, and Elisabeth Barnett (or Barnet), a respectable farmer's daughter from Auchterarder, Perthshire. His principal biographer, James McConechy, a surgeon who followed Motherwell as editor of the *Glasgow Courier* (see Motherwell, *Poetical Works of William Motherwell with a Memoir by James McConechy Esq.;* Robertson 4/1662), offered a brief historical and landed pedigree for his subject, asserting the age of his surname—referring to the holy well of or to the Virgin Mary—mentioning that his mother had inherited two thousand pounds and that his ancestors "may" have owned a small estate with a mill on the river Carron in Dundaff, Stirlingshire (with records dating back to 1629), and dedicating the edition to a "kinswoman" of Motherwell, a Lady James Campbell. Having located him in the Scottish historical landscape, McConechy turned briefly to his early residences and education to flesh out the background from which he came.

As an aside, let me say that all subsequent biographical sketches have been based on McConechy's work. Clearly McConechy had literary proclivities and had probably first met Motherwell when he contributed to the *Enquirer,* a Glasgow periodical McConechy edited. Their association continued as McConechy wrote for the *Paisley Magazine.* Manuscript letters that McConechy probably solicited prior to writing the biographical introduction to the new edition of Motherwell's poetry are instructive, revealing exactly the kind of contradictory information one might expect: some said Motherwell had been a mediocre student entertaining others with fabricated, medievalesque tales; others said he was at the top of his class. One writer claimed he wrote ploddingly, another that he excelled in extemporizing. He was either subdued or lively in social situations. His dress was merely neat or, alternately, had become quite "dandified." The biographer, of necessity, selects to "fabricate" coherence: McConechy did so, as do I.

Motherwell's father left Stirlingshire around 1792 for Paisley, but by 1797 he was married and in Glasgow for his third son's birth; he was most probably the "WM" employed at "G Auchinvole (or Auchinvoll) & Co," ironmongers, that is, dealers in iron, hardware merchants, Gallowgate. Sometime before 1805 the family moved to Edinburgh. There William is said to have studied until 1808 with one William Lennie at a school in Crichton Street, near George Square, together with Jeanie or Jane Morrison, the daughter of an Alloa brewer and cornfactor, who became, so the story goes, the subject of his best-known poem, written some years later. Accounts have him attend the High School in Edinburgh briefly; if so, his study there was interrupted by his father's "business reversals" as early as 1809, his mother's death in 1811, and his father's return to Kilsyth in Stirlingshire with his sister Amelia. As a result of a series of familial crises, young William was sent to live with his uncle, John Motherwell, a propertied Paisley ironfounder; he remained in Paisley for almost twenty years.

From a contemporary perspective, it is sad to contemplate Motherwell's situation—without a mother, separated from his father, without independent financial resources, living with and thus seemingly dependent on a successful uncle. Yet he seems to have adapted to a situation that was undoubtedly quite normal; and between his fourteenth and twenty-first years he took a

William Motherwell, by Andrew Henderson

number of steps, or was led to take a number of steps, that positioned him well.

Accounts of his early life in Paisley are a bit contradictory: he may well have studied with John Peddie and been one of three Dux (prize winner) boys at Paisley Grammar School; there are, however, no extant records of prizes prior to 1820 and this honor may have been given him ex post facto as an attempt to provide a suitable academic pedigree. At the Grammar School, he would have received an elementary classical instruction, with Greek in the fifth year. It seems almost certain that at fifteen, in 1812, he was apprenticed for a four-year term to the sheriff clerk's office to learn the legal profession, with hopes of "shining at the bar" (Robertson 4/1662, Andrew Paterson). Perhaps it was there, coming face to face with old documents, that he developed his interest in antiquities; early on he was given the task of copying materials, surprising his superiors with facsimile reproductions complete with illuminated letters (Brown, *History of the Paisley Grammar School*). And he may well have used the same artistic bent more privately: "The walls of the water closet were covered with Motherwell's caricatures . . . and also with rhymes and mock heroic speeches—full of wit and talent equal to anything in Punch of these days" (Robertson 4/1662). He was also an active participant in several intellectual clubs, including the Literary Institution and later the Paisley Philosophical Institution, for which he prepared a number of essays for presentation after 1814, when he was seventeen, on diverse topics: "Benefits of the theatre" (he was in fact an amateur actor), "Causes of the present distresses of this country" (Motherwell pointed to the agricultural sector), "Difficulty of writing essays," "Importance of literary institutions," "Remarks on brevity," "Essay on love," "Essay on emulation," "Moral tale in rhyme entitled 'Miss Tabby and her Cat,'" and a review of a work entitled "Tales of my Landlord" (this was most probably Walter Scott's latest production, published in 1816, a four-volume work containing *The Black Dwarf* and *Old Mortality,* and it suggests that Motherwell and his contemporaries were well acquainted with the most recent publications) (Paisley Literary Institution Minutes 651.77). In addition to presenting various papers, Motherwell also served the Literary Institution in a number of official capacities; he was a "mover and shaker," even submitting a proposal for ladies to be admitted to hear the discussions. His presumed precocity, however, is belied by several incidents: on 21 December 1814, he and one Warrand Carlile were called down for "laughing and talking about affairs wholly foreign to the nature of this institution," and on one occasion he was fined for "being guilty of some impropriety of speech" or for having "inadvertently pronounced a word which by the Regulations was finable" (Paisley Literary Institution Minutes). Yet his commonplace book, his tool for self-understanding, for 1815 shows him grappling with a number of questions and exploring his environment. He heard the influential divine Thomas Chalmers speak, he mulls over the value of literary society where he can practice speaking and where the participants can inspire one another, he thinks the theater is not evil, that there is value in travel. By 1817, he was secretary of the Paisley Burns Club during the presidency of his friend R.A. Smith.

The years 1818 and 1819 show him entering the adult arena, living in Glasgow and receiving mail in care of "Messrs. McLaren & Motherwell, Iron-mongers, Trongate." He spent a year or part thereof at Glasgow College studying Greek and perhaps Latin with the goal of becoming an advocate. He is listed on the matriculation list in Greek for 1818 as number 10042, Gulielmus Motherwell; his father was there identified as a Glasgow merchant (Addison, *Matriculation Albums*, 301). And he won a prize in Humanity Class VIII for the best abridgement of Cicero on old age in English (Addison, *Prize Lists*, 202). Among his papers is a draft letter to a Professor Walker thanking him for his tutelage, promising to study the ancient languages, but telling Walker that it is only prudent to leave (Robertson 9/1207, 21). On 4 March 1818 Motherwell wrote Robert Walkinshaw Jr., Sheriff Clerk of Renfrewshire, accepting a deputeship, though he writes it will retard his university studies and literary endeavors. He tells Walkinshaw that the position will give him the "grand *sine qua non*"—money—and enable or speed his independence. He expresses his desire "to raise myself in society" and confesses, "I am ambitious to excell, and would like to reach the summitt of my profession" (Robertson 9/1207, 20).

He had been, of course, pursuing his literary endeavors, if indeed that had become his chosen profession, all along. He had contributed to a Greenock publication, the *Visitor,* with which he became associated when he "went to Greenock for 4 wks—officiating as clerk for Mr. Jackson who was confined to his lodgings on account of indisposition" (Robertson 4/1662, Andrew Paterson). One of the literary miscellanies of the day, it hoped "to produce one hour's occasional relief from the cares of business or the lassitude of Ennui." His poem "The Parting," about the calmness of the actual parting but the heartbreak experienced later, is attributed with the initials "WM," the usual manner of attribution when fabricated names such as Gregory Doggerel, Leonora Daemon, and Metrical Gander were not employed. In 1818 he published a pamphlet under the name Ephraim Mucklewrath (referencing the insane preacher from *Old Mortality,* the work he had so recently discussed in a public paper) favoring mixed-sex dancing in answer to Matthew Bramble's "Hints to Young Ladies of Paisley, on the Winter Assemblies 1817" (the pseudonym here referencing the irascible but lovable Welsh country squire from Thomas Smolett's *Humphry Clinker*) and helped Robert Watt with a massive gathering of data for the *Bibliotheca Britannica; or a General Index to British and Foreign Literature,* published in 1824. As member and officer of the Paisley Philosophical Institution, he gave several essays, one on metaphysics, two on the Scottish language—a nationalistic interest also exhibited by his involvement in the movement to put up a monument to the memory of William Wallace. Yet there was a lighter, fun-loving side that could parody the club institution; he and a group of friends played with the idea of a Confederated Club of Convivial Callants to involve writing literature and essays for a periodical to be called the *Magazine of Science* and to include parodies and scatological material, all of which would be offered in a very pompous tone—no doubt the collaborative fantasy of a convivial evening (Robertson 9/1207, 23).

And then there was the social side of life. In a letter to George Miller, High Street, Paisley, he expressed the hope that just the two of them would accompany the ladies, and he attached a poem:

> Lyke twa amorous knichles
> > We'll fa laigh on our knees
> . . . .
> Then we'll ride east & we'll ride west
> > And ride both north & south
> Wi sic braw ladies we sall hae
> > O' joy an unco fouth. (898978–ALS 1817/1818)

Motherwell was clearly known as a poet and was already setting verses to music for R.A. Smith, with whom he had begun a correspondence after Smith moved to Edinburgh; through the years their letters became more and more familiar. By 1819 he was critical of his own ability to find original words on certain topics: "Subjects of this kind are grievously trite, and one is reduced to pitiable shifts indeed to conceal, or in part hide by inversion, and odd collocations of words, and new combinations of verse, the jejuneness, and commonplaceness of the sentiments and ideas" (Robertson 3/1222, 6).

He was also, almost incidentally, sheriff clerk depute of Renfrewshire. As such Motherwell worked under a sheriff clerk who in turn worked for a sheriff, the legal and social elite of Scotland, or his depute, an advocate with three years' experience, the "judicial and administrative representatives of the national government in the counties" (Whetstone, *Scottish County Gov-*

ernment, 3–5). The sheriff clerk maintained records, "handling of the proper writs, records, and correspondence of the court" and "authenticated contracts and documents." Paid from fees, the sheriff clerk was often quite well off and was "totally in control of his own establishment. He paid all his own expenses and had complete authority over his assistants." Chief among his assistants was the depute, whose duty it was "to assist them and to act during necessary absences" (ibid., 10, 125, 19, 1). This, then, was Motherwell's position in times that were hardly propitious.

Paisley was at the center of the changes that were taking place and was the third largest city in Scotland, after Glasgow and Edinburgh. As a weaving and manufacturing center whose population increased threefold between 1750 and 1821, Paisley was suffering from "severe and sustained unemployment" (Devine and Mitchison, *People and Society,* 261), unable to employ all those who had come there with high hopes and unable to prevent many of the least skilled from being replaced by mechanization of the weaving process and the highly skilled from being replaced by the less skilled. There was then a growing gap between the haves and the have-nots, a separation of management and workers, a great deal of down-classing or class realignment as the Industrial Revolution dealt a blow to the earlier artisanal collectivities. Concern and frustration led to riots and finally to labor organizations. Paisley was the center of radicalism and reform no doubt in part because of the high percentage of literate weavers who became spokespersons for both themselves and the other trades. Uprisings like the so-called Radical Wars reflect some of the tensions about class divisions and conflicting expectations. The handloom weavers were particularly affected. They had felt they were independent, the equivalent of middle class, but had become alienated from the newly arising and small middle class. They, as artisans, had lost ground, were receiving lower wages, had far less buying power than before, and were losing their relative independence in controlling the speed and duration of their work and the concomitant ability to maintain salary levels. Many of them had already experienced the shift from the land and agriculture into the more urban, artisanal culture with apprenticeships and skill levels governed by the trade. Now management was coming in and taking over the decision-making process, controlling everything, setting wages, putting an end to the relative autonomy of the weavers, and even replacing some of them with less-skilled workers. The weavers and workers were not alone in thinking that something had to happen to relieve the situation: "In Renfrewshire, the trade unions and middle classes, as well as the Whig gentry, made common cause in the great reform demonstrations" (Devine and Mitchison, *People and Society,* 304). On 20 April 1820 there was a grand rising in Paisley, and Motherwell was caught trying to keep order or was merely present but attired in a way that distinguished him from the Radicals. Early biographers claim that when he was caught by the rioters and almost thrown in the river, whatever liberal sentiments he may have had vanished, marking the birth of a conservative, very much against the Radicals, who were taking matters into their own hands. Whatever its origins, his position of record remained consistent throughout his life: he opposed the "positive" parliamentary response, some ten years later, to such uprisings as those in Paisley, the Reform Bill of 1832. And in the course of the next decade he began to feel less and less at home in Paisley, no doubt in part because his political ideas and cultural interests were not in keeping with the majority.

Being sheriff clerk depute provided him with a living, but he made his life elsewhere in a myriad of pursuits, always with literary activities dominant. In the year when gas lights and a newspaper first came to Paisley and in which the Battle of Bonnymuir saw weavers and factory operatives rising up to protest their economic situation only to be suppressed, Motherwell was engaged in more pacific pursuits: he was celebrating the artistry of the region. He wrote the introduction and notes to *The Harp of Renfrewshire* (Glasgow: William Turnbull, 1820). Including 275 pieces, only 74 of which were published for the first time, the reprints were justified thusly: "[A] good song, like a good story, may be twice told, without deterioration in any degree from its interestingness and intrinsic merit" (*Harp of Renfrewshire,* vi). Motherwell's introduction gives a mini-chronological history of poetry in Renfrewshire, beginning with Sir Hugh Montgomerie of Eglinton, mentioned in Dunbar's "Lament for the Makaris." Aware of the work of local poets circulating orally in delimited locales, he describes the works of such near-contemporaries as Alexander Wilson and Robert Tannahill, asserting that "while our language lasts, and music hath any charm, their names will be remembered." He takes issue with the practice lately popular of standardizing orthography, for "nothing is a more palpable error than moulding the Scottish language into English forms of spelling, and nothing can be more absurd, since thereby its true pronunciation is inevitably lost. . . . Scotland may part with her language, perhaps as tamely as she yielded up her parliament, and surrendered others her dearest rights" (ibid., xxvii, xlii). By twenty-three, he was already an avowed cultural nationalist, antiquarian, and certainly a regional apologist.

He contributed some of his poetry to the *Enquirer,* probably the "Sonnet to my Own Heart"—beginning "Submit, rebellious thing, quiescent be!"—not listed in his collected works but attributed to WM (other attributions were to such fanciful personages as Isabella Meekly and Maria Testy), and most definitely a balladlike piece, "Clerk Rychard and Mayd Margaret," subsequently published as "Clerk Richard & Maid Margaret" by George Thomson (1823) with music by R.A. Smith. And he began a correspondence with the Edinburgh bookseller David Laing on books and ballads and mutual enthusiasms that lasted until the end of the decade. He did not, however, neglect his civic duties: he joined with other men in organizations such as the Renfrewshire Yeomanry Cavalry and the Paisley Rifle Corporation. These were associations for the protection of the civic peace in the absence of the regularly constituted forces, then fighting in the Napoleonic Wars; they might be called forth to suppress various risings against the status quo. Their members were volunteers, largely propertied men who paid for their own uniforms and equipment (Clark, *Paisley*). Said to be a "passionate admirer of the military art" (Robertson 4/1662), Motherwell, as sergeant of the Rifle Corporation, provides a humorous account of one night's guard duty, written as "mock" report for Capt. Archie MacAlpine. The report begins by describing a noise made by a large rat that frightens three mice to death; this occurrence stimulates a lively conversation about traditionary beliefs. Motherwell's report—with careful indication of the exact time for certain occurrences—also includes a poem, "Guard Room Musings," which incorporates this "devil may care" stanza:

> Oh merry is a soldier's life
>> And void of care and sorrow:
> He lives to day, nor cares a fig
>> For what may hap tomorrow. (Robertson 9/1207, 1)

A commonplace book (Robertson 28/1210) written early in the 1820s, focuses on things literary but offers intimations of other concerns. He pronounces religion, philosophy, and literature lasting pleasures and records his views on religious wars: "[N]o wars are more sanguinary and exterminating than those which originate from a difference in religious opinion." Not until the end of his life does religion, in general, seem to recapture his interest; otherwise there are few records of church involvements or attendance aside from his going to one of Chalmers's services in 1818. Mostly he records his thoughts on topics such as the value of early poetry, which he refers to as the "first vehicle of human thought," further asserting that

> few studies are more fascinating after a short time's applica-
> tion and none perchance accomplished with more solid

advantages and edifying results than that of the ancient poetry of a country. The philologist is thereby made acquainted with the gradations and changes the language of that country has undergone from its first formation until its latest improvements—the philosopher is thereby enabled to trace the progress of human intellect from its first rude efforts to its more exalted and perfect performances—the moralist is thereby furnished with means to ascertain what effects different circumstances have wrought in the opinions and judgments of men—the historian is supplied with hints and sketches of the prevalent fashions[,] vices[,] follies[,] manners[,] literature and domestic relations of Society in these distant periods of which no other record remains[;] and the man of taste and the Critic are put in possession of materials by which the[y] can speculate & generalize with more certainty on the greater part of the subjects most intimately connected with their respective pursuits.

There is something for everyone, it seems, in studying early poetry: for Motherwell, it was a way into ballads, a frequent topic of his reflections. He muses on the aesthetic qualities of examples such as "Clerk Saunders," which he calls "a ballad of uncommon beauty and unaffected pathos. The scene when the seven brothers discover the unconscious lovers asleep in each others arms is managed with inimitable art and displays an intimate knowledge of character[,] nature and feeling."

The 1820s and Motherwell's twenties are dominated first by ballads and second by the periodical press—*Minstrelsy: Ancient and Modern* published in 1827 and the *Paisley Magazine* begun in 1828—but these were not his only activities in the literary vein. Insight into his own attitudes and his own poetry writing is found in the extensive correspondence with R.A. Smith: Smith had left Paisley for the capital city to continue his musical activities but frequently importuned Motherwell for words to go with his tunes, not always the easiest of tasks. Motherwell complains of his failure to create verses and describes the aborted process: "I am cramped every way when I have to write to a given tune and a given measure. . . . The better part of last Sunday I devoted to the task. With a laudable diligence I scratched my head and bit my pen[,] invoked all the benign shades of such defunct scribblers as my memory supplied me with and smoked sigars even to sickness in order to assist me in this minervan birth, but alas there was no true conception" (Robertson 3/1222, 15). It was an explanation in his characteristic lengthy phrases, without expected marks of punctuation, but his verbose prose did not keep Smith from asking for help again and again. In fact, he also asked Motherwell to write the preface to volume 6 of *The Scottish Minstrel,* hinting at what he had in mind: "Do for gods sake make out a Preface[;] we must wind up the matter decently and brag of course of the many fine airs introduced and saved from oblivion" (Robertson 3/1222, 13). The latter phrase was undoubtedly "tongue-in-cheek," for elsewhere Smith had admitted his penchant for "inventing" original "national" airs: "I think, if I keep in Spirits, that I will make some notable discoveries of melodies, not yet even in *embryo existence.* But this is a tale that 'must not be spoken'" (Robertson 3/ 1222, 33). Then he suggests that Motherwell make up a review of his singing book; while he, Smith, likes flattery, he suggests this more for Motherwell's fun: "A little amusement of this kind helps wonderfully to keep up the Spirits in this envious and backbiting world" (Robertson 3/1222, 33). Giving some hint about the character of his social life, Motherwell responds to one of Smith's requests by saying he'll get to it when he gets rid of his interminable headache, a seasonal disability: "At this Season few of the Goodfolk here recover their sober sense, till about a week after New Year's Day" (Robertson 3/1222, 1). Smith and Motherwell exchange information about mutual friends and song lovers, such as Peter Buchan, whom Motherwell proclaims "has done more than anyone I know to collect the ancient traditionary ballads of Scotland" (Robertson 3/1222, 60). Smith strokes Motherwell's vanity by telling him that he has heard his song "They come! The Merry Summer months" sung and "highly spoken of in Edinburgh" (Robertson 3/1222, 64). And it was Smith who showed Motherwell's song texts to George Thomson, compiler of upscale miscellanies; this led to Thomson's importuning Motherwell to produce texts for his various collections as well. He asks Motherwell for a version of "Gil Morris" *if* it will fit on one page: "In the event of my giving [printing] it (with the music, which I have, beautifully arranged by Haydn) I would of course mention it as yours" (Robertson 9/1207, 73). On another occasion he asks Motherwell to write a text for him, although he already has one in hand: "If I could obtain a Song to my liking for this pleasing Air, I would supersede the verses to which the foregoing belongs without hesitation" (Robertson 9/ 1207, 75). Motherwell was busy then writing his own poetry as well as writing song texts to go with melodies supplied by Smith or Thomson. And beginning in 1824, he was involved in preparing, serially, a publication that was completed in 1827—his ballad magnum opus.

His *Minstrelsy* did not begin as his project at all, but as a collaborative project for which he was to be one of several contributors. Early on he tells

R.A. Smith, "This is a work into which I find myself lugged will I or nill I. The fact is I was to have only now and then assisted a little. . . . At the conclusion I hope you will be as good as your word touching diverse melodies for sundry ballads" (Robertson 3/1222, 25). Finally it was Motherwell's chance to turn to Smith for help. Throughout the process of working on the *Minstrelsy* he used R.A. Smith as a sounding board: he describes his collecting experiences, some more successful than others. He was *almost* successful in collecting "Jamie Douglas" in a brothel: "You may fancy to yourself how confoundedly queer I felt to be discovered in a whore & Drunkard. I bolted off like a shot and never had courage to look in upon her again. So much for the history of ballad hunting. Not many would suffer this martyrdom of reputation for the sake of an old song" (Robertson 3/1222, 26). Clearly he liked describing such escapades to Smith and felt comfortable making fun of himself; he referred to the introduction as "that pro*found Treatise,*" that "elaborate Discourse" in which "the whole art & mystery of Balladry will be therein most delectably explained" (Robertson 3/1222, 50).

Smith, while clearly his closest friend and confidant in these matters, was not his only unofficial adviser on ballad questions. He turned to a number of other, recognized traditional ballad and song enthusiasts as well. His brief correspondence with Walter Scott is often thought to have been pivotal for Motherwell's editorial practices, for Scott admitted that he thought he probably did wrong in editing when he responded to Motherwell's somewhat contradictory letter and request for help. Writing on 28 April 1825, Motherwell waffled, "[I]f perchance any such copy [of Gil Morice/Child Maurice] may now in your possession it would in all likelihood serve to correct some evident errors which occur in this one [included with the letter], and which though trifling I would rather wish to have it in my power to amend by the assistance of other recited copies than trust to my own judgment in doing so. Other copies too may possibly supply preferable readings in many places, and contain additions of material moment. . . . As it is of some importance to preserve these remnants of ancient traditionary song in the exact state in which they pass from mouth to mouth among the vulgar I mean to get this ballad inserted in a small 4^{xo} collection of Ballads now in the course of publication by John Wylie & Co. of Glasgow" (copy, FMS Eng 862). Motherwell's uncertainty about whether to amend or print as found led to Scott's confession and may have helped convince Motherwell to opt for the more pristine approach in the concluding sections of the *Minstrelsy,* which was published in fascicles. There are also exchanges—of texts for their respective collections—with C.K. Sharpe, the Edinburgh antiquarian to whom the *Minstrelsy* was dedicated and who was called the friend or

enemy of everyone in the city. Motherwell tells Sharpe that he has "dragged
. . . [Andrew Blaikie] once more off with me to the woman's house where I
got him to prick down the tunes" (25241.56f) and says that "the recovery of
these reliques of traditionary Song is a favourite study of mine and nothing
can confer a higher favour on me than a communication on this subject from
you" (Robertson 9/1207, 44). Virtually alone among the ballad editors and
collectors, Motherwell recognized that the texts were sung; perhaps his song-
writing experiences as a practicing poet made him more receptive to this
realization than the other editors of the day. And in correspondence with the
Edinburgh bookseller John Stevenson, who served as a conduit for all sorts
of information between enthusiasts, he sends proverb information and a variety of references for George Ritchie Kinloch.

The *Minstrelsy* also stimulated a long and increasingly expansive correspondence with Peter Buchan whose enthusiasm for verbal arts almost
knew no bounds. Buchan's collecting activities and hiring of others to collect for him in the Northeast clearly influenced Motherwell as he sought
more and more to gather new versions from oral tradition for the collection
whose editing he had inherited. Motherwell's review of Buchan's *Gleanings of Scotch, English, and Irish Scarce Old Ballads, Chiefly Tragical and
Historical, &c, with Explanatory Notes* (Peterhead, Scotland, 1825) in the
Paisley Advertiser (26 Aug. 1826) is extremely laudatory and no doubt paved
the way for mutual admiration. Motherwell begins by saying how pleased
he is to see such a work, collected and recovered from "scarce sources" and
making available the "primeval poesy of our native land," mostly in the possession of the older generation, every day dying: "The changes every day
effects on the domestic habits, tastes, pursuits, manners, and modes of living of all ranks of society in the present generation, seem decidedly inimical
to the preservation and transmission of Oral Song." Perhaps using this response to a similar collection as rehearsal for his own "pro*found Treatise,*"
he goes on to say that "Ballads are the peculiar property, as well as, they
may be emphatically termed, the poetry of the people—they have grown up
amongst them with their growth, and strengthened with their strength—apparently more the product of the Universal mind, than of Individual genius."

Motherwell began the correspondence by writing for Buchan's advice, for information regarding various texts, in a somewhat apologetic tone.
Buchan's warm response to his queries laid the groundwork for a continuing
correspondence and friendship: "You seem to think it troublesome for me to
give you any information upon these subjects, but I tell you I glory in such,
and will be at all times happy to communicate anything worthy of your
notice upon your own account as an antiquarian" (25263.19.6f). And he sends

along a text of the "Earl of Aboyne," saying the singer knew nothing about the song so the notes are "imaginery"! Motherwell responds by arranging for a local bookseller to stock *Gleanings,* helps gather subscriptions to pay for the work, and offers advice on publishing Buchan's vast collections of traditionary material as well as on Peter's lifelong search for a better position. In subsequent correspondence, Buchan complains of the expense of his collecting activities and tells of starting to gather narratives and off-color songs not fit for publication. He sends Motherwell a collection of half-penny stall ballads he purchased from local sources. Motherwell suggests that he consider selling some of his manuscript material to solve two problems: the disposition of his collections and his need for money. Additionally, Motherwell gives Buchan an update on the progress of the *Minstrelsy* and even suggests that he send his old beggar down to Motherwell so he can have his tunes recorded. "Devil a thing can I pick up in this miserable hole," he complains (MS 20.5.4, f26).

At a meeting with R.A. Smith, Peter Buchan, John Stevenson, and Alexander Ramsay on 20 October 1828, probably another convivial, male gathering, Motherwell and his friends wrote and executed a humorous testament confirming Motherwell's musical aptitude or, rather, lack thereof: "Appeared William Motherwell who solemnly affirms and Declares that God not having blessed him with a Voice or an Ear he is ——ly incapable of singing any Song Holy or Profane for the Delectation of any Christian Competitors. And this in Truth" (Robertson 1/1208, 10). Motherwell was always willing to laugh at himself and his endeavors, often going to elaborate lengths to parody his own literary proclivities. In 1824 he probably wrote and published *Renfrewshire Characters and Scenery: A Poem of 365 Cantos,* supposedly written by one Isaac Brown, a muslin merchant who seldom attended to business and drew pictures of friends and wrote rhymes for lovers—like, perhaps, Motherwell himself. The book was printed, according to an elaborate introduction, by one Cornelius MacDirdum, to pay off Brown's debts, its weight, if measured as muslin goods, making it a bargain. The poetry itself is accompanied by copious notes, for poetry, MacDirdum/Motherwell says, is a hazy form of discourse and needs a prose balance; furthermore, all books need many notes. The poetry provides a poetical map of the area and the notes reveal the local history. In poking fun at himself and his own activities, he is also exhibiting local pride. And in a somewhat later manuscript, perhaps a draft for a column in the *Paisley Magazine,* Motherwell offers a poetic, satiric evaluation of a critical analysis of a poem—the critic named Doltmannus, supposedly writing on the life of a monk, Slenderwitticus, beginning

> The Poet of himself, to himself, or concerning Himself
> Ye rhyming fools, ye hare-brained asses
> Ye dull disciples of Parnassus
> Who dribble and bedirt your linen
> The narrow gates of fame to grin in. (Robertson 10/1208, 16)

Sometimes he pokes fun and laughs at himself; sometimes, no doubt, he hopes to fool others in passing off supposedly arcane or antique materials as his own. Sometimes he fosters ambiguity around authorship, as in *Certain Curious Poems,* supposedly by one James M'Alpie, said to be a seventeenth-century personage. This work was printed in thirty copies, and perhaps destined, as other works published in such small printings, to become collectors' items with an aura of mystery surrounding their origins.

Even while the *Minstrelsy* was consuming much of his energy, Motherwell continued other creative endeavors. But his ballad enthusiasm was special and led him outside books and old manuscripts into contact with people: Motherwell became a collector of ballads. His Ballad Manuscript may well even record his development as a collector (McCarthy, "William Motherwell"): the first sixty pages include material destined for an unpublished collection; the next two hundred focus on variants of texts, with the last half of the manuscript focusing on the performers, including names, places, and dates, in addition to the texts. His manuscript Ballad Notebook (copy [the original is lost], 25242.16), more informally recording his activities in 1826 and 1827, contains a potpourri of information relative to his ballad enthusiasm. He lists expenses: to pay singers who are living "in great poverty," to hire Thomas Macqueen to collect for him, to bring Mrs. Storie to Paisley so that her tunes can be taken down. He offers a list of singing women, giving their names and addresses, and writes out songs and comments, sometimes making a note where other printed copies appear. There is a draft of what became his "elaborate Discourse." The notebook also includes a list of subscribers he acquired for Buchan's *Gleanings;* a diary of a trip he made to Tobermory (on the Island of Mull), Oban, and Inverary; and descriptions of miscellaneous traditional lore. And references to other traditional practices appear elsewhere: in one of his commonplace books there is an entry titled "Memorandum as to funerals in Paisley—took down from Sheriff Clerk of Renfrewshire, Mr Walkinshaw, who remembered it from his youth." Such accounts lie buried in his copious manuscript records. The ballad materials, the result of systematic study, were published in *Minstrelsy: Ancient and Modern* in 1827, the same year he agreed to give an essay to the Paisley Philosophical Institution "on the historic and Romantic Ballads of Scotland"—very likely an oral version of his "pro*found Treatise.*"

In the course of his collecting and gathering of materials for the *Minstrelsy,* he gathered songs that did not find their way into that work because, most likely, they were not considered "proper" for polite consumption. He describes this collection in several places, although it was probably never published. He called it "The West Countrie Garland" in a letter to R.A. Smith, adding that "the contents would not do to be extensively circulated" (Robertson 3/1222, 26). Elsewhere he calls it "The Paisley Garland" and describes his plans to publish it in an edition of fifty; present taste being different, these texts, he avers, not printed before, nevertheless mirror the past (40: 4).

Motherwell found time to contribute to the *Paisley Advertiser,* a conservative newspaper begun in 1824 of which he was part owner even before he became editor in 1828. Perhaps in connection with his "real" work, he translated and deciphered charters relating to law cases against the town council and made a plan of fifteenth-century Paisley. But most important, in 1828 he, together with some friends, began the *Paisley Magazine.* Intended to complement the dominant Tory/conservative magazine of the day, Edinburgh's *Blackwood's,* and rival the more progressive *Edinburgh Review,* the *Paisley Magazine* was intended to put Paisley on the literary map. Such magazines provided relevant reading material for the rising middle class. As virtual editor and dominant contributor, Motherwell put an enormous amount of energy into this endeavor, using it as a vehicle for publishing his own work, though, like so much material in the contemporary periodical press, unattributed. Claiming to print "curious intelligence . . . regarding the topography of this town and neighborhood, ancient customs, manners, traditions, local anecdote &c," the *Paisley Magazine* printed reviews—sometimes extremely harsh; essays on various subjects, such as Motherwell's own on traditional songs; poems; and editorial humor, as in "A Friendly Notice to Correspondents with which the Public Has Little to Do Unless It Likes." The magazine ran for thirteen numbers and then ceased. Perhaps Paisley's middle class was not large enough to support such a publication. Perhaps the conservative political cast that surfaced from time to time did not sit well with Paisley's middle class, more Whig than Tory. Whatever the cause, the failure of the magazine clearly underlined the limitations of the Paisley environment for Motherwell. He already had been complaining about the lack of receptivity to intellectual and artistic work in Paisley; in 1826 he had written R.A. Smith, "I do heartily loath and abominate this villainous hole which in fact affords no excitement to exertion and is equally barren of commendation when any thing like exertion is made"

(Robertson 3/1222, 45). And in another letter to the same recipient he offers a variation on the same theme: "[R]eally the vexations of this weary & perplexing life are multiplying so around me that I am heart-sick and do loathe their embraces as I now do many things else. I wonder what I am doing staying in this detested hole—for it is a place where no person of Heart or Understanding can find community or feeling or live happily. Devil take it. But this is foolish" (Robertson 3/1222, 50). The failure of the *Paisley Magazine* was perhaps the final straw; his attempts to put Paisley on the literary map were ill-received, his regional loyalty was not supported. In 1829 he left his position as sheriff clerk depute; it may be that his work for the *Paisley Advertiser* was time-consuming and adequately remunerative, or it may be that conditions in the clerk's office were unacceptable: some years later there was an extensive investigation of the unaccountable delays getting work done, trials heard, and so on, going back to the period of Motherwell's employment (HO 102/44). In 1830 he got his chance, left Paisley for Glasgow, and became editor of the *Glasgow Courier:* his editorial work for the *Paisley Magazine* and the *Paisley Advertiser* had paid off.

Even before taking up the very public position of editor of a major Tory newspaper in the West of Scotland, however, Motherwell was well known, perhaps so well known that both his politics and his song-writing proclivities had been satirized in the *Scots Times'* column devoted to Glasgow and the West—"Noctes Sma' Westianae" (a takeoff no doubt on *Blackwood's* famous "Noctes Ambrosinae"):

> "A song?" exclaimed all at once, "what song? pray let us hear it." "Yes, the song, the song," shouted the whole Sma' West at once. The musical member made excuses, spoke of the illegibility of the MS., talked of its being found in a tattered state near Hutchesons' Bridge. Of his want of voice, and a thousand other accompaniments of singing, but finally, after a little persuasion, he trolled out, though not with the effect of a Vestris or a Foote, the following ludicrous ditty. (no. 221, 3 Oct., 308)

Later in October 1829, he may have been satirized as the Baron o' Mearns, who led a band of hired porters in preventing the Whigs from interrupting a Tory gathering against reform. If these references are indeed to Motherwell, his penchant for old song and his lack of musical aptitude—already recorded in the testament signed by Smith, Buchan, and others—and his established and rather vocal political positions indicate considerable public knowledge of this man from Paisley about to enter the political arena as critic and commentator.

If Paisley was in a bad way early in the nineteenth century, the situation in Glasgow was worse. The population of the city doubled every twenty years between 1780 and 1840, creating "very severe problems of health, sanitation and poverty" (Devine and Mitchison, *People and Society,* 41). Yet the urban area and the mechanization of a number of industries, including linen manufacture, served as a magnet. By 1841, a decade after Motherwell's arrival in Glasgow, a third of the population was made up of in-migrated Irish Catholics who found themselves ghettoized in poor neighborhoods, looked down upon by some for their religious beliefs and related social practices, and employed in manual labor, especially the manufacture of linen. At the same time, the urban context fostered the rise of a middle class living by "the application of intellect and direction rather than practical skill of physical effort" (Devine and Mitchison, *People and Society,* 110) with leisure and enough excess money to devote to various forms of consumption: Motherwell, for example, built a remarkable library with ancillary collections of coins, ancient armor, paintings, and engravings that took twelve days to sell after his death. The number of newspapers expanded during this time as well: they served as mouthpieces for class concerns and interests and facilitated awareness of similar publications in other towns and regions, to an extent solidifying on regional and national bases a sense of class consciousness. When Motherwell became editor of the *Glasgow Courier,* he became de facto a spokesperson for the Tory position: politics became much more central to his everyday activities.

As editor of the *Courier,* a thrice weekly publication, Motherwell took almost immediate steps to expand the paper's coverage of books and poetry, focuses that had been central to the *Paisley Magazine.* Like other newspapers of the day, the *Courier* contained a mix of news, often culled from other periodicals closer to the news sources (a forerunner of the syndicated news services), and a hefty amount of local interest material, including home remedies and gossip. There was a very clear editorial voice, more prominent than in the other Glasgow papers of the time, supporting the Crown, the status quo, and other Tory positions. During Motherwell's five-year tenure as editor, he had ample occasion to develop the Tory position on the Reform Bill of 1832—opposed—and to take periodic potshots at the Whig government, often referring to the Whigs as "the Incapables."

Early biographers suggest that Motherwell was out of his element in Glasgow, that his journalistic activities kept him from other pursuits. The evidence is to the contrary: he was galvanized by the Glasgow experience; it gave him a position from which to "preach" Tory positions for and to a constituency that had considerable power and influence. There was then a circle of like-minded persons, enough to support a newspaper; in fact, there were two Tory newspapers at the time. Being in Paisley, a Whig stronghold, and serving as sheriff clerk depute had probably muted his overt political involvements. In Glasgow, he was free and clearly called on to assert his positions, not only through editorial selection and statement but also by personal choice of political affiliation. In 1833, he joined the Orange Society, which was gaining considerable strength in Glasgow in response to the influx of Irish Catholic workers. An avowed Protestant and royalist organization, it was formed, according to a *Courier* article in 1835, to counter the rise of Catholicism, out of a fear of Catholic hegemony and possible persecution of Protestants, because of the political influence of priests, and out of concern that the Catholic Irish would gain too much control in the House of Commons. Serving as deputy district master, Motherwell was called to London in 1835 to testify before a House of Commons Select Committee established to investigate the role of the society in the rising sectarian tension; the committee concluded that the Orange Society was indeed fueling factionalism.

Motherwell's anti-Catholic stance was not an anomaly and needs to be seen in the context of the time. Linda Colley offers the convincing thesis that anti-Catholic sentiment and the wars against Catholic powers were the central forces that forged a British identity, an identity stridently Protestant, even among those who showed no signs of religious practice or overt belief. In addition to this sectarian perspective there was the economic reality: in areas most affected by Irish Catholic immigration, Glasgow and Paisley being prime locales, the largely young and unskilled Irish put enormous pressure on the Scottish working class, who they were likely to displace in the job market. Catholic emancipation in 1829 could not undo decades of belief in Protestant right and ascendency.

Motherwell's political beliefs and activities seem to have gone on parallel with his poetic and editorial activities. He continued to contribute to the periodical, literary press; to edit works; and to write all manner of essays in addition to his poetry. Being in the city expanded his opportunities and contacts. Almost immediately he fell into various social groups, such as the Hadgis Club, of which he was "Chief Molluk," joined by Robert Peacock, John Howie, P.A. Ramsay, Andrew Henderson, and Alex Tennant (Robertson 10/1208, 17). He was active in the Maitland Club, a nationalistic book club, like the Bannatyne Club, devoted to publishing materials relating to Scotland. He supported the nomination of a friend of George Ritchie Kinloch's

for membership and in turn asked for Kinloch's support for his friend
Campbell. He also edited for the Maitland Club "Rob Stene's Dream," a
manuscript of a late-sixteenth-century satirical poem in the Leighton Library, Dunblane. The poem was filled with invective against the character
and conduct of John Maitland, Lord Thirlstane, chancellor, who was pro-
English and forced to retire only to be reinstated and to accompany James
VI to Denmark to get his queen. In an 1831 letter to G.A. Gardiner (501
4196, 17), Motherwell indicates that he is working on a study of the Sempills,
an early literary family. By 1832 he was collaborating with James Hogg on
an edition of Burns, and he may well have begun a life of Paisley poet Robert Tannahill, later completed by P.A. Ramsay. In addition, he intended to
write an introduction to the *Memorabilia of the City of Glasgow from Burgh
Minute Books* with notices of history and manners by one James Hill, which
was first published in the *Courier.*

One of the crowning achievements of the Glasgow years, however,
was the publication in 1832 of a collection of his poems—*Poems, Narrative
and Lyrical*—a collection subsequently edited in 1847 by McConechy and
reprinted multiply with various alterations both in Boston and the West of
Scotland, attesting to the esteem with which his poetry was held, especially
at midcentury. Another achievement of 1832 was the establishment with
John Strang, Thomas Atkinson, and J.D. Carrick of the *Day,* said to be the
first daily paper in Scotland "to be ready, like the Spectator and Rambler of
yore, to make its appearance at the breakfast table, every morning of the
week except Sunday." The *Day* was an important outlet for Motherwell's
"literary" endeavors, though again there are no attributions. In addition to
poems and epigrams and rhyming fun—

> Says Tom, "of drink it is a rule,
> To change the wise man to the fool."
> Now, all Tom's friends most gravely think
> Tom need not fear a drop of drink! (*Day,* 43)

> Quoth Tom, my book is full of *fire,*
>   It *sparkles* like a jewel,
> Yes, cries his friend, that's truth entire,
>   It is the *best of fuel.* (ibid., 75)

—supposedly chosen by the "Council of Ten" (ibid., 245–48), who decided
whether to print or burn, the *Day* included Motherwell's *Memoirs of a Paisley Baillie,* an account of the wisdom of a fool. The Baillie may owe some-

thing to John Galt's Provost Pawkie, whose pompous self-importance is laid before us in all its transparency; Pawkie is mocked, undermined by his own thoughts, words, and deeds, as is Motherwell's Baillie. Said to have been a manufacturer, the Baillie was clearly a laughing stock, misunderstanding events. Motherwell has him seek refuge in the garden on washing day in search of robins: he looked kindly on them because of their role in the "auld ballat," that is, "Babes in the Wood," where they had covered the abandoned babies with a blanket of leaves. Such references to Motherwell's own other interests, ballads, as well as to other examples of intertextuality in the *Day,* as in the gossip column—"What sad cholera times we live in!! It is also said that Baillie Pirnie left Paisley yesterday, for Seester' Place, Gourock" (referring again to his fictional character) (*Day,* 108)—reveal a playful facet of his character. And an anonymous piece on the price of matrimony for established men—"break off from my jovial companions. I was to quit all my evening clubs, all the theatres—and never more visit any public place of amusement" (no. 57)—may also express his sentiments and those of his editorial associates.

Motherwell also contributed to *Whistle-Binkie: A Collection of Songs for the Social Circle,* to *Tait's Edinburgh Magazine,* and to the *Laird of Logan; or, Anecdotes and Tales Illustrative of the Wit and Humour of Scotland.* The latter, edited by J.D. Carrick and Andrew Henderson, included a number of reprints of Motherwell material. Additionally, Motherwell wrote an introductory essay for Andrew Henderson's *Scottish Proverbs* deemed by *Tait's Edinburgh Magazine* "worthy of himself and the subject" (1:648). In fact, his lengthy essay follows the same pattern employed in the *Minstrelsy,* offering a rather elaborate historical survey of studies of the proverb; the essay gave Motherwell the chance to use material he had begun to develop and publish in the ill-fated *Paisley Magazine* and to pay Henderson back for helping him with the *Minstrelsy.*

The Glasgow years then were a continuation, even an intensification, of his previous activities with the significant addition of his very public role as editor of a Tory newspaper and the chance that gave him to speak out against, for example, the Reform Bill, and for what he saw as loyal organizations, such as the Orange Society. The 1832 parliamentary reform bill was an attempt to change the political system from within, to extend suffrage to more men; it sought to incorporate some of those whose status and autonomy had been radically effected by the erosion of older patterns—agricultural and artisanal. And the bill might be viewed as a parliamentary response to the widespread fear that if something were not done to expand the voices of the underrepresented, there might be a revolution in Britain to parallel the

French one. In spite of its total opposition to the bill, the *Courier*—Motherwell—responded magnanimously to its passage. Throughout his tenure as editor, reports of the Irish Catholic situation were published: early in 1832 the *Courier* records that "the North of Ireland is now in a state of almost open rebellion" (2 Feb.), that "nothing can be more fearful than the present state of Ireland, torn as it is by contending political and religious parties, and destitute even of the shadow of an energetic government" (4 Feb.). In 1833, commenting on parliamentary action, the *Courier* records that "there is no denying the fact, that there is a lavish expenditure of the public money for the dissemination of the tenets of the Roman Catholic Church, while every discouragement is given to Protestant institutions connected with the education of the people, and the propagation of the true Gospel" (26 Mar. 1833). His personal response had been to join the Orange Society, described in the *Courier* as "a strictly Loyal and Constitutional Association, founded upon a Protestant basis[,] . . . opposed the extirpation of Protestantism in Ireland" (12 Mar. 1835). As deputy district master, Motherwell testified before a House of Commons Select Committee in a brief appearance on 31 August 1835. His biographers claim he fell apart under testimony and returned to Glasgow a beaten man; they may well have been embarrassed by his involvements and used his untimely death so shortly after the London episode as ex post facto suggestion that Motherwell did not know what he was doing when he got involved in the Orange Society. The published records (House of Lords, *XVII 1835 Reports/Committees no. 605*) reveal only that Motherwell was not a particularly forthcoming witness. No one thought to ask why he had joined in 1833.

Shortly after he returned from London he wrote his friend Charles Hutcheson, thanking him for writing an editorial for the *Courier* while he was away and reporting that he didn't like the "incessant whirl of Cabs and Omnibusses" (98559) he encountered south of the border. The *Courier* account of the House of Commons hearings is clearly Motherwell's, measured and full, with no evidence that he had lost his ability to deal rationally with either his own experience testifying or with the question of the Orange organizations (19 Sept. 1835).

Certainly Motherwell's sudden death the first of November, in his thirty-eighth year, may well have led friends to search for a reason, and the presumed trauma of the London experience and testimony were seized upon as explanation. The official cause of his death was listed as apoplexy; and thirty-eight was near the average life expectancy of the day (Devine and Mitchison, *People and Society,* chap. 1). Motherwell was buried in the Glasgow Necropolis on 5 November. The obituary in the *Courier* mourned one "whose energetic spirit sustained for several years the reputation of one of the oldest Newspapers in Scotland—and whose genius added not a little to the literary character of his native country" (2969 Ry II d 17). Glasgow's *Arbus,* representing the political opposition, nonetheless confirmed the esteem with which he was held: "This hurried and inadequate tribute is paid to him by me who, decidedly opposed to him on public grounds, and placed in immediate collision with him, was yet proud to call him his friend, and laments his loss" (2969 Ry II d 17). It was almost twenty years before a marker was raised over his burial spot, although legend has it that someone marked the spot periodically with flowers: was this one of the women he would not marry for fear of loss of freedom and male companionship? The tombstone, when put up, was a Gothic-style temple built over a foundation stone that included copies of Motherwell's works. James Fillans, Paisley artist and friend of Motherwell, sculpted a bust in addition to reliefs depicting scenes from Motherwell's works: chivalrous figures in combat over/for a "ladye" fair, representations of "Jeannie Morrison" and "Halbert the Grim," both of whom figured in his poetry. William Kennedy, to whom his volume of poems had been dedicated, provided the epitaph on the pedestal base:

> Not as a record he lacketh a stone!
> Pay a light debt to the singer we've known
> Proof that our love for his name hath not flown, with the frampe (lamp?)
>   perishing
> That we are cherishing. (Robertson 3/1222, 69)

In the year after Motherwell's death, several posthumous publications appeared, including a foray into the Gothic—"A Chapter from the Unpublished Romance of 'The Strange and Delectable Story of the Langbien Ritters, or the Doomed Nine'"—in the *Scottish Annual.* The chapter deals with two old men who have been turned into trees to protect them from the destructive force, to no avail. The trees/men are cut down and blood spurts out, revealing their true nature and objectifying the destructiveness of the interlopers. Perhaps this episode sums up Motherwell's own political perspective, providing a metaphorical denunciation of all the forces he saw altering, and thus destroying, the physical, intellectual, and social landscape he valued. Although he personally benefited from many of the changes—he acquired a degree of class mobility, he was given the right to vote, he achieved a measure of recognition—in almost every one of his involvements he exhibits a degree of dissatisfaction with his lived environment, a yearning for some better past.

Interest in a putative past was something he shared with others of his time and place: it was in a way nationalistic, but in a cultural rather than political sense, sometimes foregrounding and emphasizing selected aspects from the past for artistic rather than political inspiration. It was also an antiquarian, a Tory-embraced, concern: societies (the Society of Antiquaries of Scotland in 1780) were established to study the past, its history and artifacts; the building of Edinburgh's Register House late in the eighteenth century (designed by Robert Adam) provided and still provides a place and space for history's remains (Lenman, *Integration and Enlightenment,* 132–36). This nexus of interests in the "rusty" and "musty," in the "material remains and oral remembrances," suited Motherwell and provided a conceptual as well as real haven, bringing together men "unified by sheer delight in learning and exhuberant talk of intellectual dispute" around Scotland's past (I.G. Brown, *Hobby-Horsical Antiquary,* 42).

Motherwell's life spanned thirty-seven crucial years: the moment during which the Industrial Revolution was shaking up the established order, when the Reform Bill (including male suffrage) was under consideration, when the middle class was rising, when the artisanal class was losing status, when printing was becoming cheaply available, when commerce and capitalism were beginning to grow, when pastoral and agricultural pursuits were losing their dominance in the Scottish milieu. Motherwell was very much a part of that milieu, participating in several distinct yet overlapping fields— literary and journalistic, political and religious—sites of contestation in one way or another at that moment in time. Thus his life and activities become a way of reexperiencing, in as much as one can from this present vantage point, some of the issues and conflicts in the West of Scotland at the beginning of the nineteenth century—from one participant's own point of view.

Politics

DEATH OF MR. WILLIAM MOTHERWELL, EDITOR OF THE GLASGOW COURIER

The warfare and political strife so long waged between us and Mr. William Motherwell, Editor of the Glasgow Courier, is now for ever at an end. He was cut off suddenly by a stroke of apoplexy on Sunday morning the 1st of November curt. at the age of 35. Many hard blows had been exchanged between us during the last four or five years; but we cannot accuse ourselves of entertaining any personal *malignity* towards him or any other man. It is true we thoroughly detested his political principles, or rather the principles he professed to adopt; but we often envied his talents, and wished they had been employed in a better cause. When he assailed us, we never allowed him to escape for it. We always gave him a Roland for an Oliver, and it was sometimes bitter enough. Yet we all along entertained a suspicion that he prostituted his talents on the Tory side, because he was employed and specially *paid* for so doing. If left to the freedom of his own will, he would, we think, have been a Radical! His *heart,* we are sure, never lay in the Tory cause; and our reason for saying so is, that some years ago, and prior to his connection with the Glasgow Courier, he wrote the Prospectus of a Monument to the Memory of the illustrious Sir William Wallace, full of the most generous and patriotic sentiments that any Radical of the present day could indite. We perused the original manuscript of it two or three years ago with much pleasure. We have since often wished to lay hold of it, to bring we own, the blush to his cheek, and to confound the Tory friends by whom he was latterly surrounded.

We war not with the dead, nor do we flatter the living. We are content to pass over many of his insulting philippics against the Reformers of Glasgow, individually and collectively. But truth compels us to say, that his conduct in constantly mouthing religion with politics—in running down Reformers as infidels—in taking all the sanctity to himself—was, to say the least of it, (and especially to those who had an innate knowledge of his character, as we really pretend to have in some points,) most

hypocritical and disgusting. By these means, however, he became
the pet of many of our Established Clergy; they actually looked
up to him as one of their best champions. Accordingly, we are
well assured, that, on the day of his death, the most zealous
among them, viz. The Rev. Dr. Muir of St. James', preached a
sermon to the effect, "that while some (Peter Mackenzie & Co.
but no *name,*) was allowed to stalk abroad, and scandalize the
Church, that the Lord, in his providence, had that day taken away
(Mr. Motherwell) one of her chief supporters."

Since, therefore, the Clergy are in that pathetic strain—and far
be it from us to blame them for it—we earnestly hope they will
attend to the wants of the innocent and helpless children he has
left behind him, under circumstances of the most unfortunate
nature, and which would be altogether indelicate and very
unbecoming in us to allude to farther at present.

We best honour the memory of William Motherwell, by telling
these homely truths of him. Let the Tories be thankful we end it
as we do. He was a clever fellow. Peace to his memory!
—*Loyal Reformer's Gazette* 6 (1835–36): 70–71

THIS OBITUARY STATEMENT APPEARED in the pages of the *Loyal
Reformer's Gazette* and more or less concluded a long series of references
to Motherwell and to the *Glasgow Courier,* which he edited between 1830
and his death in 1835. The references to Motherwell and the *Courier* began
shortly after Motherwell took over his editorial duties and focus particularly
on the issue of the Reform Bill of 1832 and the Irish question. At first
Motherwell was not named but referenced: "[H]e is a strange sort of fellow
this same *Courier;*—does he imagine that the sensible part of *the* population view the present aspect of affairs through the same time-serving tele-
scope as himself, that he writes such balderdash; or does he suppose that
even the few who read his lucubrations are ignorant enough to be gulled by
such mendacious ranting?" (1 [1831]: 143). Responding to the perceived
slanderous words of the *Courier,* the *Loyal Reformer's Gazette* struck back,
calling the *Courier* "that *infamous, rascally,* and *contemptible* publication[,]
. . . the Editor of which has done all in his power to administer to the foolish
prejudices and vulgar appetites of his *numberous* . . . reforming, but *woe-
fully ignorant,* patrons" (2 [1831–32]: 264). By 1834–35, Motherwell is being called "Wee Mothy" and mocked: "Mothy being such a pure character
himself" (5 [1834–35]: 150–52); then he becomes simply the *Moth* ("he
calls us names, and we are only giving him a dish of his own sauce"; ibid.,
276–77). Motherwell, described as "stroking his huge whiskers, on which,

we understand, he prides himself more than his lines to Jeanie Morrison, declared that 'since his connection with the Press, he had never told a lie to serve a purpose; he had *endeavoured* to tell the truth, and, by reason and argument, convince men of the sincerity of his opinions'" (ibid.). The *Loyal Reformer's Gazette* responds with the blast, "How many Tory *fibs* has he told since he managed the *Glasgow Courier?* . . . Is it not the fact, that he is the *hired* scribe of the Tories, paid at so much per annum, for writing in favour of them, and their party and principles, through thick and thin, right or wrong?" (ibid.). And, in general, the *Gazette* thought very little of Tories, describing the generic Tory in a poem as a "political drone, that lives, at his ease / On the honey that's gather'd by hard-working bees" (2 [1831–32]: 139).

The obituary notice comes then out of a four- or five-year opposition to Motherwell, the Tory position on the reform bill, and other issues of the day, and it suggests that Motherwell's position and political views were recognized, that Motherwell had indeed become a political figure.

The *Loyal Reformer's Gazette* summation provides an intriguing "statement." On the surface, it tells little about Motherwell except as political opponent. And yet there is an enormous amount of information, or perspective: Motherwell was an accomplished man, even a friend, but definitely a representative of an untenable political position; the writer even points to his presumed Radical leanings. The penultimate paragraph raises questions about his personal circumstances—had he fathered several illegitimate children?—that are impossible to answer. Finally, the author of this recollection, undoubtedly the editor, Peter Mackenzie, names Motherwell a Tory but questions his real commitment to the conservative position and underlines the fact that he was a *paid* editor of the paper. No mention is made of Motherwell's antiquarian activities, his editing of or writing of poetry; here he becomes only a political figure. What is clear is that Motherwell and his political views were well known among the politically aware, those engaged in taking sides, in factional scheming, those interested in political opinions and party connections. Motherwell was in the thick of things and recognized as such.

The *Loyal Reformer's Gazette,* in suggesting that Motherwell was a paid Tory, in hinting at his nationalistic sentiments evidenced in his support for a commemorative statue of William Wallace, seeks to reveal the inconsistencies of a man who may very well have been, as some of his friends and apologists suggested, in over his head as editor of the *Courier* and spokesperson for the political conservatives. Whatever the truth may be, Motherwell's positions probably more nearly represent the ambivalence and inconsistency typical of many persons. It is possible, for example, to justify and/or explain his allegiance to the British crown and his Scottish chauvinism as aspects of the cultural muddle, or reality, of the times and characterize his response as a kind of pragmatism: accepting the political union of Scotland with England as a fait accompli but anxious to preserve the cultural aspects that identified Scotland as a distinct country, with a particular people whose history and traditions deserved to be preserved. Christopher Harvie and others have criticized this "cultural" nationalism as "noisy inaction": it might conversely be called a realistic response to the situation—much as the French in late 1990s at once anticipated the coming European Union while stressing French cultural qualities, focusing on the cuisine of a "mythic" earlier time, seeking to preserve *the* real, the antique, the old methods of baking and preparing bread in the face of possible political homogenization.

It is perhaps worth exploring Motherwell's seemingly dichotomous position further. As a presumed conservative, Tory participant, Motherwell supported the monarchy, affirming "principles of loyalty to the Crown and unaffected love and veneration for the Laws and Constitution of the country" (*Courier,* 15 Apr. 1830, 1). The very existence of two major parties keys differences of perspective, but it does not reveal what was undoubtedly a polyglot reality, the even greater variety in political perspectives held by the relatively few who were privileged enough to be active in that arena. There was no consensus—then or now. Motherwell favored the status quo, accepted the hierarchy of power, and looked to the past rather than to the future for models. Like his near-contemporary, the popular divine Thomas Chalmers, and his wish/plan to recreate parishes, small whole communities of face-to-face and supportive interaction, Motherwell sought an organic community. His yearning for Gemeinschaft drew, then, on a localized version of the "good old days" syndrome and involved a backward glance to an imagined small, homogeneous, harmonious, unchanging community united by shared custom and tradition. Such idealized glances at a fabricated, idealized past occur throughout history—in Scotland and elsewhere—when change and dislocation threaten the status quo. Interestingly, this kind of stance has often been dismissed even before it can be interrogated, as in Douglas Gifford's introduction to volume 3 of *The History of Scottish Literature,* when he describes the "parochial and sentimental yearning for a lost or imagined community" (7). This was, however, a widespread kind of nationalistic fervor, and Motherwell's perspective offers a useful example of a type of "cultural politics" that included a devotion to Scotland, its "uniqueness," its "particular" history, and its qualities—including its literature and certainly its language.

In an undated manuscript, "Essay on the Scottish Language," which may have been a copy of one of his early presentations to a club in Paisley as a young man, he articulated the close connection between language and country: "But love of our country is inseparably connected with the preservation of its language, and when the latter is discarded and disused, the former must inevitably decline and ultimately die within us." He goes further, asserting that "our vernacular language is daily loosing ground amongst us" and that "nowadays everything Scotish using a pretty phase current in the land of Cokaigne is *wastly wulgar.* Hence Scotish patriotism, virtue, talent, integrity[,] honour[,] morality[,] must all, in this refined age, be exceedingly vulgar and unfashionable." Motherwell laments this, suggesting that it is through language that one can gain insight into "the manners and modes of thinking peculiar to our Ancestors, but what is perhaps of more solid utility, access is had to the stores of ancient lore and the riches of the language of former times are unlocked" (Robertson 10/1208, 1). And it was exactly those stores of earlier lore and literature that occupied him at many points in his life, artistic materials he sought to preserve before the changes being wrought pushed them into oblivion—for the present was not deemed conducive to their continued existence and/or production.

Admittedly, the focus on the past, real and/or imagined, in some ways seemed to obscure the present or led to a very selective field of vision. Motherwell, like many of his contemporaries, seems to have been all but blind to—certainly silent on—the realities of life in Glasgow: the dreadful poverty, the horrendous living and working conditions that plagued the third largest city in Britain. That the view and analyses of Glasgow were subject to alternate perspectives should be obvious, and depended on where one "sat" in the cultural landscape. The industrialists saw Glasgow and the times as one of expansion writ with a capital E: the development of the shipping industry, the dredging, deepening, and "improving" of the Clyde; the rise of shipbuilding and development of trade in cotton, iron, and coal; the establishment of a number of institutions, such as the Hunterian Museum and prisons (a "positive" response to the increase in crime, accompanied also by the institution of a police force?); the addition of new university subjects; the introduction of street lights; the taking of salmon from the River Clyde to grace the dinner tables of the well-positioned. Another viewpoint might focus on the real human conditions, particularly the flight of many persons from the rural, agricultural environments into an urban conurbation whose industries could not expand quickly enough to absorb the new human "tools." With the population expanding and the oversupply of labor came enormous degradation, poverty, and squalor; tenements, erupting everywhere, became festering grounds for typhoid and cholera, where drink became almost the only solace. The population had exploded: in 1831 there were, according to Cleland's statistics (*Enumeration of the Inhabitants,* 34), 202,426 inhabitants, of whom 33,259 (30,032 married men, 1,790 widowers, and 1,437 bachelors, including Motherwell) were counted as householders and gained the right to vote after passage of the Reform Bill of 1832. With this reform Motherwell himself became eligible to vote, and yet he opposed enfranchisement, in general, in his public pronouncements.

Thomas Hamilton's Cyril Thornton records his view of Glasgow, and it is not a pretty picture: "long and hideous suburbs by which Glasgow is on all sides surrounded" (79); "it was not until the fifth day, that I beheld the high black towers and spire of the Cathedral, overtopping the dense volumes of vapour that lay spread like a canopy above the city. Glasgow had evidently received a great increase of population since I had last seen it. The dirty and miserable suburbs by which it is surrounded, now extended a mile or two further into the country, and the smoke of innumerable coal-works and factories, which had sprung up on all hands, infused a new and uncalled for pollution into the atmosphere" (403). Later recorders are clear in their condemnation: "But Glasgow above all, especially in the centre of the old town covering the area within a half-mile radius of Glasgow Cross, exhibited in the first half of the nineteenth century the most revolting conditions of life to be met with in the whole of Great Britain" (Handley, *Irish in Scotland,* 239).

And further, describing the very area of Glasgow known (and lived in by) to Motherwell, James Handley writes in *The Irish in Scotland:*

> Glasgow in the nineteenth century was the most densely populated area, computed at 5,000 to the acre, in the United Kingdom. In one small rectangular section in the heart of the city, bounded on the east by High-street, on the west by Candleriggs, on the south by Trongate and on the north by Stirling-street, the population exceeded that of several Scottish counties. No proper system of drainage or removal of refuse, an imperfect supply of water from the more or less polluted river that flowed through the city, no privies, or a few that women and children could not use, no baths or means of bathing even in the houses of fairly well-to-do. . . . It was into this congested city that thousands of Irish poured and added to the already terrible congestion. (240)

Glasgow Cross

Trongate, site of much commercial activity in Glasgow, including Robertson's bookshop

High Street. Motherwell was born on the corner of High and College

Glasgow College, across the High Street from where Motherwell was born; he
attended for one session in 1818–1819

Glasgow College Gardens

View of Glasgow Cathedral from the Washing Green

It is often said that when one lives "in" pollution, one does not see it, and surviving illustrations offer an almost pastoral view of the heart of Glasgow.

This is not to say, of course, that Motherwell was unaware of the situation in which he lived, but rather to suggest that, on the one hand, he accepted it, and on the other, he categorized it. Many of the incomers, many of those who peopled the tenements, many who lived in desperate poverty were Catholics—refugees from Ireland. And, in general, he was against them: perhaps their religious affiliation coupled with their country of origin precluded their ever becoming Scots; Catholicism, as an international persuasion, and thus Catholics themselves, owed loyalty to the pope and therefore were assumed to vote according to "his" precepts. In other words, the poor, often Catholic immigrants were a threat to the cultural idea of Scotland, tied as it was at that point in time to Protestantism (specifically, Presbyterianism) and, in Motherwell's mind, to inherited cultural practices, which included the singing of songs and ballads but particularly the use of the good Scots language. He was indeed against their migration to Glasgow, to Scotland from Ireland; he was against government support and the development of houses of worship. Undoubtedly he saw "them" as a threat to his idea of Scotland. If they were among the poor and the unenfranchised, he would rather blot them out than ameliorate their situation. So largely, the poor qua poor in Glasgow were not in his line of vision: they were to him a double pollution—the pollution of poverty and the pollution of religion.

Whatever Motherwell's personal beliefs were, he clearly entered into the political debate and took certain positions that can only be considered conservative. And his positions were predicated on his own preferences for the status quo and his reluctance to change, whether or not he was paid to support those positions. And there was plenty of change to resist; Harvie suggests that the magnitude of what was going on might be described as "baffling" (36). Two areas, already alluded to, deserve further elaboration because they were issues of the day, Motherwell decidedly had views about them, and, interestingly, he "felt" them both professionally and personally. They are, of course, the Reform Bill of 1832 and the Irish Catholic issue, which came to a head in his personal experience in the Orange Society, that "loyal" Protestant and secret organization.

The Reform Bill of 1832 was about enfranchisement, about who could vote, and may well have been stimulated or necessitated by the unrest resulting from massive industrialization, the changing social environment (which seemed to reconfigure the class situation), and a resulting economic climate that was increasing the number of the "have-nots" at rapid pace. The governmental response was to begin the process of bringing those persons into the political process, even—as incorporation often does—to co-opt them. I say begin the process because the resulting enfranchisement largely affected the rising middle class, individuals such as William Motherwell himself, who, by the passage of the bill, was enabled to vote directly, for the first time, for representatives to the House of Commons. Records in fact show that he used that right, casting his two votes for both the winning and the losing of the four candidates.

The reform bill, then, was especially about direct election of representatives by male householders. The editor of the *Loyal Reformer's Gazette,* Peter Mackenzie, was one of Glasgow's leaders in supporting the bill. In general, the members of the House of Lords were against it because its passage would cut into their inherited privilege—that is, the right, collectively, of a privileged and, of course, male elite to determine whom the representatives to Parliament might be. And the *Courier* lauded the Lords' position: "The British Constitution is yet safe. We refer with pleasure to the stern and uncompromising attitude which the hereditary guardians of the Crown, and of the institutions of this country, have assumed at this peculiarly critical and threatening time" (8 Oct. 1831). The eventual passage of the bill was, however, momentous for Scotland: it raised Scottish representation in the House of Commons from forty-five to fifty-three, but more important, it gave the right to vote for those representatives to a much larger percentage of the population. Prior to the bill, it is said that one in six hundred in Scotland could vote: the corresponding figure for England was one in thirty! No wonder the Scots felt disenfranchised: they were. Harvie underlines the enormous significance of this change by providing a comparative analysis. "[T]he years," he says, "from 1832 to 1835 saw a formal extension of political rights in Scotland far more drastic than the results of the French Revolution of 1830. . . . The French electorate had increased from 90,000 to 166,000; the Scottish electorate from about 4,500 to 65,000" (*Scotland and Nationalism,* 83). And Mackenzie describes what, from his perspective, was a triumphant response to the passage of the bill: "exceeding great joy in Glasgow to all classes, excepting those who were inexorably wedded to the old close-burgh system, and could see nothing in the least degree defective or wrong about it" (229). The passage of the bill led to a momentary decline in conservative strength, and I.G.C. Hutchison notes that Tories "were subjected to virulent and passionate hostility" and were identified with "oppression and injustice" (*Political History of Scotland,* 2, 3).

It is hard to pinpoint Motherwell's objection to the reform bill by which he personally profited—unless, on the one hand, it was his duty to support the Tory position or, on the other, he really did see its passage as a threat to Scotland. He may well have feared its assimilationist potential—a byproduct of industrialization as well. In the *Courier,* he asserted, "Reform means Revolution" (3 Mar. 1831); and he felt things were going well. Expanding on this declaration, he said, "[I]t is not a reform conceived in the spirit, and suited to the practice of the constitution, but it is a reform which will unsettle all law, trample on all right, and confiscate all property in the country. To a wise, temperate, and strictly just reform, and correction of existing abuses, the country is not indisposed; but to a reckless uptearing of all ancient landmarks, privileges, and chartered rights, every intelligent mind and loyal heart in the community is opposed" (8 Mar. 1831). It is hard to know exactly what he refers to here, but certainly his sentiments are hyperbolic. And there were those of his day and time, in addition to Mackenzie of the *Loyal Reformer's Gazette,* who saw that; one opponent wrote a satirical poem about Motherwell's political pretensions, mocking his presumption that he could denounce the government. Motherwell is the "little bird"; the government is the eagle:

A tomtit once, a little bird,
But full of high conceit,
Attacked an eagle of the sun,
A bird of claws and weight.

Quoth Tom, "The eagle is a fool,
And stupid eke is he;
He wears a wig, he cannot sing,
Nor twitter tweedle-dee.

"He sits upon a pack of wool—
I perch upon a tree;
Tho' petty scribblers sound his praise
He'll never match with me." (Alison, *Anecdotage of Glasgow,* 276)

Motherwell, clearly, did not convince everyone, and his positions made him ripe for such jibes. And yet, once the bill was passed, he could write a somewhat gracious, if pragmatic, response: "Since our Constitution has been changed, we hope, as friends to our country, that, in its new shape, it may prove permanent—that it may bring with it all the blessings and all the happiness that its friends have predicted of it—and that it may work well for the glory and prosperity of the Empire at large, and the conservation of those great interests in Church and State, so essential to the well-being of our social fabric" (12 June 1832). When problems were discovered with the bill and its enactment, Motherwell, perhaps predictably, returned to his critical stance: "The 'confusion' which has arisen amongst the unhappy Ministers upon discovering that their fine Reform Bill will not work—that it is in fact impracticable—is rendered 'worse confounded' by the further discovery that it cannot be amended in the present session of parliament" (12 July 1832).

Almost immediately, Motherwell shifted his attention elsewhere: he emphasized another cause, with multiple implicit ideological agendas concerning Scotland, her established church, her special national qualities, and the state of her economy and government. The issue large enough to contain these concepts was the Irish Catholic question. The Irish incomers, seen as a group with none of the subtleties of differentiation employed, represented a threat to the Scottish worker; their very presence was seen as an erosion of Scottish culture; and the propagation of their erroneous religious persuasion was feared as a "monstrous usurpation" (*Courier,* 19 Sept. 1835). Opposition to Catholic emancipation was a very loaded issue and one to which Motherwell brought both professional and personal involvements.

The pages of the *Courier* had long reported the "disturbances" in Ireland, the Protestant/Catholic imbalance there, and included criticism of governmental actions in support of the Catholic establishment. Motherwell's positions are predictable, anti-Catholic, and antigovernment: "That the Protestants are inferior to the Roman Catholics in number, there is no attempt to deny; yet the preponderance is not *so* great as to prevent the moral superiority of the former, from making them more than equal to the physical superiority of the latter" (21 Jan. 1832); "There is no denying the fact, that there is a lavish expenditure of the public money for the dissemination of the tenets of the Roman Catholic Church, while every discouragement is given to Protestant institutions connected with the education of the people, and the propagation of the true Gospel" (26 Mar. 1833).

The issue was both national—in the sense of affecting the entire British Isles—and local, that is, Glasgow-specific. In the late 1820s, culminating in a bill in 1829, George IV had agreed to support Catholic emancipation: the removal of limitations to their participation in the life of the nation. Extended, these provisions provided support for Catholic organizations. Popular responses show that there was not unanimous support for these measures. While the more enlightened citizens might have been in favor of universal liberty and supported this governmental shift in policy, many of those most affected by the policy were virulently against it, signing petitions—some nine hundred in all—holding open meetings, and making loud pronouncements against the proposition. Handley concluded that "the attitude of the majority of Lowland Scots towards the Irish immigrant was one of settled hostility. This hostility was due to economic, political and religious reasons. . . . But most of all in Scotland the Irish were disliked because the religion of the vast majority of them was execrated by the native" (*Irish in Scotland*, 287). The West of Scotland, Glasgow especially, was the seat of much opposition because many Irish Catholics were in their very midst—in 1831 some 35,554 of a population of 202,426 (Cleland, *Enumeration of the Inhabitants*). Competing for jobs, mostly as laborers, and other scarce resources, Irish Catholics were the particular target of those who feared personal displacement, who resented the possibility that they might be replaced by an inferior people possessed of different manners and customs, including a disregard for the strict observance of the Sabbath. Others reviled them as "idolators" and feared that, if enfranchised, they would vote as a block, following priestly and papal instruction, thus destroying the balance between church and state that had been one legacy of the union of the Parliaments of 1707. Their presence, too, evoked the long history of religious conflicts and anti-Catholic sentiment recorded literarily in John Galt's *Ringan Gilhaize* (1823). Opposition, then, might be based on economic, religious, or even nationalistic grounds: Irish Catholics were clearly not Scots.

The *Courier* also reported frequently on the activities of the secret

Protestant organization most identified with the anti-Catholic sentiments, the Orange Society. Founded at the end of the eighteenth century in Ireland, the society's mandate was to find ways to quell the rise of Catholicism, to suppress any thoughts of emancipation, and to maintain Protestant hegemony. The *Courier,* known as "the instrument of Orangism in Scotland" (Handley, *Irish in Scotland,* 299), credited the Orange Society with safeguarding Ireland for the British Empire: "Had it not been for this sincere and Protestant brotherhood, the Established Church would have been utterly destroyed, and the darkness, bigotry, and cruelty of the Church of Rome reigning triumphantly in its stead" (12 Mar. 1835). A summary description of the society's role also appeared in the *Courier:* "In short, the Orange Institution is nothing more nor less than a strictly Loyal and Constitutional Association, founded upon a Protestant basis, banded together to support the laws, and defend the Institutions, Civil and Ecclesiastical, of the Empire; and because it has done so most effectively, and opposed the extirpation of Protestantism in Ireland, it has been maligned by Roman Catholics, and those Destructives who would like to see anarchy prevail over order, error over truth, and civil strife and bloodshed usurp the place of tranquility and social happiness" (12 Mar. 1935). These supportive words may well have been both professional and personally felt, for Motherwell himself had joined the organization in 1833.

Motherwell was not the only person outside of Ireland to be a member; there were individual lodges with their particular memberships in a number of areas where the conflict was felt personally. Glasgow, with its large numbers of Irish Catholic incomers, was one of those areas: in 1833 a gentlemen's lodge had been established—the Royal Gordon Lodge, with the Duke of Gordon as patron—with a goal of making the Orange Society an ultra-Tory or reform party (McFarland, *Protestants First,* 57–61). Members of the more typical lodges were elected; they were Protestant and loyalist, and for the established churches, the Crown, and hereditary ranks and distinctions. Furthermore, they pledged to obey the lodge and their superiors, to protect the constitution, and not to participate in political or Jacobin groups that sought to eradicate civil and religious institutions. Perhaps even more significant to the individuals involved, members pledged to help Orangemen in need, to do business with them first, to help others, and to encourage in general the adoption of Orange principles. Finally, they pledged not to divulge the signs, passwords, declarations, or activities that were prominent in the meetings without permission. An extract from the declaration of membership, which was taken while holding the Bible in the right hand, clearly articulates the ideological perspective of the group:

> I solemnly declare by this holy evidence of truth, that I am a
> believer in the Protestant faith, and that I consider the support
> of the Established Churches of Great Britain and Ireland and
> the maintenance of the rights of the Crown to be essential to
> the welfare and good government of this Kingdom: I solemnly
> declare my abhorrence of all political designs which tend to
> impair the glorious constitution given to us by our illustrious
> deliverer William the Third, of all levelling doctrines which
> have for their object to destroy the influence of hereditary rank
> and the distinctions of society, and of all revolutionary innova-
> tions which are calculated to seduce our countrymen from that
> loyal and constitutional spirit which has ever been the proud
> characteristic of the British people. (XVII 1835 *Reports/
> Committees* 605, no. 3318)

Motherwell did more than join this organization: he became one of the leaders, serving as a member of the Council of the Imperial Grand Lodge and
deputy grand master for Glasgow. Thus he redirected his anti–reform bill
crusade locally, saw the poor in the person of the Irish Catholic incomer, and
would get rid of them: they represented a "hypothetical" dilution of ethnicity,
of Scottishness, as well as a "putative" dilution of religion, the established
church.

Because of his active role in the Orange Society, Motherwell was called
to London to testify before a select committee of the House of Commons at
the end of August 1835. The committee itself was investigating the degree
to which the Orange Society was detrimental to the peace of the land as well
as the degree to which the organization had infiltrated the army. Perhaps the
committee was responding as well to the rumor that the Orange Society was
plotting to replace Princess Victoria with the Duke of Cumberland, their
English grand master, and thus secure Protestant hegemony and defeat any
ideas of Catholic emancipation (Handley, *Irish in Scotland,* 309). The committee concluded that "the existence of the Orange Lodges, their meetings,
possessions, and proceedings, have roused an opposition on the part of the
Catholics to protect themselves from the insults offered by the Orangemen"
(XVII 1835 *Reports/Committees* 605, Report XXV) and called the society's
influence "baneful and unchristian."

This was Motherwell's first trip south of the border and must certainly
have been a dislocating and stressful experience. His actual testimony yielded
little information: he explained that in his role as district master he had sought
to bring some eight or nine lodges under control, he had suspended some

lodges for not paying dues to the central office, and he had "expelled a great number of immoral and dissolute characters" (XVII 1835 *Reports/Committees* 605, no. 3352). None of the lodges with which he was personally connected, he declared, had been involved in any of the public disturbances the committee saw as clear signs of trouble. Motherwell suggested that the Orange Society was really a defensive organization, established in response to the loyal Catholic organization and its members referred to as "Ribandmen"— a parallel secret society whose members, interestingly, were denied the sacraments by the Catholic Church. He also admitted having no personal contact with the "Ribandmen," though he suggested that other members in his lodges would have been in a better position to provide information about them "because they mix with the same class of people" (XVII 1835 *Reports/Committees* 605, no. 3148), his response distancing himself from the majority of the membership, as, in fact, many members of the Glasgow Orange lodges were Protestant Irish. When asked if any of the members of the lodges under him had given money in support of the Irish Conservatives, if there had been a collection made, Motherwell's terse response, affirming one oft-repeated national characteristic, was, "No; Scotsmen are not very ready to part with their money."

The bulk of the recorded questioning of Motherwell focused on the declaration made by members. The extract below suggests the tenor of Motherwell's testimony:

> 3411. What distinction do you make between that declaration, which it appears you take in your lodge, and an oath; it is a very solemn declaration?—Yes, it is; it is such as an honourable mind would not break, I think; but still, a cunning casuist might find means for evading it.
>
> 3412. On what ground do you consider that it is not binding on a man's conscience, the same as an oath?—You do not swear to it.
>
> 3413. Do you not, in the courts of Scotland in general, hold up the hand, and make a declaration in a form like this?—Yes; but I have heard a person who made an affirmation say very differently when he held up his right hand, and swore in the presence of God.
>
> 3414. This declaration comes very near it?—It comes very near it, I confess.
>
> 3415. It commences, "I solemnly declare by this holy evidence of truth?"—In Scotland, when we swear we say, "I will depone;"

> we make a distinction between a deposition and a declaration;
> if it is on oath he depones, if it an affirmation he declares.
> 3416. Wherein is the difference?—I am not such a casuist as perhaps
> would distinguish completely the difference; I should always
> tell the truth, whether upon oath or not upon oath.

Some later biographical accounts say that Motherwell was out of his element at this hearing, that he broke down; the actual proceedings give no hint of this, and, in fact, Motherwell's testimony is not unlike that of others called before the committee. Perhaps they were all reluctant witnesses, sensing for the first time, during the hearing, the full nature of the Orange Society. Or perhaps they weren't asked the right questions; for example, Why did you join? What does the Orange Society mean to you? Joining the Orange Society may have been a mistake—as some of Motherwell's friends asserted. Motherwell might well have thought that it would offer the organic and whole community he mentally projected on the past, with its self-help, group ethos. He may well have thought that Catholicism was a threat to the status quo, to his idea of Scotland. His scant two years of membership, however, do not seem to have offered anything but distress.

However, a letter written from London to one of his colleagues, who was covering for him at the *Courier,* gives no hint that he was in any distress:

> I have to return you my most heartfelt thanks for your
> Editorial labours on the Courier. My stay here has been much
> longer than I expected or had provided for. Two days I have
> been under examination and I am detained over this day in
> order that I may correct the notes taken by the Short hand
> writer.
> With regard to London I am quite tired of it. I have seen
> a few of its sights and heard not a few of its deafening sounds.
> Sharp ears and quick eyes a stranger ought to have for if not on
> the alert he is sure to be caught in the incessant whirl of Cabs
> and Omnibusses and made a turnation smash of as the Yankee
> says. (98559)

And the subsequent, published account—one of the *Courier*'s few cases of genuine eyewitness reporting from the capitol—is clear and evenhanded, prints part of the report of the committee, and provides a history of the society. The oath, it seems, prior to 1821, included a declaration to support the

Crown only as long as it supported "Protestant ascendency" and refers to William III, Prince of Orange, as "our glorious deliverer" (19 Sept. 1835). The article goes on to report that the select committee had concluded that approval, support, and leadership for the Orange Society by nobility, such as the Duke of Gordon, and other highly placed persons, including no doubt at the bottom end of the hierarchy individuals such as William Motherwell, encouraged the ordinary person to commit to an organization that, at least theoretically, allowed them to sit as brothers with their "betters" and thus be influenced by the anti-Catholic views promulgated. The latter had led to riots, conflict, and disturbance of the peace. The article does not respond to or critique the report. Elsewhere in the same issue of the *Courier*, however, there is an article titled "Glasgow Great Protestant Meeting" that describes a meeting at a church, led by clergymen, that discussed the reasons for the rise in Orangism and Protestant anti-Catholicism: the general growth of Catholicism and the concomitant need to "rescue [them] from error"; the fear of Catholic hegemony and thus persecution of Protestants as had happened, according to the article, in Ireland; the anxiety over the influence of the priest in secular matters; and the concern that the House of Commons was giving Irish Catholics too much power. Finally, the meeting called for Protestants to unite in response to this threat (19 Sept. 1835). And in October 1835 a Protestant Association was founded in Glasgow (Handley, *Irish in Scotland,* 298).

Motherwell died some two months after his forced visit to London, and there was a natural inclination on the part of some friends and acquaintances to connect the two events—the experience testifying in London and his death. Whether or not there is a casual relationship, the London trip must certainly have called into question Motherwell's own professional pronouncements and personal beliefs, must have introduced an element of discomfort, confusion, concern. But if, as I have suggested, his anti-Catholic sentiments connected with his pro-Scottish core ideology, he probably was not in the process of changing his mind. What might be described as his central personal concern—an "ideal" Scotland—was clearly not compatible with acceptance of immigrants of a different faith.

Politics of one sort or another might be said to frame Motherwell's life. As a young man he had worked in the office of the sheriff clerk and had become acquainted with the writs and records—old and new—by copying them; later, as sheriff clerk depute, he attended trials and provided transcripts. He was familiar with the laws of the land and intricately involved in recording decisions made; he served as notary, authenticating contracts and documents. The sheriff court in Motherwell's time had stated court days and dealt with some criminal and civil concerns: bankruptcy, debt, marriage, divorce, bastardy, wills, and so on. It had administrative responsibilities, "executed all exchequer writs, accounted for Crown dues and duties in his sheriffdom, called jurors, received the writs for parliamentary elections and struck the fiars" (Whetstone, *Scottish County Government,* 25). It served as the link between the county and the government, called meetings, sent petitions and information to London, kept the peace, and called out the militia. Motherwell's involvement as record keeper kept him abreast of the laws of the land and the particular issues of Renfrew and Paisley, such as popular concerns about the slowness of justice, which led in 1838 to an inquiry: "that the delays to administer Justice in the Sheriff Court of Renfrewshire have been intolerably vexatious and oppressive to the Lieges for the last Twenty five years" (HO 102/44)—exactly the years of Motherwell's tenure as sheriff clerk depute. One of the complaints singled out the sheriff clerk's office for delays in and/or failure to transcribe materials. Motherwell himself, of course, had limited authority, working under the sheriff clerk and, at times, in his stead. Presumably this work was well remunerated, as the sheriff clerk and his office received set fees for certain activities: writing warrants or petitions and complaints; making copies of warrants to apprehend or incarcerate; issuing bonds or acts of caution; providing lists for trials; attending trials and writing extracts, recording sentencings, and summarizing the proceedings; keeping records; and writing letters on public business. Deeds and records were routinely marked "written by ———," then "collated by ———," which involved certifying that the document was correct. While often signed by the sheriff clerk, in 1819 Motherwell's name appears in this slot frequently: "W. Motherwell, Dep." In addition, many extant records in the Scottish Record Office from the Paisley Sheriff Court were written by Motherwell, as evidenced not only by the handwriting but also by the elaborate manuscriptlike capitals beginning documents, an unnecessary flourish that must have provided him with a break from the routine copying that fell to the sheriff clerk depute and that certainly had been his lot when, as a school boy, he was first employed in the office.

His first brush with public conflict and politics is said to have come in 1818, when a Radical meeting turned into a riot; the Radicals belonged to a developing movement to put pressure on the government to change, to repeal the Corn Laws, to lower taxes, to abolish various forms of privilege, and to increase wages. The Paisley weavers, in particular, had been negatively affected by many of the governmental policies and had certainly experienced a decline in living standard with the introduction of the power loom. John Galt records aspects of the weaver's radicalism in the "Paisley

AT PAISLEY, the twenty seventh day of October One thousand eight hundred and twenty seven years

In presence of Alexander Campbell Esq. Sheriff Substitute of Renfrewshire. At a Court of Inquest held in pursuance of the Act of Parliament 5. George IV. Chapter 74. entitled "An Act for ascertaining and establishing Uniformity of Weights and Measures" and the Act 3. George IV. chapter 12 entitled "An Act to prolong the term of the commencement of an Act of the last Session of Parliament for ascertaining and establishing Uniformity of Weights and Measures, and to amend the said Act."

The said day having been appointed, and previously advertised, for taking an Inquisition, in terms of the said Statutes, for the said County — There was produced the Sheriff's Precept for summoning Assizers and Witnesses, as usual in Courts held for the striking of Fiars of Grain within the Shire, with Execution of citation thereon: And the Jurors and Witnesses being called; the following persons were nominated by the Sheriff as a Jury for the purposes of the said

A characteristic record made by Motherwell

Bodies" section of *The Gathering of the West,* a delicious record of both collective and individual justifications for going to Edinburgh to see (and be seen) and welcome George IV. Damning, certainly parodying, with his amusing description, Galt provides throughout this and other work multiple perspectives that reveal the complexities of any cultural moment. Here he gives one view of the radicals:

> Among other extraordinary effects of the radical distemper which lately raged in the West, was a solemn resolution, on the part of the patriotic band of weavers' wives, to abjure tea and all other exciseable articles; in conformity to which, and actuated by the fine frenzy of the time, they seized their teapots, and marching with them in procession to the bridge, sacrificed them to the Goddess of Reform, by dashing them, with uplifted arms and an intrepid energy, over into the river,—and afterwards they ratified their solemn vows with copious libations of smuggled whiskey. (291–92)

Paisley was a center of much Radical reform sentiment and agitation; crowds gathered at meetings and got out of control, necessitating the reading of the Riot Act and the calling out of the cavalry. In the course of one such meeting, Motherwell, either because of his attire, which identified him as a well-off individual, or because of his employment in the office of the sheriff clerk, was tossed over a bridge, perhaps knocked unconscious, or at any rate roughed up. Whatever liberal leanings he was presumed to have had were said to have been thereby destroyed. That such encounters were not out of the ordinary is suggested by Handley: "Behavior of the grossest character was to be found among the mass of ordinary people. . . . Respectably-dressed persons were pelted in the street with garbage just because they looked respectable" (*Irish in Scotland,* 267). Perhaps Motherwell was one such victim.

Paisley in fact began to feel inhospitable to him: perhaps the Radical movement in general discomfited him. His eventual removal to Glasgow in 1830 to edit the *Courier* offered both personal and professional relief: he could leave behind his routine and unchallenging work as sheriff clerk depute and move to an environment in which he had greater scope for personal expression—though perhaps, as Mackenzie suggested in the obituary, as a hired and thus paid-for Tory voice. Glasgow also expanded his personal world, extended his circle of acquaintances, and gave him greater daily access to booksellers and literary companions, and he clearly delighted in being an insider to and commentator on the political events and issues of the day. That his political involvements created public controversy and even invective directed at him, that his perhaps ill-conceived activities in the secret Orange Society precipitated his questioning in London, must have been unsettling, perhaps even terminal. Given, however, his professional role and his personal predilections, these actions make sense within his perceptual framework. Politics, then, offered an overt outlet for the expression of his beliefs, deeply held, about Scotland and the ideal nature of society—within the party politic of Great Britain.

3

The Poet

Come with me, Melancholye,
We'll live like eremites holie,
In some deepe uncouthe wild
Where sunbeame never smylde:
Come with me, pale of hue,
    To some lone silent spot,
Where blossom never grewe,
      Which man hath quyte forgot.
          —Motherwell, "Melancholy," *Poems*

POETRY WRITING WAS A LIFELONG ACTIVITY for Motherwell and others of his generation: if not as natural as breathing air, clearly writing poems and songs was a culturally accepted and validated means of creativity. Motherwell availed himself of this resource while he made his living in less creatively satisfying endeavors. He may well have begun his most beloved poem, "Jeanie Morrison," when he was only fourteen; he was still writing at the time of his death, perhaps using poetry as a means of externalizing, in stereotypical ways, both universal and individual concerns: love, age/youth, death, envy, friendship, loss. *The Dictionary of National Biography* identifies him as poet before describing the other activities—professional and avocational—that fill out his experiences of record. Motherwell would have relished that identification.

Publishing first in a variety of periodical publications, based almost exclusively in the West of Scotland, in 1832 he brought together his personal choice of those and unpublished poems to make a volume titled *Poems, Narrative and Lyrical.* This was not, of course, a radical move: other poets, known and unknown, had sought to reach a wider public through such concentrated efforts, sometimes financing their publications through prior subscription. Motherwell was, to be sure, already known as poet, had a wide circle of literary and publishing friends, and was thus nicely situated to initiate a more formal, commercial publication: his volume was in fact published by his friend David Robertson, the Glasgow bookseller and literary patron.

But writing poetry was only part of Motherwell's literary activity; he was in a more general way involved in a crusade to raise the stature of poetry—in large measure because it was so meaningful to him. He saw literature as something that "embellishes the mind with innumerable graces[,] softens all its harshnesses—all its asperities and refines and corrects the taste"; poetry is lasting (Robertson 1210). The extensive manuscript records of his thoughts are filled with random rhymes and lines of poetry, recorded undoubtedly because they struck a chord, expressed a feeling or sentiment in a significantly memorable way. Over and over again, he underlines its personal significance. In his poem "To Poetry" he wrote, "O Poetry thou charm of life / My fortune, friend, my all my wife" (Robertson 1212). And in what must surely have been his personal belief, he quotes from "Twelfth Night" in the preface to his review of Peter Buchan's *Gleanings* (*Paisley Advertiser,* 26 Aug. 1826):

Now good Cesario, but that piece of song,
That old and antique song we had last night,
Me thought it did relieve my passion much;
More than light airs and recollected terms
Of these most brisk and giddy-paced times.

While the stated purpose of the Literary Institution, to which he belonged as a young man, was "to promote especially among its members, the theoretical and practical knowledge of literature" (R.L. Crawford, *Literary Activity*, 75), he clearly recognized that not everyone shared his appreciation of poetry. In the *Paisley Magazine* he commented that "nobody reads poetry now-a-days with comfort or edification: folks have got so bitten with Political Economy and Mechanics' Institutions, and Libraries of Useful Knowledge, and all the valuable trumpery and fiddle-de-dees of Word Philosophy and Bastard Science, that they have no leisure to brood over the flimsy cobweb sweepings of any poet or poetaster's cranium whatsoever" (19). This is another articulation of Motherwell's feeling out of step with the times.

Nonetheless, he persisted in promoting poetry. He played, sometimes humorously, with the differences between prose and poetry, as in several passages from *Renfrewshire Characters and Scenery:* "Prose is a reptile that crawls heavily; / But eagle Poesy mounts to the sky." And he could write, with tongue in cheek: "*Rhymes, like Flounces* and *Trimmings,* took the market well just now" or justify the extensive and witty prose notes to accompany rather bland descriptive poetry by saying, "The flighty and mercurial nature of Poesy requireth some ballast of substantial Prose to preserve it in *Equilibrio* otherwise it hath a tendency to degenerate into flat nonsense, or to rise up into stupend extravagance, yea, as one may say, into a sort of Lunatic exaltation fearful to behold"(verse 12, n.p., iv). Here he allowed the current antipoetry sentiments to provide a raison d'être for his antiquarian comments: fortunately, there were friends who shared his play and appreciated his fun.

Beneath such comments, however, he was deadly serious about poetry, which he saw as "the first vehicle of human thought" (Robertson 28, 1210). Such assertions link him to literary theorists of a generation earlier—Blair, Duff, Ferguson, Monboddo, Blackwell—who "maintained that poetry had been instinctive and emotional in origin, and coeval, or almost coeval, with the birth of language itself" (Abrams, *Mirror and the Lamp,* 81). Furthermore, he saw that poetry—particularly early poetry, and the ballads he printed in *Minstrelsy: Ancient and Modern,* might be taken as exemplary representatives—as an extremely important cultural and national resource. Balladry, for example, was not only "Primeval poesy of our native land" (the *Day*) but provided evidence of history, of the manners and customs of the past, much as Dr. Johnson claimed for Shakespeare: literature "holds up to his readers a faithful mirrour of manners and of life" (Abrams, *Mirror and the Lamp,* 32). Additionally, he suggested that early poetry was integrally connected with music: "All poetry hath music and all music partakes somewhat of the nature of poetry. They are twinborn and coeval. As the soul is joined to the body so are these two one" (Robertson 1210). In his random statements about poetry in general, its earliest forms, he was probably not expressing a studied opinion but found himself recapitulating some of the prevailing literary views.

His affirmation of poetry is most evident in his publishing endeavors: he played a central role in a number of editions of poetry. In 1820 he was involved in the making of *The Harp of Renfrewshire,* a celebration of regional and local poetry. And in this local chauvinism he was partaking of a widespread phenomenon: "Local attachment can be found everywhere in Scottish history" (Hart, *Scottish Novel,* 1). Motherwell wrote the introductory essay to the collection in which he offered a chronological history of the poets, the Makers, of the region, making it clear that many local and minor bards deserved notice. Paisley and environs were indeed known as great incubation grounds for poets and poetry, a recognized phenomenon articulated rather humorously in 1832 in the *Day* when, prefacing a work of poetry, the "editor" wrote that Paisley "has now, in fact, become as famous for stanzas as for silks" (247). In the *Harp* Motherwell had, of course, taken a more serious and laudatory tone: "The brilliant era—the golden age of

Renfrewshire song, now opens upon us in the persons of [Alexander] Wilson and Tannahill. Both have contributed not a little to our stock of native lyric poetry; and while our language lasts, and music hath any charm, their names will be remembered with enthusiasm and transmitted to ages more remote with the accumulated applauses of time" (xxvii). This local chauvinism showed signs of national concern/pride as well when he talked of language: "Since the Union of the Kingdoms how beneficial soever this event has been in other respects, the language of Scotland has been subjected to peculiar advantages. No longer written in public deeds, or spoken in those assemblies which fix the standard of national taste, its influence has gradually declined, notwithstanding the occasional efforts of the Muse to rescue it from total oblivion" (Robertson 28/1210). Already, in this pronouncement written when he was twenty-three, Motherwell reveals a sense of place and his opposition to change as he supports local poetry ensconced in the national language.

Several years later, he publicly championed another kind of poetry, traditional balladry, with his 1827 work *Minstrelsy: Ancient and Modern.* He saw the ballads as evolutionarily prior or early written literature and urged that they be collected and preserved for both their historical and literary importance. And his views on this early national poetry were spelled out in a lengthy historical and critical introduction to be discussed in the next chapter. In 1828, Motherwell published another work devoted to poetry, in thirty copies only, *Certain Curious Poems....*: he claimed to have found it in the sheriff clerk's office where he worked. Purported to be the work of a late-seventeenth-, early-eighteenth-century sheriff substitute of Renfrewshire, one James M'Alpie, the introductory remarks point to the slight poetic value of the poems and suggest that their local and political nature make the poems obscure and difficult to understand. Nonetheless their publication "swells the catalogue of small versifyers" of a period "peculiarly barren, so far as regards Scotland, in names of poetic celebrity." And the book could become a rare item in the book collections of fellow enthusiasts—like Motherwell himself.

Once he became editor of the *Glasgow Courier* in 1830, one of the first things he did was to expand the literary coverage—through reviews of literary works and, in particular, the printing of poetry. Poetry (and critical editorial comment) was given pride of place on the front page and was printed in a larger type. The poetry printed was not just local or national, but included English poets, contemporary poets. As early as 1828 in the *Paisley Magazine,* Motherwell had made fun of a hopeless provincial who was not aware of poetry or the range of poets, having him comment, "[T]hen they got some decent folk named in their mouths called Byron and Scott, Southey and Coleridge, Wordsworth and Wilson, Jeffrey and Lockhard, &c" (467). In the *Courier,* he sought to ameliorate that ignorance, printing poems by Scott, Hogg, Leigh Hunt, John Galt, Robert Southey, and several recent poems—"A Highland Hut" and "Mossgiel"—by Wordsworth. He also printed his own work and, in the fashion of the day, memorial poems on the deaths of poets. Walter Scott, for example, died during Motherwell's tenure at the *Courier,* and Scott's death was marked both by obituary and poem; and the pages of the paper were outlined in black, a practice begun as recently as 1817 on the death of Princess Charlotte (Colley, *Britons,* 220).

Motherwell also participated in the *Whistle-Binkie* series, begun in 1832, often critically disparaged as sentimental and mediocre literature, reflective of a degraded literary sensibility (Gifford, *History of Scottish Literature,* Edwin Morgan, chap. 18). But the works' intent was to circulate contemporary literature, and thus it represents another activity in support of native writing. More significant, canonically, was his involvement at the end of his life preparing a new edition of Burns's poems with James Hogg: *The Works of Robert Burns* (Glasgow: Archibald Fullarton, 1834–36); biographical accounts suggest that a proof sheet of a note for that work was in his coat pocket at the time of his death (Ry II d 17). The "Address to Readers," after page xii, offers a somewhat flowery summary of what is to follow: "To the whole will be appended a concise, luminous, and singularly interesting Memoir of the Poet's Life, from the pen of the Ettrick Shepherd. The Poems and Letters will also be accompanied with Critical Comments and Elucidations by the same gifted individual, while much curious, literary, biographical, and anecdotical information will be supplied by Mr. William Motherwell, whose poetic genius and extensive acquaintances with all that relates to Scottish poetry and song, have been signally evinced by the high excellence of his original poetry, and the distinguished ability with which he has edited the Minstrelsy of the olden time." Motherwell's notes, presumably marked "WM," identify personages, annotate passages, define things, give received critical views (those of Curie, of Wordsworth), provide historical references, connect Burns to earlier poets, and often provide information on the location of letters and material not earlier published. Occasionally, too, Motherwell adds a critical comment, as on the stanza from "Halloween"— which would have been of particular interest to Motherwell because of its description of traditional practices around that calendar custom—beginning "Whyles owre a linn the burnie play'd": "This stanza presents one of the most beautiful poetic pictures that ever was drawn; it is a perfect gem" (1:107). A look at the verse, number twenty-five in the poem, suggests something about Motherwell's aesthetic appreciation:

Whyles owre a linn the burnie plays,
  As thro' the glen it wimpl't;
Whyles round a rocky scar it strays;
  Whyles in a wiel it dimpl't;
Whyles glitter'd to the nightly rays,
  Wi' bickerin, dancin dazzle;
Whyles cooket underneath the braes,
  Below the spreading hazle
    Unseen that night
      (Kinsley, *Poems and Songs of Robert Burns* 1:161–62).

Elsewhere, commenting on Burns and traditional song, he offers a more critical view, no doubt again derived from his own thorough study of the field: "the poet has had little antiquarian discrimination in distinguishing what were the genuine portions from the modern interpolations which so frequently, and so very inartificially, occur in most of our old Scottish Traditionary ballads and songs" (Hogg and Motherwell, *Works of Robert Burns* 4:212–13). Motherwell's collaborative project with Hogg on an edition of the work of Scotland's national poet suggests that he held a position of some prominence in the literary and publishing world of the time. Motherwell had anticipated preparing editions of other Scottish poetry as well, particularly that of fellow Paisley poet Robert Tannahill; in fact, he may well have inherited materials from his early Paisley friend R.A. Smith, which in turn provided the nucleus for the edition subsequently prepared by another friend, P.A. Ramsay.

Support for poetry and poets and the writing of poetry might be identified as Motherwell's true métier. Everywhere we look we see him connected with literature, with poets: he knew a number of local poets, such as John Goldie and Robert Allan of Kilbarchan. William Kennedy, who preceded him as editor of the *Paisley Advertiser,* too, was known as a poet. John Wilson/Christopher North, the acerbic, conservative editor of "Maga"—*Blackwood's Magazine*—was an older contemporary of his and also hailed from Paisley; and it is possible that Wilson served as an implicit role model for him. Certainly Motherwell's *Paisley Magazine* was intended to offer those in the West of Scotland, in the environs of Paisley, a similar intellectual feast, including poetry, reviews, and imaginative literature. Motherwell was a member of the Paisley Burns Club, where commemorative poems were a part of the yearly round of celebrations. Literature, poetry in particular, was a much more quotidian affair for Motherwell and his circle than we are predisposed to imagine.

Motherwell has his buffoonish character Baillie Pirnie report that "books are a sort of passport to worldly immortality" (*Memoirs of a Paisley Baillie*). Clearly lots of would-be poets felt this way and sought to bring together their poems in books, hoping for just that sort of durability. The publication of *Poems Narrative and Lyrical* in 1832 and various posthumous editions of his poetry (the 1846 edition added twenty new poems, the 1849, sixty-eight additional works) were undoubtedly the sine qua non for the persistence of Motherwell's recognition as poet. So Baillie Pirnie was right on this one. Of course, among his friends in Paisley and Glasgow, Motherwell had had a reputation as poet from his youth. Charles Hutcheson, in a letter of 1846, describes Motherwell's character and versifying abilities: "In a small party in private he commanded universal admiration. The gift he possessed of extempore composition on any theme introduced commanded . . . admiration" (Robertson 1662). Motherwell's own letters suggest less facility, perhaps more anxiety over creation. In a letter to his good friend R.A. Smith, he confessed his difficulty in writing a poem to accompany a tune Smith intended to include in *The Scottish Minstrel,* how he smoked cigars until he was sick—hoping for a Minervan birth—but to no avail. On another occasion, however, he seemed more successful in commanding his creative powers: he had promised a poem for the *Visitor* and an emissary was sent to Paisley to fetch it. The poem had yet to be written. Motherwell welcomed his courier, gave him both his bed and board, retiring himself to write the poem. Successful, he is said to have succumbed to sleep with books for a pillow. And he certainly produced a number of occasional and memorial poems, including one to his *Paisley Advertiser* predecessor and fellow poet, which appeared in that newspaper.

Motherwell's first publishing venues were in the periodical press—newspapers and magazines that proliferated during his lifetime. He wrote as well for various musical collections, producing songs to order for particular tunes. His work in this vein appeared in R.A. Smith's and George Thomson's publications. In fact, his song "Clerk Richard & Maid Margaret," set to a tune by R.A. Smith, was first published in the *Enquirer* and subsequently republished in Thomson's *Select Melodies of Scotland* in 1823. As early as 1830, however, he had begun to think about bringing together some of his published and unpublished work in a book; he seems to have had thirty poems set in print. There is only one extant copy, at the Paisley Central Library (R631); the title, "Poetic Underwoods," and a final stanza are handwritten. The dedication was to his friend William Lucas, a Paisley doctor. Why this work was never formally published remains a mystery. The year 1830 was, of course, busy: toward the end of it he was serving as editor for both the

Paisley Advertiser and the *Glasgow Courier* and presumably commuting between Paisley and Glasgow. He had his hands full; perhaps publishing his small book of poetry was not at the top of his list of things to do. In 1832, once he was nicely settled in Glasgow, involved in a rich round of professional and literary activities, the project was resuscitated, in much-expanded form.

Motherwell's poetry itself offers further evidence of his antiquarian leanings, his interest in and appreciation of earlier styles and contents. In a series of poems with Norse names, he imaginatively evokes the Scandinavian presence in Scotland; and he adopts the technique of dual descriptors or kennings of Old English and Eddic literatures. The narratives recounted are not, as some have presumed, based on the Eddas, but rather only refer to the Norse milieu through names: in his introduction to the volume he asserts that they "are intended to be a faint shadowing forth of something like the form and spirit of Norse poetry." Since he had *Snorro Sturlusson* in Icelandic/Swedish and Latin (1679) in his library, it is probably safe to assume that the martial and historical accounts of past valor provided inspiration for his own projective imaginings. "The Sword Chant of Thorstein Raudi" offers a long list of tributes to the sword, to the martial and manly pursuits, which are the be-all and end-all for the speaker. Each stanza is neatly concluded with a kenning that sums up the value of the sword: it enables the conquering of land, gives its wielder power, joy, fame. Thus the sword is the author of death and destruction, which gladdens Raudi's heart and provokes the song—that is, the poem:

> 'Tis not the grey hawk's flight
>   O'er mountain and mere;
> 'Tis not the fleet hound's course
>   Tracking the deer;
> 'Tis not the light hoof print
>   Of black steed or grey,
> Though sweltering it gallop
>   A long summer's day;
> Which mete forth the Lordships
>   I challenge as mine;
> Ha! Ha! 'tis the good brand
> I clutch in my strong hand,
> That can their broad marches
>   And numbers define.
> LAND GIVER! I kiss thee.

Dull builders of houses,
    Base tillers of earth,
Gaping, ask me what lordships
    I owned at my birth;
But the pale fools wax mute
    When I point with my sword
East, west, north, and south,
    Shouting, "There am I Lord!"
Wold and waste, town and tower,
    Hill, valley, and stream,
Trembling, bow to my sway
In the fierce battle fray,
When the star that rules Fate, is
    This falchion's red gleam.
MIGHT GIVER! I kiss thee.

I've heard great harps sounding,
    In brave bower and hall,
I've drank the sweet music
    That bright lips let fall,
I've hunted in greenwood,
    And heard small birds sing;
But away with this idle
    And cold jargoning;
The music I love, is
    The shout of the brave,
The yell of the dying,
The scream of the flying,
When this arm wields Death's sickle,
    And garners the grave.
JOY GIVER! I kiss thee.

Far isles of the ocean
    Thy lightning have known,
And wide o'er the main land
    Thy horrors have shone.
Great sword of my father,
    Stern joy of his hand,
Thou hast carved his name deep on
    The stranger's red strand,

And won him the glory
    Of undying song.
Keen cleaver of gay crests,
Sharp piercer of broad breasts,
Grim slayer of heroes,
    And scourge of the strong.
FAME GIVER! I kiss thee.

In a love more abiding
    Than that the heart knows,
For maiden more lovely
    Than summer's first rose,
My heart's knit to thine,
    And lives but for thee;
In dreamings of gladness,
    Thou'rt dancing with me,
Brave measures of madness
    In some battle-field,
Where armour is ringing,
And noble blood springing,
And cloven, yawn helmet,
    Stout hauberk and shield.
DEATH GIVER! I kiss thee.

The smile of a maiden's eye,
    Soon may depart;
And light is the faith of
    Fair woman's heart;
Changeful as light clouds,
    And wayward as wind,
Be the passions that govern
    Weak woman's mind.
But thy metal's as true
    As its polish is bright;
When ills wax in number,
Thy love will not slumber,
But, starlike, burns fiercer,
    The darker the night.
HEART GLADENER! I kiss thee.

My kindred have perished
    By war or by wave—
Now, childless and sireless,
    I long for the grave.
When the path of our glory
    Is shadowed in death,
With me thou wilt slumber
    Below the brown heath;
Thou wilt rest on my bosom,
    And with it decay—
While harps shall be ringing,
And Scalds shall be singing
The deeds we have done in
    Our old fearless day.
SONG GIVER! I kiss thee.

The poem is at once backward looking—to the Norse Eddas—as well as an expression of Motherwell's own appreciation of such male pursuits as battle, the wielding of a sword. This is a bit ironic, for his own activities were more pacific and desk-bound, though perhaps his pen was his sword, certainly at the end of his life. Yet his own collection of armaments and battle accouterments, and his youthful participation in military groups, underline his fascination with battle.

Adopting the romantic interest in the poet, in poetry as a kind of reflection of the poet, it is easy to see Motherwell's poetry as in some ways revelatory, not so much telling of specifics of his life but referencing things of concern, such as the warlike, manly realms in his "Norse" poems, or the recollection of bygone days in "Jeanie Morrison," or the imitation of traditionary ballads in "Clerk Richard & Maid Margaret." "Jeanie Morrison"—a reverie on perfect companionship remembered, childhood perfection, an ideal idyll, lost—is often identified as Motherwell's best work:

I've wandered east, I've wandered west,
    Through mony a weary way;
But never, never can forget
    The luve o' life's young day!
The fire that's blawn on Beltane e'en,
    May weel be black gin Yule;
But blacker fa' awaits the heart
    Where first fond luve grows cule.

O dear, dear Jeanie Morrison,
    The thochts o' bygane years
Still fling their shadows ower my path,
    And blind my een wi' tears:
They blind my een wi' saut, saut tears,
    And sair and sick I pine,
As memory idly summons up
    The blithe blinks o' langsyne.

'Twas then we luvit ilk ither weel,
    'Twas then we twa did part;
Sweet time—sad time! Twa bairns at scule,
    Twa bairns, and but ae heart!
'Twas then we sat on ae laigh bink,
    To leir ilk ither lear;
And tones, and looks, and smiles were shed,
    Remembered evermair.

I wonder, Jeanie, aften yet,
    When sitting on that bink,
Cheek touchin' cheek, loof lock'd in loof,
    What our wee hearts could think?
When baith bent doun ower ae braid page,
    Wi' ae buik on our knee,
Thy lips were on thy lesson, but
    My lesson was in thee.

Oh, mind ye how we hung our heads,
    How cheeks brent red wi' shame,
Whene'er the scule-weans laughin' said,
    We cleek'd thegither hame?
And mind ye o' the Saturdays,
    (The scule then skail't at noon),
When we ran aff to speel the braes—
    The broomy braes o' June?

My head rins round and round about,
    My heart flows like a sea,
As ane by ane the thochts rush back
    O' scule-time and o' thee.

Oh, mornin' life! Oh, mornin' luve!
    Oh lichtsome days and lang,
When hinnied hopes around our hearts
    Like simmer blossoms sprang!

Oh mind ye, luve, how aft we left
    The deavin' dinsome toun,
To wander by the green burnside,
    And hear its waters croon?
The simmer leaves hung ower our heads,
    The flowers burst round our feet,
And in the gloamin o' the wood,
    The throssil whusslit sweet;

The throssil whusslit in the wood,
    The burn sang to the trees,
And we with Nature's heart in tune,
    Concerted harmonies;
And on the knowe abune the burn,
    For hours thegither sat
In silentness o' joy, till baith
    Wi' very gladness grat.

Ay, ay, dear Jeanie Morrison,
    Tears trinkled doun your cheek,
Like dew-beads on a rose, yet nane
    Had ony power to speak!
That was a time, a blessed time,
    When hearts were fresh and young,
When freely gushed all feelings forth,
    Unsyllabled—unsung!

I marvel, Jeanie Morrison,
    Gin I hae been to thee
As closely twined wi' earliest thochts,
    As ye had been to me?
Oh! Tell me gin their music fills
    Thine ear as it does mine;
Oh! say gin e'er your heart grows grit
    Wi' dreamings o' langsyne?

> I've wandered east, I've wandered west,
>   I've borne a weary lot;
> But in my wanderings, far or near,
>   Ye never were forgot.
> The fount that first burst frae this heart,
>   Still travels on its way;
> And channels deeper as it rins,
>   The luve o' life's young day.
>
> O dear, dear Jeanie Morrison,
>   Since we were sindered young,
> I've never seen your face, nor heard
>   The music o' your tongue;
> But I could hug all wretchedness,
>   And happy could I die,
> Did I but ken your heart still dreamed
>   O' bygane days and me!

This paean to a young schoolmate certainly has an air of poignancy about it, especially when seen against his life: a childhood relationship recalled and identified as perhaps the dominant relationship (at least admitted) of his life. But the poem expresses as well the universal wish that those with whom one has shared moments will remember those times with similar attachment; it is probably this quality that has made the poem so appealing.

Another perspective on love and relationship is expressed in his song/ imitation of balladry, "Clerk Richard and Maid Margaret," with music by R.A. Smith; this work clearly reflects his appreciation of a kind of early poetry:

> There were two who love each other
>   For many years, 'till hate did start;
> And yet they never quite could smother
>   The former love that warm'd their heart:
> And both did love, and both did hate;
> Till both fulfill'd the will of fate.
>
> Years after, and the maid did marry
>   One that her heart had ne'er approv'd;
> Nor longer could Clerk Richard tarry,
>   Where he had lost all that he lov'd:

To foreign lands he reckless went,
To nourish love, hate, discontent.

A word, an idle word of folly,
    Had spill'd their love when it was young;
And hatred, grief, and melancholy,
    In either heart as idly sprung:
And yet they loved, and hate did wane,
And much they wished to meet again.

Of Richard still is Margaret dreaming,
    His image lingered in her breast;
And oft at midnight to her seeming
    Her former lover stood confest;
And shedding on her bosom tears,
The bitter wrecks of happier years.

Where'er he went by land or ocean,
    Still Richard sees Dame Margaret there;
And every throb and kind emotion
    His bosom knew were felt for her;
And never new love hath he cherished,
The power to love with first love perished.

Homeward is Clerk Richard sailing,
    An altered man from him of old;
His hate had changed to bitter wailing,
    And love resumed its wonted hold
Upon his heart, which yearned to see
The haunts and loves of infancy.

He knew her faithless,—nathless ever
    He loved her though no more his own;
Nor could he proudly now dissever
    The chain that round his heart was thrown;
He loved her, without hope, yet true,
And sought her, but to say adieu.

For even in parting there is pleasure,
    A sad sweet joy that wrings the soul;

And there is grief surpassing measure,
    That will not bide nor brook controul;
And yet a formal fond leave taking,
Does ease the heart albeit by breaking.

Oh! There is something in the feeling
    And trembling faulter of the hand;
And something in the tear down stealing,
    And voice so broken, yet so bland;
And something in the word farewell,
Which worketh like a powerfull spell.

These lovers met and never parted;
    They met as lovers wont to do,
Who meet when both are broken-hearted,
    To breathe a last and long adieu.
Pale Margaret wept, Clerk Richard sighed,
And in each other's arms they died.

In *The Select Melodies of Scotland* version, R.A. Smith's music is included, and the text bears the epigram:

A man must nedes love maugre his hed,
He may not fleen it though he should be ded.—Chaucer

No one would mistake this for a traditional ballad of the kind Motherwell included in his *Minstrelsy,* and yet he has picked up on the fragility of love and the inevitability of death that unites the severed lovers in the end— much as the ballad commonplace that has the rose and the briar grow from the lovers' graves and form a "true love knot." And lost love was and remains a viable topic, embedded as it is in the human condition. Motherwell's responses were not remarkable, but representative.

Knowing of his preference for the past, his muted concern for an earlier golden age, his hope for organic communities, we can "read" his poetry as being yet another articulation of his dissatisfaction with the present. That said, it is important to add that Motherwell was not the only person writing ballad imitations or looking to "auld lang syne" or using references to the Norse. William Tennant's "Thane of Fife," written in 1822, for example, deals with the Norse invasions. What we see then in Motherwell's poetic

"Clerk Richard & Maid Margaret," from R.A. Smith, *The Select Melodies of Scotland.*

output is a person very much writing out of the current topics/styles/Zeit-geist, not a poetic innovator.

He undoubtedly longed to be judged a worthy poet, something more than a run-of-the-mill local versifier. The publication of a volume of poetry was his way of marshaling evidence in support of his pretensions. It seems, at least contemporaneously, to have been a successful ploy. Understandably there were local, Scottish reviews, many from the West of Scotland: the notice in *Tait's,* an Edinburgh periodical (1832, 2:540), reads, "Mr Motherwell's stray pieces, which already enjoy a most extensive and genial kind of popularity, are here collected into a handsome small volume, well fitted to occupy an honoured place in any select modern cabinet collection of favorite authors. It is needless to say how well we conceive this volume entitled to a distinguished nook." And the *Paisley Advertiser* took notice of this publication of its former editor: "Mr Motherwell promises to be a distinguished ornament of Scottish literature. His poem of 'Jeannie Morrison' is beautifully natural, the most elegantly expressed, the most replete with tender, mournful association, that we have read for a long time" (15 Dec. 1832, 1). But certainly the notice that must have most pleased Motherwell appeared in *Blackwood's.* Fulsome and positive, the review essay was undoubtedly written by Wilson, Motherwell's fellow townsperson with whom he shared conservative views. Giving the publishers as David Robertson, Glasgow; Oliver and Boyd, Edinburgh; Longman and Company, London (1833), Maga notes that "Mr Motherwell has for some years been winning his way to public favour and fame" through publication in miscellanies; that Motherwell is not part of a group; that he is provincial but not proud; that his genius is equal to that of Tennyson. Somewhat later in the essay, Motherwell is compared to a poet closer to home, favorably: referring to "Jeanie Morrison," Wilson writes that "the Pathetic—another kind of poetry in which Motherwell excels. Yea—excels . . . nor is he here inferior—we say it advisedly—to Burns" ("Motherwell's Poems," 674). Dividing Motherwell's work into three categories—war songs, lyrical pieces, and descriptions of nature—the review suggests that the poet "has been led by the natural bent of his genius to the old haunts of inspiration, the woods and glens of his native country, and his ears delight to drink the music of her old songs." Of his Norse-inspired poems, the reviewer writes that "The Sword Chant of Thorstein Raudi" is "already not a little famous—for we have heard it chanted by one who troubles not his head about poetry, but who clove skull-cap and skull of more than one cuiraissier at Waterloo" (ibid., 670, 672). Motherwell's poems, then, do what poetry should do: "[T]he better you know true poetry, the better you love it, and then best of all, when you have gotten it by heart.

Then it becomes part and parcel of yourself." Concluding an extended essay, the reviewer suggests, "'Tis one of the functions of the Poet to awaken such reminiscences"; on that note, Maga bids "Mr Motherwell and his delightful volume farewell" (ibid., 668, 681). Such notice of his work was clearly a feather in Motherwell's cap.

He continued to be remembered as a poet even in death. There was a memorial poem that includes the lines

> None saw his grim form coming, and none heard his pale horse tread—
> Alas! They see and hear them now, for MOTHERWELL is dead!
> And to yon blue o'erhanging arch, that shines celestial fair,
> His star-like spirit is away to shine for ever there! (Ry II d 17)

The *Paisley Advertiser* printed one of Motherwell's last poems on 20 May 1837, prefaced with the report that a "beautiful female had been observed planting the snow-drop and the primrose on the grave of Motherwell," fulfilling a wish expressed in one of his last poems that he be remembered in death. Some sixteen years after his death, a monument was finally raised over the site of his grave, financed with contributions from friends and admirers from near and far (Boston, New York, New Orleans). Kennedy wrote the inscription; Fillans did the sculpture depicting scenes from Motherwell's poetry (now alas disintegrated); and the cornerstone was filled with books and manuscripts, including Dr. Strang's census, *The Rise and Progress of Glasgow,* an abridgement of Cleland's statistical tables, the Western Supplement to Oliver & Boyds's *Almanac,* Glasgow papers for the day on which the cornerstone was set, and the names of the Paisley, Glasgow, and Edinburgh committees responsible for the monument and ceremony.

Yet privately, with the distance of time and occasion for reflection, enthusiasm for Motherwell's poetry, even among his closest friends and admirers, began to wane. Marginal comments on various manuscripts, made by subsequent editors of his work—P.A. Ramsay and James McConechy—are suggestive. Ramsay's are somewhat tame: "considerable pathos in this piece"; "good drinking catch, but rather artificial"; "sweet toned" (Robertson 5/1221). McConechy, however, complains—"[T]o tell you the truth, it is waery work, and consumes a plaguey lot of time"—though he still has an occasional kind word: "The poem beginning 'one dark and snowy morning': Motherwell never wrote anything finer or more plaintive than this" (Robertson 6/1223: 1, 2). In a letter to the bookseller/publisher of Motherwell's 1832 collection, Alex Campbell expressed the opinion that publishing materials as yet unpublished would only detract from Motherwell's

reputation; he went on to suggest that "there being many stately and impos-
ing verses which, when carefully analyzed and reduced to their natural elements, are discovered to contain nothing—deaf nuts—soap bubbles, gay
with prismatic hues, but empty within" (Robertson 6/1223: 4). But Charles
Hutcheson, in a memorial letter written in 1846, recalls that at least some of
Motherwell's poetry had an impact: "[F]ew compliments pleased him
[Motherwell] more than when a friend told him he had walked from Paisley
to Glasgow with a weaver, who being asked if he had ever read any of
Motherwell's verses replied—'oh aye—Jeanie Morison is battered up on
the back of the workshop door'" (Robertson 4/1662). And R. Shelton
MacKenzie, writing from London on 10 January 1847, also offers a laudatory memory: "His Jeannie Morrison is one of the sweetest lyrics I ever
knew, and I confess that I have never been able to read 'My heid is like to
rend Willie' without feeling the tears in my eyes, & the globus hystericus in
my throat" (Robertson 4/1662).

In 1897 there was a centenary celebration, and John Kent wrote a commemorative ode, for which he won five pounds, beginning

And one there is whom we would fain recall
    Back through the vista of departed years,
To see his face, or hear his accents fall
    Upon our listening, sympathetic ears.
Sweet Motherwell! Thy very name endears
    Thee to our hearts. And we have loved thee long,
Thy strain doth move to tenderness and tears,
    And checks the thought of selfishness and wrong
Thee, gentle bard, we bless for thy pure gift of song.
                           (*Motherwell Centenary*)

The 1890 edition of *Whistle-Binkie* commented that "Jeanie Morrison" and
"My heid is like to rend Willie" matched Burns in "tenderness and pathos."
Despite the fact that his name was linked with Burns and Tennyson, and
elsewhere with Gray, Southey, Wordsworth, and Coleridge, George Douglas at the end of the nineteenth century wrote, "Strictly speaking, Motherwell
is perhaps less a 'Famous Scot' than an interesting phenomenon in Scottish
letters" (*James Hogg,* 129). John H. Ingram slightly amended that assess-
ment, affirming Motherwell's position as a leading minor poet: "[H]e has
enriched British literature with poems no lover of true poesy will willingly
let perish" (Miles, *Poets and Poetry,* 188). And W.M. Parker, writing in the
Scots Magazine for 1935, comments, "Though in his original work

Motherwell is definitely a minor poet of distinction, he was also a pioneer in adapting old poetic material to new forms" (150).

Three other notices of Motherwell deserve mentioning. Edgar Allan Poe, in an essay on short poems that appeal, concludes with Motherwell's "Song of the Cavalier," which presumably met the criteria under consideration: it "excites, by elevating the soul." C.H. Herford in *The Age of Wordsworth* (1922) identified Motherwell as "a song-writer of more various accomplishments and even finer gifts" than Robert Tannahill and proclaimed his Norse poems "stirring ballads . . . worthy compeers of the Danish *Kjoempeviser* themselves" (197–98). In the same year Raymond Havens (*The Influence of Milton on English Poetry*) suggested a link between Milton's "Penseroso" and Motherwell's "Melancholye": "[I]t is pleasant to think of these lines, with their fresh fragrance, as the last and one of the loveliest flowers which the rather thorny octosyllabic movement put forth" (476). Indeed, Motherwell had two editions of Milton in his extensive library, one dated 1809, the other 1835; whether the influence is real is another question.

For some hundred years after his death, then, and after the publication of his 1832 edition, Motherwell had some currency as a poet and did in fact stand out from the run-of-the mill poets of his time, as C.R. Johnson recently suggested: "Burns and Byron are enormous influences. Scott, Southey, Campbell, Crabbe, Barton, Tannahill, L.E.L., Allan Cunningham, Bloomfield, Polwhele, Robert Anderson, William Motherwell and others were apparently quite well known to their contemporaries" (preface). Now his name is virtually absent from the nineteenth-century literary canon: he seems, then, to have been very much of his time. He was just another minor poet, but he played an active role in the early-nineteenth-century literary field—encouraging literary activity and supporting poetic production. His own endeavors were infused with and inspired by antiquarian sentiments, were filled with longings for a lost world. In this sense they form a part with other aspects of his life—his opposition, for example, to the Reform Bill of 1832—and would suggest a kind of ideological coherence. Thus William Motherwell's life and concerns, including poetry, offer one particular way into the complex and fascinating world of early-nineteenth-century Scotland.

The Ballad Errantry

The fruit of my Errantry in an obscure path hath been this little quarto.

—William Motherwell, *Minstrelsy: Ancient and Modern*

DURING THE EIGHTEENTH AND NINETEENTH CENTURIES, considerable interest in traditional balladry and song was exhibited throughout western Europe. In Scotland, as elsewhere, this interest was both antiquarian and nationalistic; it was certainly influenced by the unions of the Scottish crown and parliament with those of England and the subsequent sense of national loss felt by some. And certainly a healthy percentage of people probably felt no loss and had no opinion on the matter. But for those who did, and for those who were concerned about Scotland's loss of nationhood, loss of individuality, and loss of identity, ballads and songs, poetry in the vernacular (or in Scots Gaelic), became tangible evidences of Scotland as a cultural entity with a literature and a history, often seen as embedded in that literature. So there was a movement—loose-knit, certainly, but observable—to valorize things Scottish. The interest in Burns in Edinburgh after the publication of the Kilmarnock edition (1786) clearly derived from this form of romantic nationalism; the fascination with Macpherson's *Ossian* (publication began in 1760) exhibits another strain of the movement. The focus on ballads and songs, still transmitted orally and thus not in any real way corrupted by anglicization, or by perceived cultural change, represents another facet of this concern for preserving, before it was obliterated, evidences of a Scottish cultural heritage.

The Scottish interest in traditionary material offers a slightly different twist on the usual idea of romantic nationalism—the use of oral songs and other verbal artistic forms to assert and affirm the united roots of a contemporaneously politically divided people. Under this scenario, the songs are evidentiary proof of some prior unity and are to become the basis for forging a future state and those essential, supporting ideological tools, language and literature. The language of the oral material is thought to be closer to the ur language, uncorrupted by "divisive," separating dialects and usages; the oral literature is thought to provide the ideal basis for a national literature, having embedded within itself some ineffable essence of the "real" unity of a group of people. This form of romantic nationalism seeks to create a nation-state, using oral literature as one justification, one evidence of some earlier unity. And perhaps the term "romantic" in this formulation implies a fantasylike idea of some past that never existed as raison d'être for a hypothetical new nation-state: Germany, the philosophical statements of Herder, the songs of Goethe, the subsequent study of the German language and the collection of märchen by Jacob and Wilhelm Grimm provide textbook examples of this kind of romantic nationalism. The situation in Scotland was, of course, very different indeed: the unity had been a reality, only recently lost and peacefully at that. The interest in things Scottish was then a recuperative operation, backward looking, thus antiquarian, but clearly tinged with a goodly dose of nationalism: save what is Scottish before it is lost forever in this incredible political, societal, and cultural avalanche that is in process. One response was to become a ballad and folksong enthusiast.

William Motherwell, then, was one cultivator in this literary field that began in earnest around the time of the union of the parliaments, that is, early in the eighteenth century. For the dramatis personae of this field, or at least a preliminary list, one could do no better than to begin with the introduction to Motherwell's own *Minstrelsy: Ancient and Modern*—that "*profound Treatise*": James Watson, Allan Ramsay, David Herd, John Pinkerton, James Johnson (and implicitly Robert Burns), Joseph Ritson, Walter Scott, Robert Jamieson, Robert Cromek, Alexander Laing, David Laing, R.A. Smith, C.K. Sharpe, Peter Buchan, Allan Cunningham, and George Ritchie Kinloch are all mentioned therein as having contributed to the exploration of this national resource. Further, the introductions to some of their respective works point out the "Scottish," nationalistic impetus for interest in traditionary ballads and songs: Ramsay asserts that "their Poetry is the Product of their own Country, not pilfered and spoiled in the Transportation from abroad: Their Images are native and their hardships domestick; copied from those Fields and Meadows we every Day behold." Pinkerton added that such ballads "will be found to breathe the living spirit of the Scottish people"; and David Herd suggests that these materials "exhibit natural and striking traits of the character, genius, taste and pursuits of the people," adding that each nation has a particular musical style determined by climate, character, and government. In essence, William Motherwell agreed and began, early on, to be interested in this kind of literature, this national poetry, and the tunes to which the poems/songs were sung.

His awareness of traditionary verbal artistry, especially ballads ("the shortest definition and perhaps the most correct we can find for the Ballad is—a *Narrative* Song" [25242.16: 114]), is evidenced in some of his earliest writings, preserved in his commonplace books, in miscellaneous pages—like the ballads and songs themselves, perhaps—rescued from oblivion by the nineteenth-century penchant for keeping absolutely everything, binding it into notebooks, and awaiting the historical, interpretative glance of a later age. Motherwell's particular interest in earlier literature is both evident and vague, lumped under the general category of poetry he called "the first ve-hicle of human thought" (Robertson 28/1210) and thus a window to the past, a way to know the concerns, values, attitudes, even personages and events of bygone days. He saw this early poetry as evolving or perhaps de-volving: "[T]he once elevated minstrel in due process of time descends from his pinnacled eminence and at length enacts the equally useful though less honourable craft of hawking ballats or vagabounding through land ward touns with a fiddle in its green bag slung over his shoulder." Further, "the rude ballad singer who chaunts his sorry stave on the street to amuse the busy multitude may unknown to himself have infused the fire of song and melody of numbers in some bosom that afterwards by its power shall astonish the world." Once this poetry was everyone's, the people's property, until un-specified change made poetry the purview of the erudite, when it lost that "infinite repetition" (ibid.). Even in his early ruminations Motherwell ex-presses interest in the materials and interpretative perspectives that were to persist: this material has certain qualities, belongs to the people, contains valuable historical information, and has developed over time, but, alas, it has been infected with *change,* detrimentally. Societal change was Motherwell's greatest fear.

Perhaps Motherwell's interest in balladry and song would have re-mained this general and relatively unformed if he had not fallen in with a group of other enthusiasts planning a collaborative publication; in due time this became essentially his project, *Minstrelsy: Ancient and Modern* (1827), as other contributors and participants abandoned the work. His letter of 6 December 1824 to R.A. Smith describes this turn of events, how "the whole labour save correcting the press has devolved on my shoulders. How I am to get through with it I don't very well know but since our hand is on the oar we must een lug away as best can" (Robertson 3/1222, 25). His letters, com-monplace books, miscellaneous writing (including other ballad and song materials [Robertson 12/1217, 2]), reviews of related works in the burgeon-ing periodical press, his collecting Notebook, the Manuscript recording his collecting activities and those of his friends and correspondents, and the introduction and musical appendix added to the *Minstrelsy* after all the texts were published provide ample evidence of the making of an authority—what Motherwell himself referred to in the introduction to the *Minstrelsy* as his "errantry": an appropriate and typically metaphoric formulation to describe his activities, and very much in keeping with his chivalric and martial interests.

But his work for the *Minstrelsy* began with providing texts. In order to take control of the work, he began by exploring what had been done before, that is, getting a feel for the field. He examined the works by the enthusiasts who had gone before him, and he perused stall copies of balladry, receiving at one point a packet from Peter Buchan of items culled from sellers and shops in the Northeast by Peter and his son. He also began to talk and correspond with the experts of the day, exchanging texts and discoveries, sharing interpretative and elucidating information—sometimes historical. From time to time they talked of their sources and their experiences gathering or locating new materials and explored the proper way to present their findings to the public, especially the question of editing.

The question of editing is an interesting one, and the prevailing attitude was in favor of it, even when dealing with canonical literatures. A favorite book of Motherwell's as a young man—*Sentimental Scenes Selected from Celebrated Plays and Calculated to Promote Morality, the Knowledge of Mankind, Facility in Articulate Reading, and Gracefulness in Public Speaking*—compiled by an Edinburgh teacher of elocution, John Wilson, clearly explains the then-dominant view: "To rescue valuable gems from the rubbish with which they are surrounded; to make a collection of literary flowers from the fields of dramatic erudition.—And, to render them more acceptable to the friends of virtue, I have, without hesitation, altered improper exclamations, suppressed exceptionable phrases, and given an obvious moral construction to sentiments of dark or doubtful meaning" (iv). Wilson's approach is used on Cicero, Shakespeare, Milton, Molière, Dryden, and others, known and unknown.

The correspondence with Buchan was certainly affirming, encouraging Motherwell that others too felt such material was worthy of study. The exchange of texts was important and early on was intended to help one another find the best text possible—or provide data for the making of a composite. Something like that is implied when Motherwell wrote C.K. Sharpe on 6 December 1824 (25241.56f): "I have likewise sent you a copy of Kempy Kay which supplies a verse wanting in your copy and gives a different account, and, I think a more humorous, of the quality of yarn which his Love span." Motherwell's letter to Walter Scott (excerpted earlier) a scant six months later may show a slight movement away from the idea of compiling or collating various copies to produce an ideal version. "[I]t is of some importance," Motherwell wrote, "to preserve these remnants of ancient traditionary song in the exact state in which they pass from mouth to mouth among the vulgar" (FMS Eng 862, copy). Scott's reply, adding no new information on "Gil Morice"/"Child Maurice"—an alternate text of which Motherwell had hoped Scott would have to help him "amend"—contains the now-famous disclaimer implicitly discouraging Motherwell's intent:

> I think I did wrong myself in endeavoring to make the best possible set of an ancient ballad out of several copies obtained from different quarters, and that, in many respects, if I improved the poetry, I spoiled the simplicity of the old song. There is no wonder this should be the case when one considers that the singers or reciters by whom these ballads were preserved and handed down, must, in general, have had a facility, from memory at least, if not from genius (which they might often possess), of filling up verses which they had forgotten, or altering such as they might think they could improve. Passing through this process in different parts of the country, the ballads, admitting that they had one common poetical original (which is not to be inferred merely from the similitude of the story), became, in progress of time, totally different productions, as far as the tone and spirit of each is concerned. In such cases, perhaps, it is as well to keep them separate, as giving in their original state a more accurate idea of our ancient poetry, which is the point most important in such collections. (Robertson 9/1207, no.15, copy)

This gave Motherwell a lot to think about, certainly affirming the alternate approach he had outlined in his original letter—that is, not to amend but to keep the materials as they were collected.[1] Scott's other ideas, dealing with the changes through transmission and the potentially self-correcting and/or creative process of oral tradition, may well have encouraged Motherwell to consider the nature of oral tradition and transmission, touched on in his "*profound Treatise*" (Robertson 3/1222: 50). Since he revered Scott, he undoubtedly took his response seriously. Nevertheless, his correspondence with Peter Buchan may well have had a more profound impact.

Theirs was a continuing correspondence centered on the topic of their mutual enthusiasms for traditionary materials. Motherwell began with a letter seeking help as he began his errantry; Buchan made clear immediately (see this book, chap. 1) that nothing could please him more than exchanging materials and information with a fellow enthusiast. Buchan had lots of material on hand, the result of his own collecting and the collecting of a blind singer James Rankin.[2] He shares with Motherwell over and over again descriptions of his or Rankin's collecting and often sends along copies: "[O]ne old woman of eighty got so much into the spirit of the olden time, that, on my approach, altho' lying on a bed by the fire, and whose decayed body and limbs could not carry her to the door, sat up and repeated many fragments which I had never heard before" (25263.19.6F). Such testimonials to the living oral tradition, plumbed by both himself and his helper, must certainly have served as an example for Motherwell, encouraging him, if he was to master the field of traditionary materials, to collect himself and perhaps to hire someone to help him for pay, as Buchan had done with such evident success. Buchan's comments, dispersed throughout his correspondence with Motherwell and others, on the question of presentation of texts must surely too have influenced Motherwell, as he was coming to his "mature" position that radical editorial emendations were in fact a distortion of the lived reality of the balladry under consideration. In July 1826, Buchan writes Motherwell that "what will render it [presumably the *Minstrelsy,* which had begun to be published in fascicles in 1824] more dear to me, as well as every lover of Scottish song, is, your having given the ballads without that disagreeable and disgusting emendations and interpolations so frequently met with in works of this sort" (25263.19.6F). Buchan's words—"your having given"—suggest that Motherwell had already begun this noninterventionist policy. Probably Buchan was talking about the most recent fascicle, for the truth is that Motherwell did not come to his mature editorial position against collating and emending until late in the preparation of the texts.

Motherwell's notes to *Minstrelsy* texts provide ample evidence of his and his erstwhile collaborators' "tamperings": at page 35, describing the text of "Hynd Horn," he says, "We have been fortunate enough to recover two copies from recitation, which, joined to the stanzas preserved by Mr. Cromek, have enabled us to present it to the public in the present complete state" (later he was to castigate this very Mr. Cromek for his overkill in emending and altering texts; lxxxviii); at page 67, concerning "May Colvin," Motherwell assures us that "this ballad is given from a copy obtained from recitation, collated with another copy to be found in the Edinburgh collection, 1776." He describes the text-making process for "Johnie Scot" at pages 204–5: "In preparing this ballad for the press, three recited copies, all obtained from people considerably advanced in years, have been used. . . . As is to be expected, in all poetry which depends on oral tradition for its transmission to our own times, the copies of this ballad which the Editor has recovered do not exactly correspond with each other. Numerous, though on the whole but trivial, verbal discrepancies exist among them; and in adjusting the text, he had therefore to rely on his own judgement in selecting, what he conceived, the best reading from each of his copies." It was some seventy pages later, on pages 281–82, in writing of "Child Noryce," which he calls "the very anatomy of a perfect ballad," that he asserts a different perspective entirely: "That the reader may have no room to doubt the genuiness of a ballad for which a very high antiquity is claimed, the editor thinks it right to mention, that it is given verbatim as it was taken down from the singing of widow M'Cormick, who, at this date [Jan. 1825], resides in Westbrae Street of Paisley." And at page 291 he assures the reader that the version of "Lambert Linkin" "is given from recitation; and though it could have received additions, and perhaps improvements, from another copy, obtained from a similar source, and of equal authenticity, in his possession, the Editor did not like to use a liberty which is liable to much abuse." These last two examples are presumably the quality of texts to which Buchan was referring and represent Motherwell's informed position. This does not mean that changes did not "creep" into his texts; after all, he was a poet and his poetic sensibilities must have sorely tempted him from time to time to correct a rhyme, fill out the meter, substitute a "better" word. He came to believe, however, that wholesale reformulation, using multiple copies as fodder, was wrong and provided an incorrect exemplar of oral tradition. Buchan was certainly more correct in his words than in his actions, too, but then he was a printer and knew well the vagaries of the buying public. Ballads and songs were becoming commodities, were being affected by the rise of capitalism, were entering the world of exchange over use value.

In his epistolary exchanges, Motherwell was receiving and giving perspectives on the ballad. His interest in "good" texts, which early on stimulated his collating activities, continued, but from a slightly different perspective. His remarks throughout the early period indicate that he is particularly interested in the first appearance of a given ballad, that is, when and where it was first published, its earliest form: he tended to valorize the oldest. Yet he was interested in discovering new materials, never before published, to include in his own work or in the works of others. The idea was to gather as much of this traditionary material, evidence of Scotland's past, as possible. As a ballad fancier, he wanted to expand the canon to include new exemplars or especially good versions, so his preliminary activities in the field were to explore the published materials, to discover just what existed. And he did that as well through correspondence with others, many of whom procured their texts from manuscripts, ancient or contemporary, or earlier rare published sources. The importance of the Buchan correspondence was that Buchan was actively at work collecting and with almost each letter gave evidence of the potentialities of actual collecting to expand the canon. Knowing what had been published and said, Motherwell was then ready to go to the people in hopes of recovering materials and expanding the canon of extant Scottish ballads.

Motherwell undertook collecting activities in and around Paisley—within the region, easily reached—where he was known: Kilbarchan, Greenock, Glasgow, Largs, Lochwinnoch, Dumbarton, Newtown Green; and as it turns out, he had more success with old women, who had learned their materials as children, than with men. In fact, he referred to a group of the singers as "old singing women." As he collected, he began to be interested in the transmission route—from whom they learned the material in their childhood and when that would have been—to push the material back into the past as far as possible and thus assure its traditionary status. Two concrete records exist of Motherwell's own activities in gathering ballads and songs from live people: a Notebook (25242.16, copy) and a more formal Manuscript (Murray 501), both referred to earlier. The Notebook is a rather informal affair, perhaps not unlike today's appointment diaries, with multiple memoranda. Motherwell noted expenses of his ballad gathering: paying poor informants for their help; paying Thomas MacQueen to collect for him in Ayr, as Buchan paid Rankin—an interesting illustration of the influence of capitalism and the advent of commodification; paying to bring an informant to Paisley so that her tunes could be recorded; and so on. The Notebook includes snippets of reminders to collect this from that person, to look up another person: "Memorandum to get from Mrs. Wm Craig the song beginning

> There's bread & cheese for Musquetiers
> And corn & hay for horses
> There's fuck & sugar for auld wives
> And lads for bonny lasses." (3)

Additionally, there are random thoughts relating to traditionary materials: "Expressions common to all ancient Metrical Romances will find counterparts in our old Ballads. Thus in 'Le Bone Florena' distance is expressed by this peri-phrasis of what can be ridden 'in a long somers day' which occurs also in the ballad of Thos of Winsberry" (122). He records his idea that chronicles were broken up and circulated as ballads "sung or recited among the people of Scotland to popular airs." And he includes extraneous material like a record of a trip he took. The Notebook is a very human document.

The Manuscript, on the other hand, was a formally prepared document, written in clear hand and intended to be his record of his collecting activities, and it was undoubtedly prepared after the *Minstrelsy* was in press or had been published. It offers, as the great American ballad editor Francis James Child rightly recognized, a different order of texts from those printed early in the *Minstrelsy,* as well as additional material, his own as well as materials collected on his behalf by Andrew Crawfurd[3] and texts sent him by correspondents. The learning that was acquired in gathering the Manuscript materials was essential to his introduction.[4] The first portion of the Manuscript contains less classic and more miscellaneous material than that which was already appearing in the *Minstrelsy,* but which he intended, but seems never to have done, to publish as a small garland in a limited edition. Several manuscript versions of possible introductions to this projected collection, alternately given as "The Paisley Garland" or "The West Countrie Garland" (MS 40, 3 and 4), may well have been written simultaneously and offer an inkling of his views on the subject at that particular point in time, probably early in his collecting activities. He says that such materials would have perished if he had not gathered them while doing work of more general interest—presumably the *Minstrelsy.* The texts were gathered from manuscripts and from oral tradition, mostly from old women: he has not touched the manuscript copies, but he has put the oral versions into the presumed orthography of the times referred to in the text—assuming that their appearance in oral tradition was coterminous with the event chronicled, if indeed there were an historical happening recounted. These items are new: "[I]t may be observed that no part so far as the Editor knows has ever appeared in print or if so in the form which it now bears." These materials should be preserved, for they provide a "passing fair mirror in which much valuable information of times past may be truly and notably discovered by the ingenious"; furthermore, "every year that rolls past diminishes the chances to the Collector of Ancient ballads of adding to his stores; for, as they are to be obtained principally from the recitation of old people, these are fast dropping."

After the miscellaneous materials, the Manuscript's focus moves to an implicit consideration of variation, giving multiple versions of the same ballad before shifting to a consideration of repertoires of individual informants.[5] Clearly Motherwell's active confrontation with the ballad world gave him an entirely different perspective on the topic, its fragility, its complexity, its possessors. He provides notes and annotations to various texts, suggesting where other versions may be found, moving beyond the historical, printed sources that figured so much in the *Minstrelsy*'s notes. Discussing "Lord Jamie Douglas," Motherwell says, "I was informed by A. Lile that she has heard a longer set of the ballad in which while Lady Douglas is continuing her lament she observes a troop of gentlemen coming to her father's and she expresses a wish that these should be sent by her lord to bring her home. They happen to be sent for that purpose and she accompanies them. On her meeting however with her lord and while putting a cup of wine to her lips her heart breaks and she drops down dead-at-his feet" (345). He gives information on the source: the name of the tradition bearer, and sometimes profession or familial connection, and age; he records when he collected and where, and often adds from whom the material was learned. Speaking of "Gill Morice," he records that "this copy is from the recitation of Margaret Paterson alias Widow Michael a very old woman residing at Dovecoteha' Barhead. She is a native of Banffshire and learned the ballad there in her infancy. She mentions that she has heard it sung with many variations but this copy was considered to be the right way. It is seventy years since she committed it to her memory" (480, 4 Aug. 1826). Elsewhere he says that "Mrs. Thomson (Kilbarchan) had this ballad ["Child Morice"] at the Water of Leven Dumbarton when about ten years of age from her mother a native of the same place. Mrs. Thomson is now near seventy years of age" (171).

It is unclear whether Motherwell and other nineteenth-century ballad and folksong scholars actually made a distinction between *recitation* and *singing:* Motherwell sometimes says the informant sang or recited. From time to time he records that he has had the music recorded—of "The Beggar Laddie" "Mr. Smith took down the musick" (249)—or mentions the tune name: for "The Eastmure King and the Westmure King," he says, "This is sung to the tune of 'Johnie Scott'" (341). Sometimes he adds as well how the song was sung—for "Lady Marjory," he suggests, "O, in singing occurs at the end of the 2d & 4th line of each stanza" (1)—or describes aspects of the performance. For "Where will bonnie Ann lie," he says he got it "[f]rom a pedlar who could repeat no more of this Song but who was so fascinated therewith that in every place where he rambled he failed not to ask Where'l bonnie Ann lye in the hopes of getting the rest of the song but I never heard that his attempts to obtain it were successful. The lines within brackets are conjectural" (the latter his more sophisticated way of dealing with the urge to conflate and collate copies [109]). He offers variant titles for an item, sometimes providing background-historical information: what the motivations might be for the action, what data a missing stanza might have provided, and so on. Occasionally he notes where other or related versions may be found—as he so copiously did in the *Minstrelsy* proper—as for "The Unco Knight's Wooing": "'The Noble Riddle wisely expounded or the Maids answer to the Knights three questions' an English Ballad in the Bodleian Library Oxford is probably founded on the preceding. The english ballad has also the burden which I have heard the foregoing also sung with viz.t 'Lay the bent to the bonnie brune'" (648). He also makes comments evaluating the relative merits of versions, suggesting that one or another is a more "perfect" copy. The Manuscript might be seen as Motherwell's permanent record of his own collecting activities, recording those aspects and examples of the tradition he deemed important.

Interestingly, the Manuscript was begun after a number of sections of the *Minstrelsy* had been published, with Motherwell's careful comparative and historical notes and annotations. So the Manuscript was not the source of or a draft for the *Minstrelsy,* but rather his record of what he—and others—gathered from oral tradition, a process that began for him *after* he inherited the *Minstrelsy* project and as part of his attempt to master the subject. It can be seen, then, as evidence of his enlarged notion of the ballad—more than texts and comparative notes, the possession of real people. The Manuscript, the Notebook, and miscellaneous papers together reveal the names of many of his informants and their repertoires, which I have reconstructed in Appendix 1.[6]

The Manuscript offers a wealth of data about the materials, moving beyond the text-based approach. Yet it does not provide any overt articulation of Motherwell's expanding theoretical sophistication about this material, influenced by his active collecting in the field. For that kind of information, we must turn to the periodical press and a review of 26 August 1826 of Peter Buchan's *Gleanings,* which appeared in the *Paisley Advertiser,* and, especially, to his introduction to the *Minstrelsy,* already invoked.

Essentially, Motherwell makes three points in praising Buchan's work. First, old ballads are our earliest poetry and deserve preservation: "We have a sincere, and to some it may appear, a foolish liking for those rude old trumpet-rousing strains which stirred up the passions, and awoke the deepest and best sympathies of our forefathers. Nor do we wish to conceal the hearty and unfeigned satisfaction we feel when, in the course of our literary duties, we now and then light on spirits of a kindred mould, busying themselves in collecting, from oral tradition, or scarce sources, these interesting remnants of what we have ever looked upon as the Primeval poesy of our native land." Second, this early poetry is the product of a collectivity, the people. And third, these relics of the past are mostly gone, because of the societal changes that have affected taste; one can still gather remnants, but the times are not conducive to their "preservation and transmission." He returns to these points in his "pro*found Treatise*" with considerable fervor and with a depth that, in many ways, is quite surprising.

Motherwell's introduction, published in 1827, offers a full and rich articulation of his subject, which he calls alternately traditionary literature, vernacular poetry, and national minstrelsy. What distinguishes this kind of material is its mode of transmission—oral tradition: "a safe and almost unerring guide" (iii) that keeps the old language and holds onto the essentials of the narrative in remarkable ways, alas all too easily wiped out by the strike of an editor's pen "who may choose to impose on himself the thankless and uncalled for labour of piecing and patching up its imperfections, polishing its asperities, correcting its mistakes, embellishing its naked details, purging it of impurities, and of trimming it from top to toe with tailor-like fastidiousness and nicety, so as to be made fit for the press" (iv). Having earlier done this himself, he certainly knew whereof he spoke! While this material exhibits distinctly Scottish qualities, there is an "inter-community" (xl), especially England and the Scandinavian countries, that shares similar materials, similar story lines, and similar genres. And balladry is distinct in other ways, primarily in its rather unusual position on the borderland between oral and written literatures. Ballads were presumably composed orally, perhaps by minstrels whose names we do not know. Thus the exact circumstances and environment of their creation are unknown. Likewise we cannot say which example is the oldest because through time, in both oral and subsequent written transmission, a ballad may be contemporized and changed. The older the version, the more likely it is to have a formulaic quality that Motherwell designates as "common-places," perhaps *the* distinctive stylistic characteristic of this "curious and interesting species of national literature" (x). After the minstrels who transmitted the balladry, "succinct and veratious narratives" (xxviii), and romances, humbler retainers learned the materials and passed them on, perhaps altering the material to fit the taste of the "lower ranks" (xxix) whose "stubborn sensibilities could only be excited by narratives of real incident, suffering or adventure, distinctly, plainly, and artlessly told" (xxx). For creating the material, after this earlier, unknowable time, "a new race of ballad-writers succeeded—an inferior sort of minor poets who wrote narrative songs merely for the press" (xviii): more regular, more insipid, more contemporary materials. Such material, which he designated "lesser" rhymes, are popularly sold in the streets and include the supposed last words of criminals. Motherwell's interest is with the earlier materials and with the distinctive qualities he discerned in them.

This earlier material—"They convey to posterity, that description of song which is peculiarly national and characteristick; that body of poetry which has inwoven itself with the feelings and passions of the people, and which shadows forth as it were an actual embodiment of their Universal mind, and of its intellectual and moral tendencies" (v)—was sung and perhaps created by minstrels in the Middle Ages. Snatches are embedded in Renaissance drama; "small poets" and "balladmongers" (xl) renovated some, created new ones, sometimes printing them in Garlands, on broadsides, and finally in books. But they are still on the lips of some, especially the older members of the community. The latter source he deemed very important: not only were the old growing older, but the times too were changing, altering things and obliterating the very situation/s or contexts in which the older balladry flourished. While the original is lost, records "as they orally exist" (v) need to be made. This is particularly true for Scotland, which has not the written records of England. Not only must the material be collected, but it must be presented to the public "with scrupulous and unshrinking fidelity" (iv): "What their texts or forms originally were, we have no means of knowing; what they are now, we do know; all then which remains by us to be done, is to transmit that knowledge unimpaired, and with rigid fidelity, to posterity. By publishing in this manner, we stamp upon them all the certainty and authenticity which their shadowy and mutable nature can receive" (cii). This means, of course, that collated copies, which give "inaccurate impressions of the state in which these compositions are actually extant among us" (vi), are unacceptable. In fact, each version, and there are multiple versions of most ballads, has equal authority and is equally authentic, though there may be incredible differences between versions, the result of additions and confusions, misunderstandings, forgetting, inventing, and interpolations on the part of the possessor of the ballads that sometimes introduce so many changes that the result is almost a totally new ballad—yet recognizably related because of shared commonplaces.

Editors of this material, he can now assert, should not collate but should select "that one of his copies which appears the most complete and least vitiated" (vii). Recognizing that such demands for editorial accuracy have not always existed, he reviews earlier precedents perhaps by way of understanding his own earlier weaknesses: "At the time Ramsay published, the business of editing Ancient poesy was not well understood; nor were the duties of an Editor, in that department of letters, accurately defined. . . . In the liberties which he took with the ancient Song of his country, he has however unfortunately supplied a precedent for posterity to quote, and set an example which men of less talent, and even less critical integrity, have been eager to imitate" (lxi). He is harder on near-contemporaries such as

R.H. Cromek, whose *Remains of Nithsdale and Galloway Song,* he says, contains "[m]ore pretention, downright impudence, and literary falsehood, seldom or ever come into conjunction" (lxxxviii); in fact, Cromek's work is filled with forgeries. And Motherwell describes Allan Cunningham's editing in *The Songs of Scotland* as a "heartless, tasteless, and impious jest, . . . violating ancient song. . . . [A] wholesale mode of hacking, and hewing, and breaking the joints of ancient and traditionary song" (xcvii). These evaluative comments indicate just how far he had come in a few short years—and what he learned from his firsthand experiences of this material. Collating gives the wrong idea of the state of the living tradition. Outright forgeries are even more heinous, however, and Motherwell offers a clear condemnation of forgers, "those gentlemen who deem themselves fully better poets than ever earlier times produced; but who cannot persuade the publick to think so, or even prevail on it to read their compositions till they have given them a slight sprinkling of olden phraseology and stoutly maintained that they are genuine specimens of ancient song" (viii–ix). Motherwell is throughout making claims about authenticity, what kind of texts, and tunes, should be published; and he asserts the trustworthiness of oral tradition. His own collecting, especially, forced him to see the ballad's lived reality, to recognize the multiformity of this species of literature. His statements carried enormous weight with two major nineteenth-century scholars—Svend Grundtvig and Francis James Child. Their subsequent, near-definitive publications, *Danmarks gamle Folkeviser* and *The English and Scottish Popular Ballads,* took Motherwell as authority: they sought to publish all extant versions in copies as close to oral tradition as possible. Thus Motherwell's firsthand acquaintance with the ballad and his articulation of its features was the sine qua non for ballad scholarship in the modern sense.

Motherwell's views on balladry do not end with the question of authenticity: he talked about the ballads' reception, divisions, characteristics, and performance. He suggests that this ancient, national literature, which still lives in oral tradition on the lips of ordinary people, may once have been heard by the high and mighty in the performances of minstrels and deserves considerable attention: for one thing the people who possess the ballads hold them as true, if not specifically, generally, as records of an earlier society with more marked class distinctions. The element of truth—he uses the word "legend" to refer to the story line—he has encountered more than once in collecting: "From no discourteous motive, but from sheer ignorance of this important article of belief, I have unfortunately for myself, once or twice notably affronted certain aged virgins, by impertinent dubitations touching the veracity of their songs, an offence which bitter experience will teach me to avoid repeating, as it has long ere this, made me rue the day of its commission" (xxvii) and "The audacious sceptick, who, in the plenitude of his shallow worldly wisdom, dared to question their being matter of incontrovertible fact, I may state for the information of those who may hereafter choose to amuse themselves in the quest of olden song, would eventually find the lips of every venerable sybil in the land, most effectually sealed to his future enquiries" (xxvii). His division of ballads into two categories—"Romantick and Historick" (i)—is in a sense tied to the legendary concept: historical ballads are based on particular historical events; romantic ones could well be true but can't be traced to any particular public or private event. Nonetheless, the materials contain truth, history—thus their importance as records of the past.

As early literature, the ballads are characterized by a "venerable simplicity" (vi), which was maintained by structural qualities that helped to keep the story the same although the words might change from one authentic version to another. The ballad begins at once, creating the scene; the characters are revealed through action rather than by description; the story is always forward moving with an absence of backward glances to fill in the gaps; the story, rather than embellishments, is essential, producing a succinct account of "perfect harmony and wholeness" (xiv); many details are left for the imagination to provide; and there are no appeals to tradition to affirm the veracity of the account, as the story, as it occurs, is assumed to be comprehensible and accepted. The mainstay of these qualities are commonplaces, "identity of language, epithet, and expression" (xix): "[I]n all cases where there is an identity of incident, of circumstance, of action, each Ballad varies not from the established mode of clothing these in language" (xxi). The older the ballad, the more likely it is to be embedded with commonplaces, which not only provide ready-made descriptive qualities but also have connotative significance: "[T]he expressions of *wiping on the sleeve, drying on grass* and *slating owre the strae,* always occur in such ballads as indicate a dubious and protracted and somewhat equal combat" (xxiii). Thus the commonplaces provide a shorthand way of saying something—what Motherwell calls "brachigraphy." Burdens, too, although their significance seems now lost and they may have been fragments of even more ancient songs, probably "were a key to a whole family of associations and feelings, of which we can form little or no conception" (xxiv).[7]

The composition of ballads, often dealing with love, that "fruitful source of human misery" (xx) (was he speaking from personal or general experience?), "had been," he suggests, "reduced to a certain system" (xxiii). The structural characteristics plus the commonplaces allowed for "spur of the occasion" (xxiii) composition, serving "as a kind of ground-work, on which the poem could be raised" (xxiii), allowing a poet to "rapidly model any event which came under his cognizance into song" (xxiii). And, of course, these very qualities helped a singer hold the material in memory. What Motherwell actually describes here is an *avant la lettre* articulation of oral formulaic composition: he points out the structural and stylistic building blocks that enabled a ballad creator to compose, perhaps recompose, in performance. It may well be, in fact, that he is recording what he observed in the act of collecting this species of ancient poetry.

Virtually unique among early ballad and song students, Motherwell—perhaps again a result of his firsthand acquaintance with the living song tradition—recognized that the ballads were not poems, but songs, and that their music formed an essential component of the whole. Ballads are sung, sometimes recited; and the meter is not always regular and suited to modern taste. He calls it "licentious" (xvii), by which he means that syllables that would not ordinarily be stressed are accented. In fact, he makes it clear that the ballads "have throughout the marks of a composition, not meant for being committed to writing, but whose musick formed an essential part of it" (xvii). The actual performances are often prefaced by background information relative to the personages and places mentioned in the song; such information, provided in the past by minstrels, helped to smooth over "abrupt transitions" (xiv) and suggests that the stories were held to be true. Sometimes the prose commentary is formalized, at other times it is informal.

Having given more information, more analysis, more detailed data about this "remarkable class of compositions" (x) than any other commentator, he offers, in the second portion of his indeed "pro*found Treatise,*" a mini-history of the publication of versions of balladry as "traditionally preserved in Scotland." He surveys the published collections, cataloguing the new exemplars therein published, offering comments on the quality of the collections and providing rich notes to parallel texts or to offer historical information. In a sense Motherwell describes the folksong field, the students of the tradition, and he places himself at the end.

Predictably, he praises Scott's *Minstrelsy:* "Long will it live a noble and interesting monument of the unwearied research, curious and minute learning, genius and taste of its illustrious Editor. It is truly a patriot's legacy to posterity; and much as it may now be esteemed, it is only in times yet gathering in the bosom of far futurity, when the interesting traditions, the chivalrous and romantick legends, the wild superstitions, the Tragic song of Scotland, have wholly faded from the living memory, that this gift can be duly appreciated" (lxxix). His note for "Captain Wedderburn's Courtship" attempts to offer similar information:

> This is also inserted in Mr. Jamieson's "Popular Ballads and Songs." Few are more popular; it occurs in every assortment of stall literature. Winton is copious in his details of an attempt made by the Devil to puzzle by curious questioning, that singularly holy and wise man, Saint Serf; but as usual, the saint prevails in this combat of wit and learning. Of a similar nature is that recorded in a Gallwegian tale, named "The Fause Knight upon the road," wherein the fiend is baffled by the pertinent answers of a "wee boy," who must have been a very saint in miniature. As this ballad has never been printed, and is briefer than these compositions generally are, it is now given:

> O whare are ye gaun?
> Quo' the fause knicht upon the road;
> I'm gaun to the scule,
> Quo' the wee boy, and still he stude.
> What is that upon your back?
> Quo' the fause knicht upon the road;
> Atweel it is my bukes,
> Quo' the wee boy, and still he stude.
> What's that ye've got in your arm?
> Quo' the fause knicht, &c.
> Atweel it is my peit,
> Quo' the wee boy, &c.
> Wha's aucht they sheep?
> Quo' the fause knicht, &c.
> They are mine and my mither's,
> Quo' the wee boy, &c.
> How monie o' them are mine?
> Quo' the fause knicht, &c.
> A' they that hae blue tails,
> Quo' the wee boy, &c.
> I wiss ye were on yon tree,
> Quo' the fause knicht, &c.
> And a gude ladder under me,
> Quo' the wee boy, &c.

And the ladder for to break,
    Quo' the fause knicht, &c.
And you for to fa' doun,
    Quo' the wee boy, &c.
I wiss ye were in yon sie,
    Quo' the fause knicht, &c.
And a gude bottom under me,
    Quo' the wee boy, &c.
And the bottom for to break,
    Quo' the fause knicht upon the road;
And ye to be drowned,
    Quo' the wee boy, and still he stude.

In the "Legenda Aurea," a tale occurs of a worthy bishop who was a devoted admirer of Saint Andrew, much to the dissatisfaction of the Devil. The evil one transforms himself into a comely wench, who speedily found favour in the holy man's sight, and there is no saying but his soul might have been placed in jeopardy by her blandishments on one occasion when feasting together, had it not been for a loud knocking at the gate, which opportunely disturbed their enjoyments. On looking out, a poor pilgrim was seen beating furiously for admittance. The fiend lady afraid lest her victim should escape her machinations, stipulates that before the pilgrim be admitted, he should answer certain three questions, to be propounded by her. The pilgrim being no less a personage than Saint Andrew, answered the two first questions promptly, and the third to so much purpose, that the fiend immediately flew off in native ugliness, filling the air with horrid imprecations, whereby the bishop saw at once his imminent peril, and became still more unremitted in his devotions at the shrine of the Saint, who thus interposed in his behalf. (lxxiv–lxxv)

The concluding portions of the introduction gave Motherwell the chance to reiterate his belief that the ballads are from "high antiquity" (ciii) and that the music may well be evidence of the earliest Scottish music. Both words and tune have "passed through a process of refinement, which has militated against their individuality and primitive character" (ciii). But they are not likely to survive the current upheavals without alteration—"the rapid decay of much that we have been accustomed to love and venerate" (cii). He continues, "The changes which, within this half century, the manners and habits of our peasantry and labouring classes, with whom this song has been cherished, have undergone, are inimical to its further preservation" (cii). Motherwell, of course, is drawn to the material as both history and art, but also as symbol of the past, as holdout against the changes he does not like, as prima facie evidence of what is in danger of being lost forever. Thus he concludes his "trial-run" in the ballad field, his "errantry" (civ), begging the indulgence of the "courteous reader" (cv), a holdover from the oral world of closer connection between performer/singer and audience, and quoting from Hill's *Physiognomy* (London, 1571): "I referre me wholy to the learned correction of the wise; for wel I wrote, that no treatise can always be so workmanly handled, but that somewhat sometymes may fall out amisse, contrarie to the minde of the wryter, and contrarie to the expectation of the reader: wherefore, my petition to thee, Gentle Reader, is to accept those my traveyles wyth that minde I doe offer them to thee, and to take gently that I give gladly, in so doing, I shall thinke my paynes well bestowed, and shall bee encouraged hereafter to trust more unto thy courtesie" (cv).

This disclaimer is particularly apt, of course, in an ironic way, for the texts they introduce, but in fact conclude, were largely the result of the editorial principles he writes so persuasively against. Thus Motherwell's introduction, written after the work was actually completed, ought really to be styled an afterword or conclusion because, as I have suggested throughout, it sums up all that he learned in the course of working on the *Minstrelsy,* the collaborative effort that became his individual project. As a summation it describes editorial procedures that, as we have seen, were in fact violated at every turn until late in the preparation of the texts for the collection. The introduction, then, might be seen as a correction or, put more colloquially, a "do as I say, not as I do."

This editorial waffling certainly vexed one of the most meticulous of ballad scholars, Francis James Child, who valued Motherwell's work and thought of him as an authority. Nonetheless, Child repeatedly comments on the discrepancies between Motherwell's source and the Manuscript texts. For Child, the published texts in the *Minstrelsy* provided the avenue into an exploration of the sources *behind* that work; he had copies made of materials that reflected Motherwell's growing knowledge of the field—the Manuscript of his and others collections, the Notebook—and he acquired various letters as well as material published in the *Paisley Magazine.* Motherwell's materials, which Child designates as "hitherto unused" and "much the most important" of new materials uncovered, provide 225 versions of 108 Child numbers; and Motherwell's texts are frequently privileged: his title is used sometimes even though his text is not the A version. Yet still Child frequently queries Motherwell's texts: "Motherwell professes to copy the ballad from Herd's MS. by way of supplying the stanzas wanting in Scott. There are, however, in Motherwell's transcript considerable deviations from Herd, a fact which I am unable to explain" (*English and Scottish Popular Ballads,* vol. 5, 218, no. 50) or "Motherwell's ballad is 'traditionary' to the extent that it is substantially made up from traditionary material. The text of the recited copies is not always strictly adhered to. The fifth stanza happens not to occur in the text used, but may have come in in some other recitation obtained by Motherwell, or may simply have been adopted from Ramsay. The last three stanzas are from recitations not preserved in Motherwell's relics" (ibid., vol. 4, 104, no. 204). Behind Child's queries lay his suspicion of Buchan as well as Grundtvig's assertion of the validity of Buchan's texts and his acceptance and affirmation of Motherwell as an expert.

Motherwell's "pro*found Treatise*" confirms his acquisition of a broad and deep knowledge of balladry—its qualities, histories, distinctiveness— and exhibits a grasp of the subject chosen, narrative songs, which remains a definitive statement. Motherwell's introduction exists in a number of versions that show him grappling with the complexity of the subject matter, how best to articulate the natural dynamic nature of the material while condemning the editorial interventions that in fact only continued that dynamic, but a dynamism introduced in writing rather than through oral tradition, that "unerring" source. Appendix 2 offers a look at two draft versions of Motherwell's discussion—preserved at Pollok House, Glasgow—together with the final published version, and illustrates the process of sharpening his points and clarifying his positions fully: expansion was clearly the technique as he offered, for public scrutiny, his concluding thoughts on a subject on which he had become a recognized expert.

When the *Minstrelsy* was finally published as a book, when the individual fascicles were bound together, the introduction was placed first before the texts, which were at once an object lesson on how not to prepare texts and the heart of the matter. The texts, which more nearly reflect what he had learned, which provided the basis for his introduction, are, of course, those contained in his manuscript.

If the introduction provides in actual fact a summation of what he had learned, the addition of musical examples and their introduction might be considered a part of those conclusions, another example of what he had learned in the process of selecting, frequently collating and editing, and collecting the texts that are the core of the *Minstrelsy.* He began his study as a person interested in literature, national literature—the older and more antique the better. What he learned in the process of the textual exercise he and his friends had begun and several so cavalierly abandoned was that at best the ballads are sung. So after the work proper was concluded he made sure that a section titled "Musick" corrected the view of ballads as poetry, providing a "specimen of the description of melody to which a great number of the early traditionary ballads of Scotland are still chaunted by the people" ("Musick," xxiv). His prefatory paragraph shows his cognizance of melodic variation from verse to verse—thus he prints the text that was sung to the tune printed—of which there are thirty-three: "The following tunes having been taken down from the singing of particular verses in the respective ballads to which they belong, and these verses having sometimes happened not to be the initial stanza of the ballad, it has been deemed advisable to print the precise verses from the singing of which the several tunes were so noted. This is rendered the more necessary as some tunes are given to which no correspondent ballad will be found in this collection, while others refer to sets of a ballad different from those which it contains" (ibid., xv). The tunes were transcribed from singing by Motherwell's friend Andrew Blaikie when singers were brought to Paisley for that purpose. The "Musick," added, like the introduction, after the work proper was completed, records a number of tunes from singers whose texts were recorded for Motherwell by Andrew Crawfurd between 1826 and 1828 (see Lyle, *Andrew Crawfurd's Collection*) and enter the *Minstrelsy* only in the final significant stages, when Motherwell was preparing the introduction, appendix, and "Musick." Naturally, some of Crawfurd's materials are included in the Manuscript. Crawfurd's own substantial work, only recently published, then is another result of Motherwell's errantry—seeking out help from others in mastering the subject.

As a good knicht, his interest in ballads and songs did not cease with the publication of the *Minstrelsy* together with the introduction and "Musick," though other activities and interests took priority. Yet various manuscript essays and the pages of the *Paisley Magazine* show evidence of his continuing interest in this species of literature. In a holograph draft of an essay titled "Early Historic Song of Scotland" (Robertson 10/1208, 7), Motherwell gives the narrative ballad pride of place as the "parent of every other kind of poesy." Reiterating points made in the *Minstrelsy,* he suggests that each country's ballads are distinctly marked and serve "in elucidating many isolated points of national history." This material is held in memory by rhyme and music. Then he bemoans the fact that written materials are privileged, lauding the "imperishable memory among a people the mass of whom is strictly speaking unlettered." He goes on, however, to characterize what may happen in oral transmission when he suggests that "in its course it might either have been polished by continual attrition or broken or polluted according to the nature of the channels through which it had to pass." Narrative songs may be historical or "imaginative," but not all songs are narrative: there are as well songs of sentiment.

Despite his focus on ballads, on narrative songs, Motherwell had been, almost from the beginning, interested in all traditional song, a category that includes the ballad, as well as other vernacular cultural expressions, such as customs and proverbs. The famous Manuscript includes song material both in the paginated portion and in the initial unnumbered pages. The ballad may well have been the "hegemonic" category after Scott; and the *Minstrelsy* continued that trajectory. But when that work was concluded, Motherwell resumed the more catholic position, shared with singers and listeners alike, and talks generally of song. One manuscript account deals with "An Attempt to recover Ancient Song" and touches on songs of sentiment: "In lyrical productions few countries surpass our own. These as illustrating national character[,] national manners[,] language, feeling and peculiar trains of thought and fancy and all that confers an individuality upon the universal mind of a particular race are of deep interest and in a philosophical and historical point are of the first importance" (Robertson 6/1223, 5). Songs in general become the focus of a series of articles in the *Paisley Magazine,* which was Motherwell's creative focus in 1828, the year after the publication of the *Minstrelsy.*

The series, called simply "Scottish Song," continues his interest in looking for and printing things that haven't been published before, that is to say, haven't been recognized as exemplars in the informal canon of Scottish materials begun in the *Minstrelsy.* He names broadsides as a legitimate source, one he doesn't count, properly speaking, as publication. And he suggests that a single example may seem insignificant but its value may be raised when seen as part of the whole of traditionary song. He prints new examples, from broadsheets, from recitation, sometimes commenting on the tune. Above all, he urges collection.

Elsewhere in reviews and editorial comments, Motherwell expands on the value of collecting, on gathering this material from whatever sources, expending less time justifying such endeavors, though from time to time he returns to that concern: "[O]ur understanding may be enlarged, and wits whetted, by studying the genius and extracting the marrow of the literature of our ancestors" (*Paisley Magazine,* 250–56). He praises the publication of ancient materials that has been undertaken by the Maitland and Bannatyne Clubs. But collecting from the lips of persons is particularly urgent: "[W]e deem it the duty of everyone who has the least unpublished scrap of traditionary on his memory, to get it committed to print in some shape or other" (ibid., 321–22). Under the topic "A Friendly Notice to Correspondents, with which the public has little to do Unless It Likes," he pushes, among other things, his own hobby horse, a bit humorously. In talking of a poet who submitted a poem to the magazine, he writes, "[I]f, in the place of writing original verses for us, he would employ himself in endeavouring to procure a few old traditionary songs of that neighbourhood. . . . [C]ould he get these as also some short rhymes of place and persons. . . . It is of use to collect and preserve these rude ditties of our forefathers" (ibid., 163). Here, of course, there is the sense that he is casting a wider net.

Scattered throughout the *Paisley Magazine* are further thoughts on the actual process of collecting. In a review of Thomas Lyle's *Ancient Ballads and Songs* (London, 1827), a work with many shortcomings in Motherwell's view, he reiterates the importance of gathering ballads and songs over other recuperative activities: "They deem, (and we are partly of their mind ourselves,) that to recover the fast-decaying memorials of the passions, feelings, and imaginations of earlier races of men, is a more important acquisition to human knowledge, than to delve through the entrails of the earth, for the purpose of finding the grinder, or may-hap the jawbone of some huge monster" (17–18). Then he describes what may well have been his own experience in that gathering process:

> We see—(observe 'tis only in our mind's eye, we see—nothing
> more, for we do not wish to mislead sober-thinking people,)
> the patient, weariless, enthusiastic, single-hearted Collector of
> Oral Song, in earnest confabulation with blind fiddlers and
> lousy mendicants, and diligently committing to writing their
> valuable recollections. Or we see him wandering from glen to
> glen, and from cot to cot, in some remote upland district or
> pastoral parish, a perfect personification of the agreeable, to
> each great-grandmother or bed-rid beldame he can there worm
> out. How slily he ingratiates himself into the confidence of this
> one, by replenishing her snuff-box; how beautifully he fills the
> pipe of a second; how adroitly he presents a third with a small
> modicum of tea or sugar; and mark, when the shrivelled lips of
> the Sybil will not open and pour forth its oracular responses,
> how, with a desperate resolution and flushed brow, he extracts
> from his tender purse, its one solitary coin, and rapidly
> transfers it into the paralytic palm of doting and avaricious

age. But the dark side hath yet to come. The literary gamester, who has thus risked his last shilling on one throw, finds, when too late, that her memory is a sieve—her mind shattered—her songs of the days of other years gone with her youth—faded away with the joys and hopes of that glad season.(18)

Perhaps there is here a bit of condescension for those who possess the material, a snobbism that may well derive from his Tory, classist position. There is certainly a bit of parody and self-criticism paraded as well. On a more serious note, he gives his idea of the kind of fieldwork one should undertake before making generalizations about anything—embedded in negative criticism of Robert Chambers and his *Picture of Scotland:* "A long residence in one place, and an intimate acquaintance with the peasantry is necessary, before we can hope to fish out all the curious and wonderful oral narrative that that *country-side* contains" (472–82).

In a review of Peter Buchan's *Ancient Ballads of the North of Scotland,* Motherwell returns to ballads but continues to talk about collecting. For the first time, he underlines that this material is both national poetry and national music. Since the ballads are sung, their tunes must also be collected— unfortunately Buchan didn't: "Ballads, to be felt thoroughly, must be sung. . . . [T]heir airs have preserved them" (643). Of course this material wasn't recorded earlier because they "were in every one's mouth, and chaunted around every hearth, and at every sport and pastime of the people." Then he sums up what a collector should do: "The whole duty of a collector of traditionary ballads is to print them exactly as they were said or sung to him; to mention the district of the country where he recovers the version, and to abstain from all conjectural emendation on the text" (657). Buchan, he says, does this. The review becomes an occasion as well for him to reiterate some of the points he had made in the introduction to *Minstrelsy,* especially on the subject of commonplaces—"identity of expression, where identity of action occurs"—an example, perhaps, of "their perpetual poverty of invention, but which we believe was a device, ingenious as it was judicious, to fix them in the memory of the people, as well as to assist the professed minstrel on those occasions, when circumstances might call on him to produce extempore narratives of passing events" (660). He praises Buchan for publishing many new ballads, new versions, which might result from "making one ballad to suit many persons, and many occasions by a slight change of name and locality" (660).

Motherwell's move to Glasgow, his role as editor of the *Glasgow Courier,* did not, of course, take him completely away from such literary pursuits. Never again, however, did the ballads and songs of Scotland play such a dominant role in his activities and thinking. They nevertheless remained something very much in his mind, something every Scot was presumed to know, a body of shared reference. This is evidenced in an article printed on 27 March 1830 in the *Courier,* recording the parliamentary postponement of the question of Jewish emancipation. Until their emancipation, the Jews could not acquire or hold property, such prohibitions being but one example of a long history of discrimination contained even in oral tradition: "[T]he cruel slaughter of Hugh of Lincoln is only remembered in faded chronicles or legendary ballads."[8] For Motherwell, ballads contained valuable history. They were, in fact, cultural and symbolic capital—a given. He helped preserve them and to make and keep them known.

5

The Death of Literature

Some critical readers cannot imagine it possible, that any thing
good is to be found in the pages of a Work which is of local
origin.

—Anonymous, *Visitor*

THE NINETEENTH CENTURY SAW the expansion of the periodical press
and journalism, stimulated by a multiple factors: increasing literacy, the
French and Industrial Revolutions, the rise of the middle class and leisure
time, and the availability of cheap paper made from wood pulp. It is likely
that periodicals and newspapers were more important than books and
"reached a broader cross section of society and had a richer diversity than
monographs" (North, *Waterloo Directory*, 9). The writer of these words further clarifies: "Just as periodicals and newspapers are greater in volume than
printed books, they are arguably more influential in the nineteenth century.
For instance, they were the primary mode of entertainment and communication before the age of radio, television, telephone. Inexpensive, readily folded
up, and easily digestible in small bits, for many people they were more attractive than monographs" (9). Astute commentators suggested, however,
that the knowledge communicated in small dribs and drabs was superficial
at best, implying that periodicals were contributing to the death of literature
(*Visitor* 2 [1818]: 22). Journalism, then, might be identified as a democratiz-
ing agent that made news and information on aspects of culture widely available. Newspapers and magazines commodified news for wider distribution
than that afforded by earlier elite or hegemonic forms of communication,
which had kept news and knowledge largely in the hands of the powerful
few. As such, journalism—cheap print—might be seen as an aid to "suffrage," in the enfranchisement of a wider circle of "knowers," of citizens.

For known and unknown—would-be—writers alike, the periodical
press (and I speak here particularly of the magazine format, the annual, rather
than the more frequently published newspapers, printed weekly, thrice
weekly, or every day) offered something else: the tantalizing possibility of
publication. The more prestigious exemplars even paid authors though ma-

terials were not always attributed. And Scotland's periodical press often represented a Whig/Tory political perspective/ideology, sometimes exhibited in a contrast between the expression of Enlightenment ideas of reason, progress, the new and nostalgic utopian visions—two competing or alternate perceptual frameworks in the early-nineteenth-century Scottish milieu.

The early giants of the periodical press were the *Edinburgh Review* and *Blackwood's*—the former founded in 1802 and the latter in 1817 (see Gifford, *History of Scottish Literature,* chap. 10); their target audience was the "intellectual and bourgeois community." Later in the century, working-class publications arose, becoming, according to William Donaldson, an "agency for disseminating culture." In between the early and well-known Edinburgh periodicals and the later working-class publications, there were many similar publications—certainly in the West of Scotland, in and around Paisley and Glasgow—that were directed toward a middle-class population and can certainly be read as evidence of literary vitality. Some were published annually, others on a monthly basis; many had short lives—several years, thirteen months, one or two numbers. New ventures, however, continued to replace those that failed, attesting to literary interests if not to the durability of particular publications.

These publications provided the first media outlets for Motherwell, and they remained important means of publication throughout his life: he contributed to them, edited them, and created them. He offered a cogent reason for their existence in his commonplace book: "One of the most striking advantages of a periodical miscellany is the shelter (if we may use the expression) such a publication affords to those fugitive thoughts[,] broken hints &c. which occasionally start in the mind of the man of business as well as the scholar and which for want of such a depository would be lost forever. In them many a valuable observation may be found[,] many an excellent hint extracted amply sufficient to compensate for the labor of searching them out from the rubbish and dust where they lie hidden" (Robertson 28/1210). In searching for such memorable pieces, however, it is not always possible to identify the authors, as pieces were routinely published without attribution. Early on, Motherwell's contributions were poetic, in time expanding to include reviews, prose sketches, and other miscellaneous writing. It may be that his first appearance in the periodical press was in a Greenock magazine, the *Visitor, or Literary Miscellany,* in 1818, which ran to two volumes. Intended "to amuse during long nights of winter" and to include "biography, essays, narrative and tales, moral pieces, historical and descriptive, criticism, miscellaneous, humorous, poetry," the individual contributors are identified only, if at all, by initials and amusing pseudonyms like "Metrical

Gander." There is an interesting anecdote recounted in a folder of obituary pieces at the National Library of Scotland (2969 Ry II d 17) about a promised poem on Loch Lomand for the *Visitor* alluded to earlier. A Mr. Turner came from Greenock to Paisley to get it. Motherwell told the courier to eat his meal and sleep in his bed: the poem would be ready in the morning. Turner supposedly left Motherwell sleeping, fully clothed, on the floor in front of the fire, with books for a pillow—but the poem was finished.

Marginal attributions in one of the many Robertson manuscripts (Robertson 1221/5) suggest that Motherwell also published in the *Enquirer,* a Glasgow publication that appeared for parts of 1820 and 1821: "Sonnet to My Own Heart" beginning "Submit, rebellious thing, quiescent be!" is signed "WM" (154); and "Clerk Rychard and Mayd Margaret" (247) is probably his as well. Few materials are attributed except by humorous noms de plume.

Undoubtedly Motherwell's peak periodical experience was with the *Paisley Magazine*—his dream offering to his adopted town. In many ways it was a public version of his own private interests, expressed in a variety of holograph commonplace books (for example, Robertson 1210/28 and 1212/ 15) in which he recorded ruminatory poetry, ballads, critiques of published work, and sketches on various topics, such as criminal law, the government, taste, religion, literature, Scots language, and the development of poetry. Similar materials were planned for the *Paisley Magazine,* which was financially backed by a number of his literary friends and acquaintances: printers, booksellers, writers. First conceived as an annual—an approach deemed overused—the final plan was to offer in twelve installments "curious intelligence . . . regarding the topography of this town and neighborhood, ancient customs, manners, traditions, local anecdote &c" (52) to a thousand subscribers from whom submissions would be welcome. The goal of this new publication was "to create a longing for literary enjoyments, not fully to gratify that longing" (178); the thirteenth and last issue is even more explicit that the hope had been to improve taste (535–36) and concludes fearing failure in the "Postscript Valedictory": "[W]e leave them (some Readers) to the uninterrupted enjoyment of that intellectual gloom which we strove to dissipate with our ingenious speculations, research, industry, and fancy . . . 'ART HATH AN ENEMY CALLED IGNORANCE' says Ben Jonson, and we should be sorry if, in relation to this valuable miscellany and our townsmen, the saying found an application" (692).

The magazine was aimed at a local audience, with regional and Scottish focus; the writers too were drawn from the greater Glasgow and Paisley areas. There were no nationally prominent figures like those who regularly contributed to the *Edinburgh Review* and *Blackwood's.* Prose tale, poetry, facts on local history, and correspondence provided a structure to showcase Motherwell's own interests (as well as those of his friends, supporters, and contributors). Amusing editorial opinions appear throughout the thirteen numbers. He can say that "reviewers are the caterpillars of literature. They farce their lean ribs with flesh peeled warm from the bodies of other men of happier condition. . . . The ambition of the Reviewer is to shew himself off—not to make appear the learning or genius of the author" (175); but this does not keep Motherwell from writing and printing his own reviews. Two are particularly telling, touching on favorite hobbyhorses—oral traditions and poetry.

Motherwell's review of Thomas Lyle's *Ancient Ballads and Songs* (1827) begins gently, questioning the sanity of collectors who are "most kind-hearted men, but not quite sound in their upper works" (17); but they are not as bad as poets whom he says are as "mad as march hares." He bemoans the fact that poetry is not appreciated. Having made his general introductory comments, he dismisses the book in question as useless balladry and worse poetry: the author gives no information about the supposed manuscript; there are no tunes; the texts are "altered and improved"; the original poetry is awful. He concludes, "We have read much good, bad, and indifferent in our time, but we are free as honest critics now to say, that we have rarely met with more pitiable, trivial, brainless, blunderings, and futile attempts to rise in what our author calls the *Parnassian scale*" (27). The ballad scholar and poet displays his mettle.

Yet his review of the twenty-five-year-old Paisley weaver-turned-soldier William Crawford's volume of poetry—*The Fates of Alceus; or, Love's Knight Errant, An Amatory Poem in Five Books, with other Poetical Pieces, on various subjects* (Paisley, 1828)—offers encouragement, though he doesn't quite think the materials at hand work. He praises Crawford for returning "to an earlier age for his copies" and makes no bones about his appreciation of local things: "Whatever is of local origin, hath a tye on our sympathies, so long as we breathe in the same atmosphere" (158). Here Motherwell is local apologist.

There are no attributions in the *Paisley Magazine,* but subsequent colleagues and friends have identified the various authors in an annotated copy. In Motherwell's case, some of his materials can also be identified because they were later published elsewhere. A case in point is a moralizing fictive work, "The Doomed Nine, or the Langbein Ritters: A German Legend," concluded posthumously in William Weir's *Scottish Annual* in 1836, which had at one point been offered to *Blackwood's.* The first two installments appeared in the *Paisley Magazine,* an early example of the serialization of fictive works, which Donaldson has described for working-class materials later in the century and which became a marketing ploy, whetting the appetite for the next episodes, though it is doubtful that Motherwell's serial would have captured the imagination of readers in quite that way. The first segment sets the narrative "in the pleasant simple days" of the past, which were interrupted by the ritters, the personification of evil. Each year the ritters pledged before a stone to Odin to do evil and especially to kill the one thing they loved: they were in the service of death. The second episode describes the return to the "simple days" with no signs of the ritters and focuses particularly on two old men, whose surviving children have married, producing grandchildren who brighten their days. The old men live near ancient elm and ash trees, which even the ritters have respected. The episode concludes with signs that the ritters are returning and a voice telling the old men to hide behind the trees. The third segment, published after Motherwell's death and called "A Chapter from the Unpublished Romance of The Strange and Delectable Story of the Langbein Ritters, or the Doomed Nine," tells that the old men had become part of the trees. On their return, the ritters sense negative responses from the trees and cut them down, surprised by the groans and blood that result.

Prefiguring or affirming the weather as topic for conversation, Motherwell's "Cool Thoughts for a Sultry Day" describes an ideal way to spend a summer day: in a cave, reading and drinking. Elsewhere describing six days in the Highlands on *Shanksnaigie,* that is, on foot, with friends and reflecting on the lack of intellectual interchange, he sums up his thinking: "Summer is no time for either talk or study. Winter, surly winter, with its sleet, and shower, and snow, and frost, is the only time for devouring books, for enjoying the conversation and society of friends, for vigorous study, and lastly, we should perhaps have mentioned it firstly, it is the only portion of the year when a good dinner more than music hath charms to soothe the breast of savage or saint. . . . O there is nothing comparable to this self-abandonment, this implicit up-giving, unconditional surrender of the soul to the beauties, sympathies, and delights of material creation" (533). In the former he yearns for reading, especially old books with old wine, believing that "our understandings may be enlarged, and wits whetted, by studying the genius and extracting the marrow of the literature of our ancestors" (253), a sentiment somewhat contradicted in the latter, where he says "devouring" of books and good meals belong to winter, not summer. These sketches or personal ruminations exhibit the contradictory quality of conversation to be sure, yet they also reveal something about the man: the importance of reading as a mechanism for improving oneself, his delight in the pleasures of drink and food.

Traditional practices and verbal habits inherited from the past are subjects of innumerable articles. The magazine featured a series on Scottish song; the first segment is devoted to a call for preservation of all songs, even fragments, in order to get a sense of the whole body of material. Some songs were suppressed by religious conflicts, which makes their recovery difficult. Then he prints a broadside, said to be sixteenth century, that deals with the good old days, when presumably songs and ballads were integral parts of life:

> Now worse & worse the world grows ay,
> No Betterment appears to be
> The nearer hand the Latter day,
> The more mischief doth multiplie
> O thou that reign'st in Persons Three,
> Whose Power doth all things contain,
> Grant us to rest in Peace with Thee,
> *From this worst world that e're was seen.* (265)

In another article, he offers a collection of proverbs from 1585 that prefigures the introduction he wrote for Henderson's collection of proverbs; in both he quotes D'Israeli extensively. One article is devoted to Dugald Graham (1724–1789), the Glasgow bellman whose creative works were enormously popular among peddlers. Motherwell suggests that a history of "vulgar" or popular literature would be useful, including such chapbooks as those attributed to Graham, because they play such a significant role in "forming the mind of the people" (n.p.).

He includes his own poems, as well as those of others. His "Joys of the Wilderness" (437) longs for peace and tranquility in nature, away from strife: "From Worldly guile, from Woman's wile, and Friendships brief and cold." It is tempting to read this autobiographically. And in some ways the entire thirteen-month existence of the *Paisley Magazine* was intimately tied to Motherwell's life and interests: it became a showcase for his concerns. Its failure to capture the loyalty of the Paisley "bodies" was a disappointment and must have confirmed the discomfiture he already sensed about the environment and its receptivity to literature. It did not, however, end his involvement with the periodical press. Nor did it go without notice: the *New Statistical Account of Scotland*'s volume on Renfrew-Argyle says the *Paisley Magazine* was "characterized by talent and varied local information . . . as favourable specimens of the periodical and ordinary literature of Paisley" (299).

Motherwell continued to contribute materials to similar periodicals, such as *Tait's Magazine,* published in Edinburgh in 1832; his most acclaimed poem "Jeanie Morrison" appeared there under the title "I've Wandered East, I've Wandered West"—the first line. Notice was also taken of the publication of Henderson's *Scottish Proverbs,* for which Motherwell had written an introduction: "We could sit and laugh by the hour over these quaint traditionary jokes. . . . Motherwell's preface is worthy of himself and the subject." *Tait's* also offers positive notice of the publication of Motherwell's poems. The year 1832 was a busy one for publications: together with his friends John Strang, J.D. Carrick, and Thomas Atkinson, and others of the so-called Rumblegumpy coterie, he began something between a magazine and newspaper trusting that the urban environment would be more receptive. The *Day,* an announcement read, "will be published, in fools cap folio, Price one Penny, By John Wylie, Bookseller, Argyle Street, A Daily Paper of Literature, Politics, Fine Arts and Fashion." The publication had pretensions to be like London's *Tattler* and "like the Spectator and Rambler of yore, to make its appearance on the breakfast table, every morning of the week except Sunday." Rather than original pieces, much of the *Day* involved reprinting selected articles that met the journal's goal: "The leading object of this Publication will be to pour forth, through the Cheapest Channels, wholesome political and moral principles; humorous and novel essays on the vices, follies and fashions of the age; honest and dispassionate criticism on Books, Art and the Stage, well-chosen extracts or abridgements of English Belles Lettres, past and present; a succinct catalogue raisonée of all literary and scientific novelties; and, in fine, occasional specimens of Glasgow gossip and West-country tittle-tattle. In addition to these, will be regularly given, a list of Births, Marriages and Deaths, the Tide Table at the Broomielaw, &c &c" (2 Jan. 1832).

There is often a playful quality under Glasgow gossip: "We are credibly informed that certain *ladies* appear at the breakfast table with their hair *en papillottes.* Such a species of dishabille, it is hoped, for the future, will disappear before the arrival of the 'Day'" (36). In fact, the gossip column allowed some amusing intertextuality, as in the reference to Motherwell's fictive character Baillie Pirnie, whose "Memoirs" were first published in the *Day.* Moved outside the literary frame and inserted in the gossip column, Pirnie becomes a means of satirizing a common response to the cholera epidemic: "What sad cholera times we do live in!! It is also said that Baillie Pirnie left Paisley yesterday, for Seester' Place, Gouroch" (108). Elsewhere Paisley is described as "that hot-bed of poetical genius" where "there are more verses manufactured . . . than in any other of the British empire" (247).

A column called "Ourselves and our Letter Box" describes a "Council of Ten" who decide what to print, sometimes voting to "burn it!" This council or club may well have been modeled on the editors of the *Spectator,* which also supposedly included a Mr. Spectator as the *Day* had a Mr. Day, or Mr. Every Day, or, finally, Dr. Didimus Day. Whoever the "Council" was, they enjoyed their collaborative endeavor and offered a magazine tied to the West of Scotland, but outward looking, more urbane, even cosmopolitan. The magazine's folding after one hundred and twelve issues gave the council a final occasion for satiric amusement, as in the 30 June 1832 announcement "Death of Dr. D. Day" and the plans recounted for a public funeral:

> It is with much pain we have to announce the sudden demise of Dr. Didimus Day, who, last night, expired at his mansion in Miller Street, at the goodly age of 112. To a most kindly and gentlemanlike department, he united the most versatile power of mind. He was at once a dramatic and lyric poet, a biographer, a satirist, a wit, and a man of *vertu.* He was a profound scholar, and a modern linguist of the very first order, having given proofs to the world of an acquaintanceship, not only with the tongues, but with the literature of France, Italy, Spain, Germany, Persia, Arabia and India. To these high literary qualifications which have spread his fame far and wide and brought celebrity to his native city, he added so many amiable social qualities that it has been resolved to give him a public funeral, and this morning, the following programme of the procession was agreed on, which is to take place on Monday:—

> Six Mutes, three and three.
> Band of Music, playing, "Oh, the days are gone"
> Ten Leeries, with torches lighted, preceded by the City Laureate,
> singing, "Oh 'The Day' is gone down o'er the Baltic's broad billow."
> The Secretary of the Commercial and Literary Society, in deep mourning.
> Followed by the Members—The Editors of the different Newspapers, arranged in the following order.
> Reformers' Gazette and Ursa Major.
> Free Press and Trades' Advocate.
> Chronicle and Scots Times.

Courier and Herald.
Stationers' Company, headed by two rival Bibliopoles,
bearing Gumphions.
Mr. John Finlay, carrying a bannar with "The Day"
reversed.
The Architect, bearing a plan of the Monument to be
placed in the Merchants' Park, with the following
EPITAPH
Both clouds and sunshine linger'd o'er his name,
Exalted now beyond the reach of Fame:
Reposing here, beneath this verdant lawn,
He knows, for him, no Brighter "Day" can dawn.
THE BODY
Editor of "The Day" as Chief Mourner.
Pall Bearers.
The Council of Ten, followed by the Contributors.
Baillie Pirnie on Horseback, followed by Aunti Pyet in
a Sable Coach.
The Original Publisher of "The Day," followed by the
leading
Members of the Drunkmakers' Society.
Rejected Contributors in plain clothes, while the
Procession closes with Mr. John Graham, Printer,
bearing a banner on which is inscribed
FINIS

In Paisley, Motherwell had committed himself to the *Paisley Magazine,* no doubt hoping that it would enable him to focus on literary matters. After its demise, he had a chance to become the editor of the *Paisley Advertiser,* which had been established in 1826. The news account of the dinner on the departure of William Kennedy, the former editor, hints at Motherwell's position and offers an account of his public persona. Kennedy, referring to the current topics in the news as "two or three wars . . . and Europe in a state of combustion, and the currency question as problematical as ever," suggests in glowing terms his successor's abilities: "[I]f solid and extensive information—a genius of first-rate power—and a heart honest as the steel of Damascus [Damocles?], constitute a perfect Journalist, then the Proprietors of the Paisley Advertiser may double their Subscriptions as soon a they please." For his part, Motherwell offers his promise: "What I can do, I will do, conscientiously, fearlessly, and honestly, not allowing private feeling to interfere with the upright and ample discharge of that duty, which an impartial journalist owes to the public. My hand is now on the stilts of the plough, and when like my friend I resign them to another, it shall be my proudest boast, and my brightest solace, if, on retrospection, I find that the furrow I have described, has at all approached the straight and undeviating line which his masterly hand has traced out for my feeble imitation" (*Paisley Advertiser,* 5 May 1828). This journalistic experience between 24 May 1828 and 9 October 1830, together with his role as editor of the *Paisley Magazine,* must have provided the necessary qualifications for his subsequent career as newspaper editor. And both these publications probably offered financial remuneration that, in the case of the *Paisley Advertiser,* allowed him to resign from his position as sheriff clerk depute, a repetitive and routine job that must have frustrated his creative and literary interests.

The *Advertiser* had been "markedly Tory" (Cowan, *Newspaper in Scotland*) even before Motherwell's editorship, and he clearly honed his invective prose in that context: "[T]he Irish blister is gathering, and must be lanced ere long" (5 July 1828). It was characterized in the *New Statistical Account* (7:299) as "[a] very respectable weekly paper . . . published every Saturday morning, has survived considerable opposition, and promises to maintain its present position from the fairness of its details, the soundness of its principles, and the judgement and good sense which generally characterize it." Motherwell and his predecessor Kennedy continued to be connected in the *Advertiser's* pages, even after leaving their posts as editor. In 1837, for example, poems by both men appeared in the "Poet's Corner," prefaced with a note attesting to the appropriateness of associating the two "in that paper whose destinies each, for a season, so ably and so honourably wielded. The health of the one, and the memory of the other, are never forgotten, and never omitted here, when festive parties assemble to honour poetry, literature, and genius" (20 May 1837). The Motherwell poem there reprinted from the *Glasgow Constitutional* is the one he is said to have written only several days before his death:

> When I beneath the coal red earth am sleeping,
>> Life's fever o'er,
> Will there for me be any bright eye weeping
>> That I'm no more?
> Will there be any heart still memory keeping
>> Of heretofore?
> When the great winds through leafless forests rushing,
>> Like full hearts break;

When swollen streams, o'er crag and gull gushing,
   Sad music make,
Wilt there be one whose heart despair is crushing,
   Mourn for my sake?
When the bright sun upon that spot is shining
   With purest ray,
And the small flowers, their buds and blossoms twining,
   Burst through that clay,
Will there be one twill on that spot repining
   Lost hopes all dye?
When no star twinkles, with its eye of glory,
   On that low mound,
And wintry storms have with their ruins hoary
   Its loneness crown'd,
Will there be then one versed in misery's story
   Pacing it round?
It may be so but this is selfish sorrow
   To ask such need—
A weakness and a wickedness to borrow
   From hearts which bleed,
The wailings of to-day for what to-morrow
   shall never need.
Lay me then gently in my narrow dwelling—
   Thou gentle heart;
And though thy bosom should with grief be swelling,
   Let no tear start—
It were in vain, for Time has long been knelling—
   Sad one, depart!

Motherwell carried his own interests, such as poetry—his own and that of others—over to the journalistic work successfully, expanding the literary contributions, using humorous anecdote and descriptive squibs about local customs and traditions as filler. Most of all, journalism enlarged his own horizons, placing him in a politically charged context and offering new challenges. Several contemporaries, ruminating on his life and work after his death, felt the move to journalism and Glasgow were incompatible with his literary interests. Evidence suggests, however, that for him the move, especially the physical move to Glasgow, was altogether positive: he found a circle of like-minded friends with whom he continued to initiate new projects of a literary nature; he achieved public recognition as an Editor of a major urban newspaper; he had moved up the next step of the ladder; he was "making" it in the emerging capitalist economy, in an urban environment.

The *Courier* had been established in 1791 and continued publication until 1865. Identified as "a distinguished and aristocratic newspaper" (Tierney, *Early Glasgow Newspapers*, 6–7), a "newspaper of some distinction" (Graham, 22), the *Courier* Motherwell joined as "A Notable Editor" (Tierney, *Early Scottish Newspapers*, 6) was one voice for conservatism when popular opinion is said to have been more progressive and liberal, radical even; nonetheless, "he advocated the cause which he conscientiously believed to be the true one with dauntless determination." Motherwell's biographer, McConechy, who followed him as the *Courier*'s editor, suggested that Motherwell's intellectual interests—"deficient in modern history and moral and philosophical science" (Cowan, *Newspaper in Scotland,* 185)—made him poorly suited for journalism, an opinion picked up by later writers on the nineteenth-century press. One of those writers, R.M.W. Cowan, goes on, however, to describe some of Motherwell's reasoned views, such as his concern for Scotland's "labouring poor" over the distant poor of the colonies. And Motherwell's predecessor, James Macqueen, was probably not ideally prepared for journalism either: he was part owner or proprietor, had managed a sugar plantation in Granada, was interested in West Africa, and advocated the rights of the West Indian Colonies. His editorship was perhaps facilitated by economic rather than intellectual/cultural capital.

The *Courier* was a respectable paper that appeared three times a week— Tuesday, Thursday, and Saturday—with a circulation of between four hundred and eight hundred by 1841. The paper was begun by James McNayr, who added his own opinions at the end of news items: "[T]he principle of neutrality in presenting news, which had been characteristic of earlier newspapers, was abandoned early in the nineteenth century. It became accepted that newspapers represented views, reflecting the political and social dimension of the day, and people began to look to the press to assist with the formation of their own opinions both on local and national issues" (Matheson, "Scottish Newspapers," 180). It may be that political bias was not new and had been established as precedent at the beginning of the eighteenth century (Ewald, *Newsmen of Queen Anne,* 5). Nevertheless, this partisan practice certainly allowed for the expression of the newspaper's "high" or extreme Tory positions, which distinguished it from the *Herald,* also Tory but more even-handed and with a considerably larger circulation number (from one to two thousand). Circulation numbers do not, of course, indicate the numbers of readers; individual issues were passed from hand to hand, thus concealing the extent to which the newpaper's influence might spread.

The physical appearance of the *Courier* was not unlike other contemporary papers. Motherwell introduced larger pages as he sought to make his mark on the standard four-page, five-column format. His changes, announced on 1 April 1830, made room for things that mattered to him—literature in addition to politics; local, national, and international "intelligence"; and so on. Happy with the changes, the issue of 15 April writes that the "Proprietors of the GLASGOW COURIER would fondly flatter themselves that the sphere of its usefulness will be materially extended, and its value as a vehicle of general intelligence considerably enhanced." He did not warn that things literary and editorial would thenceforth appear in larger type!

Motherwell's changes gave him room to make his mark, to solicit contributions, to write them himself, in addition to the ongoing process of refiguring news, which was standard fare in provincial papers: news from outside the local environment came from metropolitan papers. This meant that almost always "news" was printed at considerable time lag. Sources were seldom identified and accounts were sometimes "mutilated" in the process of summarizing, organizing, and rewriting. Part of the problem can be identified as the lack of access of Scots reporters to the Parliamentary Press Gallery until 1881 (Cowan, *Newspaper in Scotland,* 24); but clearly distance and lack of communicative technology were also contributing factors, in addition to the lack of monetary support and staff. So much of the "distant" news was patched together by the editor and any staff he might have.

The editor was aided by sub-editors or reporters; there was also a compositor who played an essential role in preparing and setting the type. Printing was usually done elsewhere, often by hand press; then papers had to be folded. Phillips, writing of the *Herald* and its Columbian Press, said that "in the hand of two hard-wrought first-class men . . . 350 impressions" could be made in an hour (*Glasgow's Herald,* 46). Interestingly, in addition to the editor, names of some compositors have survived—at least two of whom may have worked closely with Motherwell: John Moore and William Skirving. The staff size could be augmented by counting correspondents who might or might not have been remunerated for their contributions. No matter how it is viewed, however, the newspaper staff was extremely small by today's standards and might have been limited to three persons working in a small space.

Even deriving the news and other information from London newspapers, the production of an early-nineteenth-century Glasgow newspaper was surely enormously labor-intensive—in the hands of four or five persons, one or more of whom was responsible for obtaining the advertising that was essential to underwriting publication, ideally a business manager. The advertisements themselves, occupying the better part of the third or fourth page, provide interesting historical and sociological data. Sales were prominently featured: of shares of the Garnkirk Railway, of Dutch flower roots, of Highland ponies, of patent medicines, of theological (as well as other kinds of) books, of properties both commercial and residential. Various announcements found a place: of publications, to creditors, of available jobs. Prominent above all were notices relevant to the shipping trade, whether for passengers or freight. Such notices were visually identified with the icon of a ship and listed familiar and exotic locales linked to Glasgow: Edinburgh, Inverary, Belfast, Liverpool, London; St. Vincent, Kingston, Trinidad, St. Thomas, and Grenada; Naples, Palermo, Messina, Trieste; Cadiz, Gibralter, Malta; Rio de Janeiro and Veracruz; Manila and Honduras; Singapore, Batavia, China; Bombay, Madras, Calcutta; Cape of Good Hope; New York. Notice of meetings and events, lectures, exhibitions, sales (of wine and coffee), performances (ventriloquist), and courses of instruction (language, calisthenics, dancing, the making of wax flowers) found their place. One small announcement noted an upcoming conservative dinner at which the editor William Motherwell and the Duke of Gordon would be present: the price, twenty shillings; the venue, the Exchange Coffee Room; the time, 6:00 P.M.

Investors lay behind the newspapers, and they were sometimes actively engaged in the business. At about the time Motherwell was working as editor of the *Courier,* both it and the *Herald* cost seven pence. This price included the hefty government taxes of the Stamp Duty (established in 1712 and repealed in 1855) and Advertisement Tax, which amounted to four pence of the sale price, that is, over half the cost.

Motherwell's predecessor had been one of the owners, a recurring pattern for other newspapers; records do not suggest that Motherwell was, although it is within the realm of possibility. Presumably, however, he was a salaried editor, not like Samuel Hunter of the *Herald,* who was paid sixty pounds, then eighty pounds, and then one hundred pounds in his thirty years as editor, which ended in 1836. However, Hunter might have received as much as one thousand additional pounds, as his share of the profits as partner. It is impossible to guess Motherwell's earnings; if he was not a partner, probably about two hundred pounds a year. If he did not have Hunter's material accumulation owing to his position as partner/editor, he certainly inherited as editor a class position.

Glasgow editors were educated, recognized figures who took a stand on the news and in turn received responses, sometimes negative and vocal, to those positions. Samuel Hunter was burned in effigy at the Cross for his opposition to the Reform Bill of 1832 (Phillips, *Glasgow's Herald,* 37). That was part of the territory. Editors were involved in civic activities, were often writers or poets, and saw themselves as public persons, paying for a listing in the Glasgow Directory. This was a high profile position. And Motherwell seems to have reveled in the public recognition.

Newspaper articles were not signed, so it is impossible to know exactly what Motherwell wrote; but it is clear that he wrote a great deal and that the paper's stance, and its format owed much to his own supervision. Certainly the paper was about news and opinions on current happenings. Partisan politics are prevalent. The Whigs come in for considerable criticism; they are called "Incapables," "dirty reptiles," and, less offensively, "blunderers": "We have the honour to announce two ministerial blunders in one day, which proves the exceeding fertility of the Whig administration" (6 Sept. 1832); "glaring instance or other of Whig apostacy of principle, of political inconsistency, of mendacity and absolute moral dishonesty" (27 July 1833). And yet the paper could also print a humorous definition of political parties taken from and attributed to the *Edinburgh Evening Post:*

> *What is a Whig?* A man who will promise to turn the moon
> into green cheese, to obtain a selfish object, and who, in the
> hour of his success, will laugh at or oppress the dupes who
> smoothed his path to power. *What is a Tory?* A man who,
> caring for what he deems beneficial to the country, neglects
> and scorns the temporary clamour of the multitude, and who,
> in the time of his prosperity, looks more to the people than in
> the period of his distress. *What is a Radical?* An honest fool,
> who theorises till his mind becomes incapable of judging
> between right and wrong, or distinguishing between *meum* and
> *tuum.*— (11 July 1833)

In general the paper expressed "loyalty to the Crown and unaffected love and veneration for the Laws and Constitution of the country" (15 Apr. 1830) and affirmed the positions of the House of Lords: "The British Constitution is yet safe. We refer with pleasure to the stern and uncompromising attitude which the heriditary guardians of the Crown, and of the institutions of the country, have assumed at this peculiarly critical and threatening time" (8 Oct. 1831).

Particular coverage during Motherwell's tenure as editor was given to the economic crisis, to questions around the reform bill, and to the debate about the Irish Catholic "problem." The paper positioned itself against free trade as "destructive to home industry and capital in practice" (24 Dec. 1831) and in favor of protectionist legislation such as the Corn Laws. It was definitely against the Reform Bill of 1832, against extended suffrage and redistricting: "Reform means Revolution" (3 Mar. 1831); "It is not a reform conceived in the spirit, and suited to the practice of the constitution, but it is a reform which will unsettle all law, trample on all right, and confiscate all property in the country. To a wise, temperate, and strictly just reform, and correction of existing abuses, the country is not indisposed; but to a reckless uptearing of all ancient landmarks, privileges, and chartered rights, every intelligent mind and loyal heart in the community is opposed" (8 Mar. 1831). Despite that denouncement, the paper/Motherwell could see humor in the situation, printing the announcement that "it has been calculated that the skins of upwards of 2000 sheep have been already consumed in the parchment used for Reform petitions" (7 Apr. 1831). When it passed, the paper hoped that indeed it would do good.

The status of "the Church," by which Motherwell and the *Courier* clearly meant Protestant and Presbyterian, continued to be problematic according to the *Courier;* and it was tied in with the situation in Ireland. Speaking of Northern Ireland, the *Courier* read, "The North of Ireland is now in a state of almost open rebellion" (2 Feb. 1832). Absolutely opposed to any government support for Catholicism—and Catholicism was equated with the Irish—the *Courier* reports that "there is no denying the fact, that there is a lavish expenditure of the public money for the dissemination of the tenets of the Roman Catholic Church, while every discouragement is given to Protestant institutions connected with the education of the people, and the propagation of the true Gospel" (26 Mar. 1833). And on 15 October 1833, quoting the *Dublin Evening Mail,* "The emigration of our Protestant brethren to the Canadas has been long deplored by all who have at heart the real and substantial well being of Ireland."

In the years after the failure to stop the Reform Bill of 1832, the paper and Motherwell seem to have adopted the Irish question, supporting the Protestant position, reporting favorably on the Orange Society: "When we see the Orange Institution attacked with tooth and nail by O'Connel and his heartless gang, we may rest assured that it is of vital importance in thwarting his seditious attempts to disintegrate and revolutionise the empire, as well as of preserving our civil and religious institutions in all their original purity[,] strength, stability, and effect. Had it not been for Orangism in Ireland, that island, long ere this would have been no part of the British Empire. . . . In short, the Orange Institution is nothing more nor less than a strictly Loyal and Constitutional Association, founded upon a Protestant basis, banded together to support the laws, and defend the Institutions, Civil and

Ecclesiastical, of the Empire" (12 Mar. 1835). And on 22 August 1835 the support continues: "The persecution of the Loyal Orangemen is continued with a bitterness and perseverance which shew us that nothing less than the total extinction of Protestantism in Ireland will satisfy O'Connel and his gang. . . . The Committee of the House of Commons, to report on the Orange Institution, is a packed one." On 19 September 1835, the *Courier* prints Motherwell's testimony before that very committee and thus offers a rare instance of firsthand news from London.

In between the news, there were amusing comments and human interest stories: "Another musical wonder has arisen in fertile Germany—a woman who plays beautifully on the piano-forte with her nose. Nobody knows what the next improvement will be; perhaps to play the harp with elbows" (5 Aug. 1830). Motherwell misses no opportunities to include references to his traditional interests, including a reference to the ballad about Hugh of Lincoln in discussing the question of Jewish emancipation. Elsewhere the *Courier* prints a health cure: "[O]ne of the most effectual means of curing a cut, bruise, or burn, is said to be the inside coating of the shell of a raw egg. Apply the moist surface to the wound; it will adhere of itself, leave no scar, and heal any wound, without pain, more speedily than any salve or plaster in the universe" (9 Mar. 1830).

The emphasis Motherwell gave to the *Courier* was, of course, an increase in coverage of things literary: reviews, commentaries on various magazines and annuals, references to literary personages, and publication of poetry. A review of William Frederick Wakeman's *Traits and Stories of the Irish Peasantry* reports that the book is "decidedly the most amusing volume we have fallen in with since the publication of Crofton Croker's Irish Legends" (2 Mar. 1833). This review is most certainly Motherwell's. He excuses himself, however, from reviewing Henderson's *Scottish Proverbs:* "A volume with which we have ourselves had some slight ado, we cannot according to the usages of the day, well make or meddle . . . [so we will] make room for the observations of a friend, who, . . . opposed to us in politics" (2 June 1832) is presumably capable of writing a positive review!

Blackwood's is frequently invoked, and there was a predisposition to be positive because of the shared Tory perspective: "The number of *Blackwood* for the present month is excellent in every particular" (5 May 1832); "Christopher North [the editor and also a Paisley man and perhaps a model for Motherwell] is beyond all question the vainest man and the most enormous egotist that ever lived; but these characteristics, which are faults in other men, are not only pardonable but even agreeable in him, as they are vouchers for the real honesty and simplicity of his heart" (25 Aug. 1832);

"We have been readers of Blackwood's Magazine since its first appearance, and, of course, many glowing Numbers have passed through our hands. We looked forward to the Number for March with no ordinary degree of interest, and now that we have perused it, we scruple not to say it is one of the most splendid that has yet appeared. The leading article, 'Shall we have a Conservative Government?' is one of the most powerful political papers we have ever read. It rivetted our attention so intensely that we devoured its contents without once moving our position; and now that we have gone over it a second time, we cannot enough admire the genius of the gifted individual who penned it" (14 Mar. 1835).

Literary figures, too, are noted. The paper, for example, records the death of Robert Burns's widow: "We love to see the homage thus willingly awarded to the relict of so magnificent a genius; but we confess that that part of our contemporary's narrative, which relates to the exhumation of the Poet's skull, for the purpose of taking a plaster cast of it for the benefit of phrenological dreamers, was peculiarly revolting of our feelings, and a species of desecration of the hallowed sanctities of the tomb that we shall ever condemn. With Hamlet, we say, our 'gorge rises at it'" (12 Apr. 1834).

Literary pride of place was taken by poetry, published prominently on the first page, in larger type. Here the poems are often attributed. There were topical poems on the death of George IV, on the French Revolution, and on Walter Scott's death; there were pieces by Leigh Hunt, Robert Southey, and John Galt; and Motherwell prints several of his own works. And there were two poems by Wordsworth, on Scottish topics, suggesting how up-to-date Motherwell was:

POETRY
SONNETS BY WORDSWORTH
A Highland Hut.

See what gay wild flowers deck this earth-built cot,
Whose smoke, forth-issuing whence and how it may,
Shines in the greeting of the Sun's first ray
Like wreaths of vapor without stain or blot.
The limpid mountain rill avoids it not;
And why shoudst thou? If rightly trained and bred,
Humanity if humble,—finds no spot
Which her Heaven-guided feet refuse to tread.
The walls are cracked, sunk is the flowery roof,
Undressed the pathway leading to the door;
But love, as nature loves, the lonely poor;

Search, for their worth, some gentle heart wrong-proof,
Meek, patient, kind, and, were its trials fewer,
Belike less happy.—Stand no more aloof!

MOSSGIEL

"There!" said a stripling, pointing with meet pride
Towards a low roof with green trees half concealed,
"Is Mossgiel farm; and that's the very field
Where Burns ploughed up the daisy." Far and wide
A plain below stretched seaward, while, descried
Above sea-clouds, the Peaks of Arran rose;
And, by that simple notice, the repose
Of earth, sky, sea, and air was vivified.
Beneath "the random field of clod or stone"
Myriads of daisies have shone forth in flower
Near lark's nest, and in their natural hour
Have passed away, less happy than the one
That by the unwilling ploughshare died to prove
The tender charm of poetry and love.

With such poems, William Motherwell affirmed his own interests, made his journalistic endeavors continuous with his literary concerns, and offered his reading public something to improve their taste, while confirming his own.

Despite the critique of several contemporaries, I think it is possible to suggest that his journalistic and editorial endeavors were in fact his métier, that through them he came close to doing what he wished. They allowed him to bring together a number of things that mattered to him: poetry and creative works in general; notice of traditional songs, sayings, and beliefs, which gave evidence of and implicitly affirmed an earlier way of life; and politics, including current events, especially those that impinged on the world he favored and would bring change. And his involvements show him participating in and relishing the activities of an expanding profession, one that played a significant role in shifting general reading from literature to ephemeral materials. His own involvement in the expansion of the periodical press and journalism show, then, another contradiction of his life: his own endeavors were part of the very changes he sought to resist.

6

Les Bons Mots

Each word that John has said to you,
To others he'll unsay.
How can he be but spare and lean,
Who *eats his words* all day?
—*The Day*

MOTHERWELL MADE A SERIOUS STUDY of ballads because a project was dumped in his lap: taking his responsibility seriously, he then went out of his way to become an expert. And he was multiply rewarded for his efforts—with positive press accounts and with election to corresponding membership of the Scottish Society of Antiquaries. His interest in ballads and folksongs must have arisen originally from his lived environment, where he heard them performed and read them in books. His interest was further piqued because he sensed that they were of the past, that the changes that were taking place in society were slowly making them obsolete, that other forms of song and entertainment were encroaching, that taste changes. In fact, it may well have been the dissonance between the old traditions and the new environment that caused him to notice them in the first place. Ballads and folksongs were not, however, the only evidences of what he judged to be a former way of life to capture his attention: he noted and noticed interesting beliefs, sayings, practices, and narratives largely because he saw them as holdovers. His interest in them sprang in part from his personal sense that life was better in a hypothetical past, that the legends, proverbs, and "quaint" sayings, the beliefs, the practices, and, of course, the ballads and songs emanated from an organic community that no longer existed.

He had a keen eye for the odd tradition, writing down a description or example on any odd scrap of paper—destined subsequently to be bound, preserved, and presented, by friends who esteemed them valuable, to Glasgow University Library—including them as part of published and unpublished compositions and records and printing them as filler in the *Glasgow Courier.* On the surface level, the existence of curious traditions made life more interesting—for himself and for others. He recorded a peculiar saying of

"Daft Mrs McKinlay": "He had neither house nor ha' coq nor chair stool nor spoon when I took him by the hand" (Robertson 28/1210) and put a proverb into the mouth of one of his own inventions, the Baillie Pirnie: "What cannot be mendit suld be sune endit" (*Memoirs of a Paisley Bailie, Day*). Both instances illustrate his interest in short verbal forms, particularly the proverb, to which he devoted considerable attention toward the end of his life.

Motherwell records narrative and legendary traditions and goes to some lengths to "correct" a tradition concerning the poet Robert Burns: a number of biographers had been misinformed, suggesting that Burns wrote negative verses about the royal family on the window of an inn in Stirling. According to Motherwell's intelligence, his traveling companion Nicol was the real culprit, and Burns took the blame to protect him. Motherwell chastises John Gibson Lockhart for accepting the common attribution to Burns (*Paisley Magazine,* 437–46). He referred to a former, widespread belief in witchcraft as explanation for nervous fits: "This day saw Robert ———son of a respectable weaver in SM Street. This boy for 8 days past has been subject to certain nervous fits. Fits which in olden days would have been attributed to witchcraft. And fits which were caused by a fright the poor boy got from an old beggar woman" (25242.16). In March 1825, he wrote down a former practice concerning the making of funeral announcements remembered by Mr. Walkinshaw, sheriff clerk of Renfrewshire, from his youth. A bellman would go about the village ringing a bell and announcing a death:

> Brethren and Sisters I let you to Wit that a worthy brother
> or Sister
> as the case might be
> B.B. died at the pleasure of the Lord
> Here the bellman took off his hat
> upon the day of——— and that his corpse lies
> here the place named
> and that he is to be interred upon
> the day & hour
> in the——— Churchyard and you are warned to attend his corpse to
>   the grave. Amen
> Take off his hat. (Robertson 12/1217: 2)

The subsequent procession was led by the bellman, ringing and tinkling the bell; followed by the male mourners and the corpse, after which came female mourners and friends. Motherwell's account provides more than text; it offers performance cues as well. Elsewhere he recorded another former practice: "*[C]urious custom* anciently when the widow of a bankrupt in Scotland wished to release herself of all claims by her husband's Creditors she danced above her husband's grave with a white stocking on one leg and a black one on the other—made her water on his grave and sang a satirical song. This was making him a dyvor—Query about this custom & the song" (Robertson 10/1208, last page).

The tongue-in-cheek record of guard duty, referred to earlier, with a group of friends—supposedly for the edification of his superior—gives a full account of what transpired between 6:00 P.M. and 6:00 A.M. and touches humorously on the subject of belief. He writes that a large rat made a noise, causing three mice to drop dead in fright, stimulating a conversation "anent super natural noises—of the influences of witches—of the truth of judicial astrology. Of the Lapis philosophorum. Of the Reappearance of the Dead. Of the physical nature of the Devil form and attributes and titles—whether he is married or unmarried—if he has any children and if they inherit the mischievous qualities of their parent—a refutation of the vulgar idea of the Devil having horns and hoofs—a confirmation of the fact of his having a tail—all men had at one time tails but were obliged to part with them at the close of the deluge. Noah and his sons towing their ark ashore used their tails as cables but they unfortunately broke off at the rump" (Robertson 9/1207, 1).

In the *Courier* he includes periodic accounts of customs surrounding holidays: at New Years, poor children go around begging for oat cakes, appropriately dressed with a large pocket. Performances by "guizards" of traditional plays are given for a halfpenny at Christmas, New Years's Day–Hogmany, and on Hansel Monday. He also reviews works dealing with traditional material—Hugh Miller's *Scenes of the North of Scotland; or the Traditional History of Cromarty* (Edinburgh: A. & C. Black, 1835)—in which he referred to Croker's *Fairy Legends of the South of Ireland,* thus making his readers aware of important publications on one of his favorite subjects. In the *Paisley Magazine* he describes the male practice of meals, between four and nine in the evening, always featuring whiskey and sometimes port: "A well-fed man nourishes no animosities." In various reviews and essays, particularly in the *Paisley Magazine,* he not only has the opportunity to note former sayings, beliefs, practices, he sometimes takes the opportunity to comment in depth about such traditions, about the process of gathering such materials. A review of Chambers's *Picture of Scotland* is a case in point: Motherwell begins by praising the work's concept—"the embodying and preserving in his narrative, all the traditionary anecdotes, legends, and superstitions, which are current regarding the localities he describes" (*Paisley*

Magazine, 473). Their preservation is clearly important to Motherwell for the historical materials they contain: "Traditions may be corrupted and disguised; but they still cleave to the germ of fact from which they sprouted" (ibid., 474). But Chambers should have included ballads; more important, he set himself up for failure by doing a superficial job: to know a place well, you have to live there for a long period of time. And Chambers, from Motherwell's perspective, did a terrible job in Renfrewshire—Motherwell's own territory: "[W]e shall convict thee of inconsistency, misrepresentation, inaccuracy, carelessness, libel, defamation, ignorance, errors without number, hasty speculation, crude observation, folly, and wickedness"(ibid., 477–78). Chambers had clearly touched a sore point and roused Motherwell's regional pride. This is particularly interesting because Motherwell had reached the breaking point on the subject of Paisley and the area: he felt it cramped his style, limited his opportunities, and wasn't receptive to the kinds of things that interested him. A native can criticize, however, not an outsider! Motherwell's general criticism and insistence that knowledge of an area took time was well-taken: it remains the sine qua non of ethnographic research.

A number of reviews and essays in the *Paisley Magazine* allowed him to delve into theoretical and methodological issues concerning the recording of extant traditions. On several occasions he suggests that people only begin collecting certain materials when they are threatened, when they are on the verge of disappearing. And he has his eyes out for areas that need to be studied. One was a category he referred to as "vulgar literature," that is, chapbooks. They played an important part in "forming the mind of a people"; he especially noted the eighteenth-century Glasgow bellman, chapbook creator, and seller, one Dugald Graham. His works continued to be sold and appreciated for "his fat jokes, and grossly indecent, though true portraitures, of Scottish life and manners" (666–71). Motherwell lists his early works and what he could discover about his life and experiences, warning that such information as he is able to provide is in danger of being lost.

In a 1831 publication of the Maitland Club, William Hamilton of Wishaw's *Descriptions of the Sherrifdoms of Lanark and Renfrew* (1710), Motherwell added an interesting appendix describing the various explanations that had been offered of the origins of a variety of so-called ancient monuments—stones of various sizes and shapes—that dotted the landscape of those counties. Surveying the stones himself, and referring to historical published records by a variety of "worthies"—a near-contemporary Semple, Wyntoun, Pennant, Lord Hailes, Froissart, Boece—Motherwell also calls upon the traditionary record with all of its multivalence and multiplicity of perspectives, that is, versions, in offering his own conjectural suggestions. Unlike some of his predecessors, he considers the potential verity of the oral accounts, even though they "run counter" to the historical record. He goes on to "contend that it is altogether improbable that such a story took its rise wholly independent of some foundation in fact. The historical facts may be disguised by oral embellishment, or corrupted by being fused with other events prior or subsequent to their own era, but they can never be wholly suppressed" (297). In giving historical weight to oral accounts, he hints at the process by which both oral and written records arise; he calls it "a species of mental alchemy, by which names, facts, circumstances, and the occurrences of various ages, are imperceptibly fused together in Time's crucible, till oral tradition streams forth to posterity a current of imperishable bronze— a mixed, but a useful and right beautiful metal" (302–3). He makes it clear to the reader that history is often silent and that oral tradition is needed to fill out the account. In knowing the past, both are needed; the oral too arose from the facts. Then he goes on to call into question the dismissal of the "traditionary" accounts just because they are not written: "[W]e deem it right to offer an apology to those rigid antiquaries, whose sympathies for by-past times are circumscribed within an alphabet of written signs, and to whom all history appears fable until it is transferred to a sheep's back, or a piece of perishable rag" (303).

Motherwell uses the appendix to extend his comments on oral tradition and its historical validity. Yet the author of the preface to the volume raises the suspicion that Motherwell penned the material himself in referring to a full-length narrative Motherwell recounts about the origin of a stone called the Palmyarm Ross: possibly this is a retelling of an historical legend although I have not been able to locate parallel Scottish texts. While the account is filled with internationally known motifs and is clearly told in Motherwell's words, I doubt that it was his invention. The legend in question, "The Story of Palmyarm Ross" deserves notice:

> A long, long while ago—tradition seldom condescends to
> traffic in precise dates—when the Kings of Scotland and
> England were on excellent visiting terms, it happened that the
> King of Scotland, with his Queen, went to spend some weeks
> of summer in the Court of England. Here every description of
> splendid pageant, pastime, and knightly entertainment,
> befitting the quality of such exalted guests, was lavishly
> displayed, and, among the rest, various martial exercises
> formed no inconsiderable portion of each day's amusement. In

the English Court there was a champion of surpassing height and strength, and so expert in wrestling and swordmanship, that neither knight nor knave, in all merry England, could match him. He was in high esteem with the King of England, who never ceased jibing the Scottish King to produce any one of his subjects who would overthrow the English champion. Irritated at these repeated boasts, the Scottish King coolly said, that next year, when his royal cousin visited Scotland, he would prove to him that the smallest man in Scotland was more than a match for the biggest born of England. Wagers were accordingly laid between the rival sovereigns, and these, as may be supposed, were equal in amount to the ransom of seven kings. All preliminaries of the combat were arranged agreeably to certain articles. These principally consisted in a condition that the champions should fight within a circle out of which neither could escape. By fire or water the vanquished was to perish. The circle was to be surrounded by a deep and broad ditch, sufficient to drown the coward who would be so base as attempt flight; and in its centre was to be kindled "a bauld bane fire," into which the victor might cast his antagonist to be consumed.

The King of Scotland had, in his pride, undertaken what his prudence told him was of difficult accomplishment. With a heavy heart he turned his back on London, and went home to find out a champion to redeem his pledge. But the fame of the Englishman had reached Scotland, and this was no ways diminished by the marvellous testimony which the King's retinue bore to the prowess of the gigantic wrestler, whose feats they had witnessed. Day after day passed away, and yet none of the Scottish knights offered to venture life and limb in the king's quarrel. In vain the King summoned his chivalry around him, and proffered vast honours to any one that would redeem the regal, and the national honour. In vain the King said he would gladly bestow on the person who vanquished the English champion his own pleasant Inch and Castle of Renfrew, where he resided, and which he loved as the apple of his eye. All were silent; they had seen or heard of the Titan to whom they were to be opposed, and already heard, in imagination, their own bones crashing under his enormous bulk.

Meanwhile preparations were making for the combat on

the Knoc, and for the accommodation of the respective Courts. A mound was raised—a deep ditch was dug around it, and filled with water, across which a single plank was thrown to give access to the combatants.

While almost in despair of finding one courageous enough to undertake the "adventure perilous," Ross, of Hawkhead, offered himself, and he was gladly accepted by the King, while all the Court marvelled at his extraordinary temerity. The eventful day at last arrived. The gigantic Englishman stood within the circle—the "bauld bane fire" was crackling in the centre—and beside him stood the comparatively diminutive, but dauntless, laird of Ross. From neck to heel Ross had clad himself in a garment which fitted tightly to his body, made of the skin of some beast, the fleshy side outermost, and this glistering and smooth with oil. The English champion smiled at his antagonist, and both addressed themselves for the combat. Deafening cheers now rent the air; the heralds sounded their trumpets; and at the signal the Englishman attempted to pounce on Ross, and truss him up as a hawk would a sparrow. Here, however, he was disappointed; for Ross eluded his grasp, and leapt clean aside. Again and again the champion of England made a snatch at Ross, but the slipperiness of his skin armour, or his agility, saved him. For a long while they continued engaged in this manner, the Englishman endeavouring to get his favourite hold of Ross, and to toss him on the fire at once, and have done with such child's play; but his attempts proved abortive. Despairing at length of accomplishing his object, the Englishman, almost breathless with anger and unavailing exertion, stood still, and invited Ross to take his favourite hold. "Palm *my* arm," said the Englishman; and Ross, who waited for such an invitation, and depended upon the strength of his grasp, and a peculiar sleight he had, immediately sprung forward, seized the Champion by his wrists, and, by a desperate wrench, dislocated them both at the shoulder joint. A scream of agony burst from the lips of the unsuspecting Englishman. Disabled in this summary fashion, he could offer no effectual resistance to his wily antagonist, who immediately made short work of him, and, with little difficulty, dragged him into the burning pile. Thus terminated the savage combat, to the immense contentment and glory of the King of Scotland; but to the inexpressible chagrin and sore dismay of him of England.

Having accomplished this splendid feat, Ross demanded the proffered reward. The King hesitated to surrender the Inch to his faithful vassal, for which, as mentioned above, he had a great local attachment. "Ross," said the King, "for this Inch I will give thee a span in any other part of my realm." "Nay, my liege," retorted Ross indignantly, "I will content me with the *inch* even now, and when I have again to defend they honour I shall expect the *span.*"

The King could not retract his royal promise; so, from that time, the gallant Ross bruiked the lands and castle of the Inch, which he had so valiantly won, and ever after he was distinguished by the soubriquet of Palm-my-arm, in consequence of the circumstance above narrated. (300–302)

The motif of a "Wrestling match won by deception" (K12) is prominent here; other relevant recognized traditional elements in this narrative are S166.3 "Mutilation: shoulder-skin torn off in wrestling"; P677 "Customs connected with dueling"; L311 "Weak (small) hero overcomes larger fighter." Motherwell's account clearly works within traditional parameters.

One issue of the *Paisley Magazine* featured a collection of proverbs from 1585 (437–46). Prefacing a list of some 232 proverbs, Motherwell's introductory comments suggest that he finds the material dry to read but recognizes their role as early literature; and he offers long quotes from D'Israeli by way of defining the materials. In some ways this was a dry run for an extended essay he would write later to preface a collection of proverbs made by his Paisley friend, the portraitist Andrew Henderson. Motherwell built upon this earlier essay for the introduction, again citing D'Israeli's *Curiosities of Literature* wherein proverbs are designated the wisdom of the ages and described as printed on large sheets and sometimes put on walls. Motherwell reprints the earlier list of proverbs. In fact, he does a miniature version of what he had done for ballads in the *Minstrelsy,* going into their history, providing a history as well of the written records of proverbs: while both introductions are early examples of serious study of traditionary materials, the proverb introduction lacks the depth and breadth of the *Minstrelsy*'s introduction/afterword.

The introduction to Henderson's *Scottish Proverbs* is a full eighty pages (abridged drastically in the 1891 edition), devoted to what Motherwell, perhaps characteristically, designates an important species of national literature: "[W]e shall ever rejoice to see additions made to the stock of our native literature" (lxxxvi). Such materials are national, "illustrative of the domestic habits, civil economy and living speech of a people" (lxxv), offer references to history ("*Peace gae wi' ye, as King James said to his hounds*"; lxxx), and reflect national characteristics ("[E]very time a Scot speaks of eating, he thinks thrice of his drink"; lxviii). Yet Motherwell clearly recognized the parallels between Scottish and other national proverbs that suggested that many of the proverbs, while existing in national redactions, were international or even universal: "[T]he identity of human nature has necessarily produced a correspondence and parallelism in the proverbs of every nation" (lix).

His focus, however, is on Scottish materials, now on the wane. Motherwell offers an outline of the published collections of Scottish proverbs, pointing especially to the role of clergymen as paraemiographers, often using the materials to "make their address to their hearers the more affecting and nervous" (*Scottish Proverbs,* xx). He describes earlier works, offering evaluative comments. Of a collection made by James Kelly and published in London in 1721, Motherwell says, "[O]f the proverb, 'I will be your servant when you have least to do and most to spend' Kelly adds, 'The true Meaning of that common Phrase *Your humble Servant, Sir*'" (xxv). Motherwell suggests that there are few Scottish manuscript collections. One was made by George Bannatyne during the pestilence (this would appear to have been a reference to a pastiche of proverbs in poetic form rather than to a formal collection); ever ready to note parallels, Motherwell appends a footnote to the effect that his own proverb essay was written during the time of the "Indian Cholera" (xxxi). Under the discussion of manuscripts, Motherwell refers again to the materials earlier published in the *Paisley Magazine,* the 232 proverbs amassed by John Maxwell of Southbar, of which number 10 is "In all degrees of frindeschipe equalitie is chieflie considderit" (xxxiv) and number 14 the familiar "Thair is no smoke bot quhair thair is sum fyre" (xxxv). The more extensive English collections are dealt with in a long footnote.

Following earlier commentators, such as Erasmus, D'Israeli, Johnson, and Aristotle, he offers succinct definitional suggestions—"*sense, shortness, and salt*" (liv), "germs of moral and political science" (lxiii), "substitute for philosophical principles" (lxv)—in general to confirm a statement. Of Henderson's collection in particular, for which his essay was written, he offers several suggestions: Henderson and other proverb editors should not censor their publications, should identify examples that are in current use, should arrange materials alphabetically rather than thematically as done in the work under consideration, and above all should offer commentary, explanations of allusions, and history. As illustration, he provides an anecdote that explains one particular proverb that averted a duel: one of the duelists inadvertently gave his rival not his calling card but a card on which was written "NAETHING SHOULD BE DONE IN A HURRY, BUT CATCHING FLEAS" (lxxiii).

Motherwell attacked the proverbs briefly, but he approached them with seriousness, bringing to bear considerable knowledge and expertise about matters traditional. This essay, together with his remarks on other traditions and his recording of them, underline his interest in elements of culture that were changing, his keen eye for the habits of the past, and his abiding interest in things that might conceivably be identified as Scottish.

Play

> The subsequent notices regarding Barochan Cross, and other
> ancient monuments in the neighbourhood of Paisley, have been
> contributed by William Motherwell, Esq. a member of the
> Maitland Club; and to whom the reader is particularly obliged for
> the pains he has taken with these romantic tales, though it may
> still be reasonably enough doubted whether they owe not more to
> the fertile pen of the writer than to the faithfulness of traditionary
> record so strenuously urged.
>
> —Maitland Club,
> *Descriptions of the Sheriffdoms of Lanark and Renfrew*

THIS PUBLISHED SUGGESTION of Motherwell's participation in literary play—that is, in the creation of fabrications and forgeries—offers an apt beginning for a discussion of his literary activities in general: they were in the broadest sense play, activities undertaken in leisure time for his own pleasure. The writing of literature, whether poetry, sketch, or essay, was perhaps Motherwell's greatest delight; it gave meaning to his existence and was his vocation, his calling. Thus it was something about which he was deadly serious. But it was also pleasure; it involved sociability, collaboration with like-minded persons, and it was, quite often, "playful." It was certainly the most significant thing in his life.

As literateur, Motherwell was very much tied to a prevailing literary tradition, some characteristics of which—the forgeries and fabrications and pseudonymous publications—seem to intensify the playful aspects of this "play."[1] At the same time he was participating in a much larger, and quite serious though unstated, inquiry about representation, about truth, about authorship and authenticity, both within and without Scotland. How is literature true? How can readers assess its trustworthiness? Such unarticulated concerns seem to lie behind some of the critical work and much of the literary practice in a Scottish historical period whose literature is often written off as uninteresting at best.

A generic shift may offer an avenue into this aesthetic morass. If poetry had been the hegemonic form earlier in the nineteenth century, and certainly in the eighteenth century, prose was gaining ground. And the shift from poetry to prose involved, implicitly, notions about creativity, about appropriate form and style, but also more basically about "truth." If poetry expressed feelings and was thus "emotionally" true, the move to prose, to more facticity, was a move that involved a different connotation of "truth," where fact might be fiction and verisimilitude might masquerade as truth. As a loosely defined genre, the "romance" may have allowed an ideal nineteenth-century literary compromise, both fact and feeling truth in a hybrid melange: blurring history and legend, reality and imagination. Such a blurred genre might be said to share much in common with the oral tale and ballad, in which talking parrots might be juxtaposed with the plausible world's facts and history to suggest a universally "felt" truth. Certainly this melange reached its written peak in the nineteenth-century literary world in the Gothic. If, as Harvie suggests (Gifford, *History of Scottish Literature,* Christopher Harvie, chap. 2, p. 25), the eighteenth-century commonsense school of enlightened reason "found fiction inherently misleading," if there was a Victorian critical debate between realism and romance (chap. 14), and if Hart's statement is understood as describing this unsettling dislocation of "truth" in the creative art—"The Scottish romancer comes to resemble the traditional storyteller, for whom the line between history and legend exists only to be blurred. The romancer does precisely what the reader of novel and history is conditioned to resist: he mingles fact and fantasy, the givens of history with the projections of imagination" (Hart, *Scottish Novel,* 146)—Motherwell's literary field was caught right in the middle of this interrogation by literary activity. Looking back we see what was happening in a way, of course, that the participants could not: there is some value to the historical perspective.

One focus of this interrogation of fact/fiction, around the boundaries of the meaning of "truth," involved the question of authorship. It is tempting to suggest that this was part of a larger cultural questioning of both national and personal identity, stimulated by the unions; such a supposition may well be worth considering in another place. Certainly there are numerous literary illustrations of the problematics of authorship. Who wrote *Ossian?* What was MacPherson's role? What about Surtees's passing off his own stuff as genuine to test the public? How about Galt's publication of *The Ayrshire Legatees* anonymously to maintain the fiction these were real letters, or Scott's publication of the Waverley novels anonymously for fear his own known Tory politics would hurt their reception and sales (something John Wilson did as well)?

I'd like to suggest three areas in which questions around authorship and a related "truth" issue, authenticity, flourished, areas in which Motherwell himself participated, and areas in which "playful" play found play. Ballad imitations are an ideal starting point, since Motherwell's antiquarian fame rests on his *Minstrelsy,* which contains perhaps several of *his* own "successful" imitations. In a literary climate, one segment of which valorized the old, the evolutionarily prior, the "ur" poetry, the ballad, imitations of the "traditional," were commonplace. Many were acknowledged and signed, but others were published without attribution. Success in passing off something as old was not a limited activity but almost a movement. Sometimes, as in the case of gentlewomen, the hiding of authorial activity behind the mask of unnamed "tradition" allowed or facilitated appropriation of a male activity. For others, this activity was "play," almost a game: those in the field, or literary circle, often knew when something was spurious. Allan Cunningham, for example, passed off his own stuff as traditional to Robert Cromek, but he was soon "caught" out, that is, his imitations were not successful. Motherwell comments on this process in his note to "Fair Annie" in the *Minstrelsy* when he points the finger at another known fabricator: "Mr Jamieson has fallen into a mistake in saying that the ballad first appeared in Pinkerton's Ballads, not reflecting that Mr. P. deserves little credit for his industry in *collecting* unedited ballads, however much he may be entitled to for his pains in *inventing* some" (327). Walter Scott may well have written "Kinmont Willie"; if so, that imitation was certainly more convincing. And he devoted the fourth and least well known volume of his *Minstrelsy* to imitations and prefaced it with an "Essay on Imitations of the Ancient Ballad." For the most part, Scott names authors for the imitations that are separated from the traditional exemplars, themselves arranged pastiches and mosaics, artfully selected composites. That the putative "true"—become the edited art—could nestle nicely with the imitations suggests some implicit dialogue about authenticity as a part of the interrogation of authorship, a blurring and/or questioning of categories. It seems curious today to consider that authorial success was sometimes measured by succeeding in not being recognized as author! One way of making sense out of this is to realize that notions of authorship were in flux; additionally, authorship was not totally unrecognized, but was known and recognized by the field, the circle, the cognoscenti, the private world of co-conspirators in fabrication.

Pseudonymous publication offered double room for play—not only concealing the author's name but also involving the fabrication of one, often evocative and/or funny, as in "Jock Clodpole," used later in the nineteenth century in the popular working-class press. Such names, Donaldson suggests, allowed editorializing behind a presumed name and thus avoided the necessity of taking responsibility for what was said and published. It might also be suggested that authorship and its meaning had indeterminate social significance—certainly in a milieu in which the anonymous and old were valorized; denial of or fabrication of authorship could then be seen as seizing for oneself and one's artistry traditional privilege, aligning oneself with the ancients. The anonymous publication of Wordsworth and Coleridge's *Lyrical Ballads* and the adoption of the old forms and stances among adherents of the romantic movement suggest the widespread use of various authorial poses, and likewise raise questions about the essentiality of authorship itself. If Carlyle's *Sartor Resartus* "purports to be a nameless editor's summary, with the help of a German colleague, of the life and theories of Herr Dr. Diojenes Teufelsdrockh (devil's dung), Professor of 'Things in General,'" and Mackenzie's *Man of Feeling* "purported to be scattered fragments reclaimed by a rather reluctant editor" (Gifford, *History of Scottish Literature,* Roderick Watson, chap. 8, p. 154), there is clearly a great deal of interrogation of authorship within a range of literature written by Scots as well: What does it mean? And what constitutes authorial responsibility? There also was a distance between the private world of the literary field, where insiders clearly knew authorship, and the public world of "fame" and, ideally, successful commodification and gain—and the possible artistic resistance to art as exchange value.

A third recurring area of authorial interrogation involved the "found manuscript" trope: an author/editor begins a work with the question of provenance, disclaiming personal responsibility. This is, he declares, something found, discovered by accident, not created, but rescued and saved; it is old, not new, and thus it deserves notice. MacPherson's claims for his Ossianic material; Scott's "disclaimer" in *Old Mortality;* Hogg's "Three Perils of Man" and his claim that it was taken from an old manuscript; the Chaldee manuscript of *Blackwood's* first issue, which scandalously satirized and lampooned the Whig literary establishment, creating a bestiary of human equivalents—all hid authorship from the public and simultaneously suggested a pedigree, an authenticity for the literary work that should make it worthy of notice. A brief notice in the *Day* of the Maitland Club, perhaps penned by Motherwell himself, describes that organization and its "archaeological" findings with benign amusement: "MAITLAND CLUB, an association which boasts about seventy members, whose bibliomanical peculiarities and propensities have excited, if not the envy, at least the sarcasm of certain of our witty wiseacres and would-be utilitarians. As we ourselves have rather a sort of *penchant,* like Lot's wife, to cast our eyes back on what the industry of such men as Scott, Thomson and Pitcairn occasionally dig out of old charter chests, and Dutch escritoires, we have prevailed upon a gentleman . . . to extract . . . a few of the more amusing pictures of Scottish manners" (115). The "found manuscript"—"old charter-chests, and Dutch escritoires"—disclaimer was another authorship "hedge," another means of not claiming responsibility for work, for fear it might not be taken seriously or might be taken too seriously and result in reprisals for "unpopular" stances. Its use offers another concrete example of the concerns about authorship and authenticity, and the "disclaimer" was undoubtedly "read" by the cognoscenti. When individual responsibility was accepted, when authorship acquired a more modern connotation, perhaps the anonymous, pseudonymous, and "found" stances were replaced by the eyewitness account, which offered a different attestation of "truth" and authenticity.

To these central concerns around authorship, I would like to add another area of literary play, the caricatured naming of characters within literary works: Mrs. Ferrier's Mrs. Gawffaw and Mrs. MacShake, Scott's Buskbody and Dryasdust. Such names—signposting a central quality of often narrowly drawn, stereotyped figures—were, of course, a literary convention, something between fact and fiction, and their creation surely offered another avenue for playfulness.

Motherwell was heir to these literary proclivities. Until he became deeply involved in ballad studies, he took enormous liberties with the idea ballad: heavily editing, collating, and even passing off his own work as traditional. He was much less likely to engage in this activity after his work on the *Minstrelsy*. Many of Motherwell's poems and sketches/articles and those of others as well were published without attribution in the periodical press; authorship was known only to the close coterie of other authors. In fact, one bound copy of the *Paisley Magazine* is annotated by hand, probably P.A. Ramsay's, sometime after the fact and illustrates insider knowledge of authorship.

Sometimes humorous pseudonyms called attention to an author's stance, as in some of Motherwell's first published works, a series of pamphlets published in 1818. Referred to locally as the Brambletonian Controversy, they concern a curious issue articulated by one Matthew Bramble, a.k.a. John Birkmyre, who subsequently became a Presbyterian minister in Nova Scotia. In a pamphlet of 1817—*Hints to the Young Ladies of Paisley, on the Winter Assemblies and subsequently More Hints*—Bramble describes the "pernicious practice now becoming very prevalent in Paisley, of collecting together a numerous assemblage of the youth of both sexes, to enjoy the pleasures of dancing" (PC862: 395). Taking the moral high ground, he urges parents to step in and forbid their daughters' attendance at the assemblies where they "meet Gentlemen with whom she is for the most part unaquainted [*sic*]." The pseudonym Bramble refers to the central character in Smollett's *Humphry Clinker,* the somewhat irritable but lovable Welsh country squire; the author of the response, presumably Motherwell, references a state of mind in the pseudonym chosen: Ephraim Mucklewrath, the extremist, insane preacher from Scott's *Old Mortality.* In his 1818 response—*An Answer to the Hints on the Winter Assemblies,* printed in Paisley by John Neilson, the publisher with whom he was to have a long social and professional relationship—Motherwell takes an oppositional stance. Anticipating his strongly articulated partisan positions in the *Courier* some years later, he begins by saying the issue is of no personal concern: he doesn't go to assemblies, nor is he on the organizing committee; he is motivated by concern for "the welfare and happiness of society—and watchfully alive, lest that happiness be embittered by the insidious approaches of the masked calumniator, or disturbed by the concealed attacks of the destroying wolf, under the peaceful and friendly garb of the lamb." He was warming up: "[P]ests of society, enemies to friendly intercourse, and innocent amusement, like this Matthew Bramble, cannot be long tolerated with any degree of patience or forbearance. . . . [W]ho made this Matthew Bramble censor-general of public morals, or prime dictator in the amusements and pleasures of this town? Self-elected! Bloated vanity, self conceit, pedantry and affectation. . . . [H]e fixes his teeth on an innocent and virtuous amusement—and attempts to tear to pieces the reputations of those whom the breath of slander till now, hath never passed." There is indeed "much wrath" in this response. The copy of the pamphlets preserved at the Paisley Central Library is annotated by Andrew Crawfurd of Lochwinnock, the mute collector of ballads and other traditional materials (see Lyle, *Andrew Crawfurd's Collection*). The final pamphlet in the series—*Cursory Remarks on the Publications concerning the Winter Assemblies,* by one Peter Plain—may well also be by Motherwell, attempting to moderate his own immoderate initial response, which is here characterized as "head-strong violence." Plain suggests that Mucklewraith may well have "frustrated his own designs"—a "bombastic verbosity" characterized by "scurrility, self-importance, and sound without sense." Affirming Matthew Bramble's well-founded concerns, the pamphlet recounts various improvements made in the assemblies, thus concluding the paper war, a dialogic discourse that reached greater, and more playful, heights in a subsequent Paisley-based work, *Renfrewshire Characters and Scenery.*

The pamphlets marked the beginning of a series of local endeavors that reflect Motherwell's appreciation of Paisley, his drawing upon the region as basis of literary works, and his very embeddedness in the area's history and traditions. His *Memoirs of a Paisley Baillie* was supposedly by one Peter Pirnie, but in reality it was fabricated by Motherwell, who may well have been inspired by John Galt. It was first published in the *Day* and subsequently a section was reprinted in the *Laird of Logan.* The central character, a bailie, or local authority, was also a manufacturer. The presumed memoirs belong to the category "wisdom of a fool." Written in a dialect orthography, the *Paisley Baillie* hopes "to enlichten all and sindry anent my manifold experiences of men and things, seasoned with suitable reflections on passing occurrents." Clearly Pirnie is a laughing stock who misunderstands events, and the humor results from the reading of his naïve and straightforwardly simple accounts of experiences rendered with no self awareness: a naïf in polite society, he misunderstands the waltz and yells out a warning to his daughter to hang on. He is sentimental, too, thinking of the "auld ballad" about "The Babes in the Wood" when he sees a robin in his garden, where he takes refuge from domestic preparations for a local ball. He values "warldly wisdom" of proverbs like "What cannot be mendit suld be sune endit." Above all, Pirnie prides himself on his local knowledge, on antiquities, waxing eloquent on local pearl fishing in Roman times, providing an etymology for Paisley: "I proved, to my ain satisfaction, that the name of the town was altered from Vanduaria to *Pax et Lex,* and softened down, afterwards, by elision, and otherwise to Paselet, Passelay, and now as it is written Paisley. . . . [T]he farrer back I gade, I universally found myself mair at hame. . . . Facts and dates are just anither term for falsehoods and errors, and a perfect down-draught to clever thinking" (294). Using the first person, Motherwell reveals the character as ludicrously unaware and thus a target for the reader's laughter—a satiric stance that, on the one hand, shows Motherwell's view of a certain provincial type, the very type perhaps who made his own residence in Paisley such a trial, and, on the other, suggests his awareness of popular valuation of exactly his own literary/antiquarian interests. Of course, the use of such a character as humorous butt is paralleled in other nineteenth-century depictions, even in Scottish literature, of the Scot as bumpkin. Long unnoticed, the Paisley Bailie accounts are reprinted in appendix 3 for their ethnographic richness, the literary connection with Galt, their status as serial publications in the periodical press, and the interesting fictive dialogue they sustain with the fact of William Motherwell, their "real," if playful, author.

Two earlier works, also in the humorous vein and mocking certain antiquarian activities, combine the pseudonymous stance with the found manuscript pretense: *Renfrewshire Characters and Scenery* published in 1824 by John Neilson and *Certain Curious Poems* in 1828. Both date from Motherwell's Paisley days and show his interest in local and regional matters—and his attempts to interest others in such things—and his ability to see himself and his interests in a humorous light. In *Renfrewshire Characters and Scenery,* Motherwell is introducer (as Andrew Wilson), poet (as Isaac Brown), annotator (as Cornelius Mac Dirdum), and printer's devil, enjoying the dialogic mode for all it is worth. The work is then, in part, poetic: ostensibly a poem of 565 cantos, though only the first part—mercifully, 43 cantos—was published. Attributed to one Isaac Brown, a linen merchant, and not a very good one, this publication was being printed, according to the preface "To the Public," to pay off his debts, Brown himself having disappeared; readers are encouraged to keep a look out for him. Nonetheless, the book should be considered a bargain—certainly when the full, anticipated work appears—if measured in weight as was the custom in the sale of muslin goods among which it was found: "I immediately supposed that it was a blanket of rich silk shawls, which Mr. Brown might have purchased, and which are much heavier than his own manufacture. I hastened to open the blanket, but what was my surprise, and also astonishment to find, in place of *Silk Shawls, Tippets,* or *Plaids,* a great mass of paper, written over, with a ticket on the top, having these words, 'Renfrewshire Scenery and Characters, in 565 cantos, written during the year 1821.'" The creditors being apprised of the discovery, one among them, "who . . . knew well about these matters, said that *Rhymes,* like *Flounces* and *Trimmings,* took the market well just now"; publication was thus undertaken by the creditors in an attempt to recoup their losses. Alas Brown had not been particularly attentive to business; he preferred to draw pictures and write rhymes for lovers, two traits, incidentally, of the young Motherwell; thus clues to the identity of the "personages" offer evidence of authorship to those "in the know." To the poetry itself are appended notes as well as a prefatory statement to the "Judicious and Reflecting Reader!" by one Cornelius Mac Dirdum. He justifies the presence of notes by asserting that poetry is a hazy form of discourse that needs a prose balance: ALL books need copious notes. He provides them in both English and Latin: "At the time I was impetrated by my respected friend, the Trustee, to pen learned adnotations upon this work, I suggested to him, in divers conferences and sociable communings, which we had on the subject, in a quiet houff in St Mirren's Wynd, that the same ought to be announced as a 'New Continuation of a late Continued, but as yet Unfinished History of Renfrewshire.' To this title the work would, with the battalia of notes, diversity of readings, emendations on the text, &c. with which I intended to fortify and ensconse it, in due time establish and vindicate its right; and, moreover, spread a wide and salutary consternation among the unweildy and indolent pens, who have essayed, but failed to produce a pleasant and profitable history of the country." And in a sidebar, in italics, is printed: *"'Tis a quiet and sequestered spot, where the contemplative have it in their power to muse on the vain and shadowy picturings of Hope, and the brittleness of human joys, over a pipe and a glass of ale"* (vi-vii). Motherwell thus delights in poking fun at the conventions and pretensions of contemporary writing and antiquarian endeavors, the very activities to which he himself aspired.

The poetry itself is descriptive, an ideal jumping-off point for the commentator, Mac Dirdum. Brown/Motherwell—as poet—gives a poetic description of the town in Spenserian stanza, perhaps reminiscent of William Tennant's "Anster Fair":

> *Paisley,* it is y'clep'd; of much renown,
> Near and far known for many a wondrous deed;
> For *turning* kings and wooden trenchers round;
> For weaving muslin webs of finest reed,
> And schemes political that *must* succeed;
> For *wealthy* tradesmen, and for *deep* divines;
> *Wise* bailies; *prudent* matrons, that take heed
> To all their neighbours' *virtues;* chief, it shines
> With writers *douce,* save when *Pap-in* their wit refines.(10)

The annotator jumps in to expound on *Pap-in:* "I would bet a groat to a sixpence, this line was written ere the fumes of his meridian tankard had quite evaporated. Of the virtues and nature of Pap-in, allow me, courteous reader, to give thee a taste. 'Tis a wholesome and generous beverage, compounded of whisky and single beer, the which is usually quaffed in wooden bickers, caups, or quaighs. . . . [T]his nectarious fluid . . . becometh sweet and pleasant, diffusing through the whole heart, a kindly warmth, tickling the spleen, and wonderfully invigorating and refreshing the head, breeding therein many pretty fancies and sage observations, worth their weight in gold. A Neophyte ought to be sparing in his libations, for it is seductive and intoxicating in the extreme. But the seasoned bag may be filled without fear of bursting" (31). Mixing fact and fun, Motherwell as poet Brown refers as well to Paisley's versifying men:

> This town is noted too, for *rhyming* men,
> Whose fame, o'er all the country wide, has spread,

It has, of living songsters, nine or ten,
And many more have been, alas, now dead;
When Milton is forgot they will be read.
There I myself, endeavour to reside,
Though almost starv'd; my ample *sign* is spread
In *Plunkin,* which runs off the Causeyside,
Where those, that lie in wait for monied merchants, bide. (11)

The annotator glosses *Plunkin:* "What the etymology of *Plunkin* is, may be difficult, for ought I know, to resolve as the etymology of Paisley itself, and that is sufficiently puzzling. Both of them might poze Dean Swift, who was fruitful enough in devising whimsical etymologies" (33). The printer's devil dismisses the poetic sentiment that Paisley was known for its *rhyming* men with an alternate perspective: "A rash assertion" (32). Elsewhere he corrects the poet's overstatements; Paisley was not really known for whaling though there were some salmon fishing boats. And the printer's devil glosses Mac Dirdum's name as meaning tumultous noise, altercation, uproar or, ironically, achievement, great deed. The poetical mapping of place and person might be seen as a joyful, playful celebration of local pride and a paean to the past, the good old days, clearly affirming Motherwell's own viewpoint:

These calculating times are not for me:
I should have lived three hundred years ago,
And spent my easy days in errantry,
As monk, or knight, to care a mortal foe.
I'd like to fight, indeed, but so and so;
With fiery dragons, and with giants grim
When others fought, I might have cried—brave!
With age, these monster's eyes would have been dim,
Ere to molest their peace, *my* heart had been in trim. (17)

The "fun" of this work is the multivocality, the parodying of serious critical fashion, and the "play" that no doubt stimulated amused and congratulatory responses from Motherwell's friends and co-conspirators: one amusing note refers to R.A. Smith's fortuitous discoveries in the Old Charter Chest of the Paisley Abbey of "some fine reliques of ancient psalmody" (47).

The audience for such works would surely have been limited: the fun was really in the knowing, in the recognition of the clues, through the approbation of friends. Some of these publications were published in very limited numbers, really for friends and co-conspirators who would enjoy the joke; and additionally they could thereby gain another rare volume for their own collections. That was exactly the tack taken in the publication of *Certain Curious Poems* in 1828 in thirty copies. Supposedly the work of one M'Alpie, the poems were found in the sheriff clerk's office—the very location of Motherwell's work for more than a decade—and a real M'Alpie had indeed been a sheriff substitute of Renfrewshire. The "found manuscript" claim, a recognized literary trope, was, in this instance, a truthful assertion. This M'Alpie had been a local poet who dealt with political matters, particularly the pros and cons of the papacy and Presbyterianism. Motherwell claims he is only the editor, that the manuscript was found among court documents, that he can find out little about the author. When Motherwell probably reviews his own edited volume in his own *Paisley Magazine,* cognoscenti, knowing of his penchant for fabrication and recognizing the "found manuscript" trope, could be excused for thinking this was Motherwell rather than a real historical figure.

Motherwell and his colleagues use humorous pseudonyms in addition sometimes to using their initials. Noms de plume from several periodicals to which Motherwell contributed offer amusing examples. In the *Visitor, or Literary Miscellany,* published in Greenock beginning in 1818, there are selections attributed to Abraham Smoothback, Leonora Daemon, Metrical Gander, Gregory Doggerel, Puffendorf, and Christopher Surlychops. In the *Enquirer,* published in Glasgow in 1820 and 1821, Motherwell published "Sonnet to My Own Hert beginning submit, rebellious thing, quiescent be!" and signed it "WM" (154). Other materials were less definitively attributed to Isabella Meekly, Maria Testy, and Jonathon Oddly.

There was clearly a lot of in-group awareness of what was going on: the Maitland Club preface that began this section clearly references an awareness of Motherwell's activities. The cognoscenti knew what one another were doing. R.A. Smith told Motherwell what Motherwell already knew, that some of his tunes were not traditional but his own, and he wrote Motherwell of having seen Allan Cunningham in London and referred to Allan's forgeries as common topic, understood activity (Robertson 1222: 42, 51). Likewise, Peter Buchan admits, in a letter to Motherwell, that his notes for the "Earl of Aboyne" were "imaginary" since the singer had nothing to say about the text (17 Jan. 1826, 25263.19.6F). And the annotations of some of Motherwell's extensive manuscript materials offer evidence of recognition of Motherwell's participation in such literary play: in one instance (Robertson 6/1223: 6), Motherwell, in talking of poetry of some antiquity, says "of the author we are unable to furnish our Readers with any notice." The marginal comment, perhaps the bookseller/antiquarian Robertson's, adds, "All this is of course a little piece of deception to make out the verisimilitude." In a like manner, one manuscript critic, pointing out Motherwell's penchant for "legpulling, a form of literary amusement in which he indulged frequently," adds that "M——— more than once produced poems under names other than his own, poems that were his own handiwork" (B/Moth).

This was in a sense public play, published; yet this same playful approach to life pervades the manuscript and holograph record: the rhyming testament attesting to his inability to sing, signed by friends and colleagues who appreciated Motherwell; the record of guard-room duty that turned a civic duty into a night of fun. Some of the holograph material, like aspects of the printed play, shows Motherwell's ability to "see" himself as others might: in letters to R.A. Smith, he "mocks" his own activity when he refers alternately to the introduction of the *Minstrelsy* as "that pro*found Treatise*" or as "elaborate discourse." One amusing example of such self-mocking and parody may well have been destined for the *Paisley Magazine*. Labeled "Poetical Department," it offers a parodic analysis of a poem written about the life of a monk, Slenderwitticus, and provides the disquisition by such learned men as Munchgulpius and Doltmannus, Timothy Twist-stave, Pretty headics, and Hartusdestillaties. The learned poem begins thus:

> The Poet of Himself to Himself, or concerning Himself
> Ye rhyming fools, ye hare-brained asses
> Ye dull disciples of Parnassus
> Who dribble and bedirt your linen
> The narrow gates of fame to gris in . . . (Robertson 10/1208: 16)

Perhaps it is better he allowed this *jeu* to remain unpublished, as evidence only now of his playfulness, his self-awareness, his amused creation of pseudonymous characters. All of this points to an attractive personality trait and helps explain why Motherwell was such a good companion within his small circle: he simply had, for the most part, an attractive and amused view of himself and the world. The fillers he either chose or approved for the *Paisley Magazine* and the *Courier* further emphasize his delight in amusing stories and activities—fabrications included—which his correspondent and companion R.A. Smith had named as basic to maintaining "the Spirits in this envious and backbiting world" (Robertson 3/1222: 33). A column in the *Paisley Magazine* is titled "A Friendly Notice to Correspondents, with which the public has little to do Unless It Likes." Saturday, 13 March 1830, there appeared in the *Courier* the following:

> The poet Harding, at Oxford, was half crazy, and sometimes walked about with a scythe in his hand, as Time; sometimes with an anchor as Hope. One day I met him with a huge brick and some bits of that upon the crown of his hat; on my asking him for a solution of his prosopopoeia, —"Sir," said he, "to-day is the anniversary of the celebrated Dr. Goldsmith's death; and I am now in the character of his Deserted Village." (4)

He had always then an eye for something to delight himself, his friends, and the public—often, of course, choosing things of enormous interest to himself, as in this humorous literary anecdote.

Writing was the central focus of his life; it was serious business. But it was also fun, sociable, a means of defusing tension, of sharing with friends. That it also can be seen as part of a larger issue over authorship and authenticity in literary and philosophical terms offers an illustration of the ways in which ordinary human beings become implicated, by their very situatedness, in concerns they neither articulate nor consciously feel.

But Who Was
William Motherwell?

[E]ach life is a whole, a coherent and directed ensemble, and . . .
cannot be apprehended except as the unitary expression of an
intention, both subjective and objective, which is made manifest
in every experience.

—Bourdieu, *Rules of Art*

BIOGRAPHICAL FACTS and public, published records aside, who was
Motherwell? What mattered to him? Where did he live and how? What were
his thoughts? Recognizing the impossibility of ever answering these questions in any specificity and with any assurance of the answers' verity (there
are, after all, many "lacks" in the written, historical record), I would like to
suggest something more about the man, and to begin to place him more
completely in the tangle of ideas that were floating about Scotland in the
first third of the nineteenth century.

There are plenty of studies that talk of specifics of history—of the
Radical risings, of the Reform Bill of 1832; there are studies as well that
generalize about the "isms" and "ologies" of the day. And there are studies
and ample allusions to the big names of the time—the Humes and Adam
Smiths, the Walter Scotts and Francis Jeffreys. The real issue before me is
how to insert one ordinary/real/middle-class person into the equation, how
to offer or to postulate a lived experience and one person's life.

I would like to begin by saying that we write of the past as though it
were coherent, unified, and knowable, when it is largely opaque. Our "histories" are only attempts at a kind of representation that serves "our" purposes
today. Recognizing my own complicity, I hope to suggest a possible truth, a
possible life, by admitting to begin with that I believe few people's lives are
as coherent as we would like to make out, though a semblance of order can
always be created by the individual(s) or those who come after. I am seeking
a kind of coherence myself: I would like to understand what made William
Motherwell tick and perhaps, in so doing, understand more fully the ways

By A. EDOUART.

WILLIAM MOTHERWELL, Poet. 1797～1835.

all of our lives are tangled and confused in the midst of competing ideas and ideologies, personal needs, and human frailties.

The past of William Motherwell's experience might well be depicted, from a twentieth-century perspective, as a struggle within the politico-cultural milieu between Tory and Whig, conservation and reform, nationalism and internationalism, past and present—the classic struggle within fields of power. We can identify, more or less, certain figures with certain positions. As useful as such retrospective generalizations are, they probably obscure lived reality, the ordinary human situation. So I would hope to be able to recreate a semblance of some of the swirl and confusion of available ideas, the resources for forming positions and identities, following Williams, if you will, or more explicitly Bourdieu's *habitus* (the "semi-learned grammars of practice" [*Outline of a Theory of Practice,* 20] or the range of ideas and beliefs that both structure and generate practice and are held by persons occupying similar social space). I seek to recover some of the available structures of feeling that gave birth to, facilitated, enabled in myriads of ways real human responses and actions. I would hope to suggest William Motherwell's *habitus.*

Certainly the unions of the seventeenth and eighteenth centuries (of the crowns and parliaments) form a backdrop to any discussions of Scotland's status in the nineteenth century—and by extension the situation of her citizens. The curious position of having "national" educational, legal, and religious structures without a government has been identified by some as an issue; this lack of government, by extension, led to a muting of nationalism or national feelings and refocused such feelings on cultural rather than political manifestations. A nation without a government, a nationalism without goal and without the underdevelopment Tom Nairn insists nationalism needs suggests an anomalous situation. The fact, however, of prior independence, of a cultural heritage, however valued, must be said to have formed some sort of structure of feeling, some kind of sentiment, and it was clearly an available conceptual area for those with the inclination and leisure for such reflection—and that surely was not everyone. In fact, it would be fair to say that such a reflective stance was most surely available only to the landed and professional classes, to the elites and to the rising bourgeois middle, and to those few "lads-o-pairts" who seized the equality of opportunity to move up the class ladder at least enough to reflect on such non-immediate issues.

For some folks, ideas about Scotland led to overt concerns over Scotland's nineteenth-century national dilemma, her political status; for others, probably the majority, the notion Scotland conjured up implicit feelings of belonging, of connection to the history and past of locale and place without much concern for larger state apparatuses. In general, ideas about Scotland were connected to other "ideas" in the tangled *habitus* Motherwell experienced. Sentiments of national identity linked to the past (to the records and artifacts of the past) combined easily with antiquarian appreciation, study, and recovery of times past, sometimes couched in nostalgic longings for that past. This nostalgic, pro-Scottish—though not necessarily felt as anti-union or British—antiquarian perceptual framework might well encompass a number of different strands of nineteenth-century Scottish thought. It certainly could include ideas of an organic, whole society, a utopian past of the kind Chalmers used in his articulation of a godly Commonwealth as well as related ideas derived from dreams of a more unified, rural, whole, supportive community "felt" to have been a part of the agrarian past. It is easy to see how such notions, such ideological nexuses for perception, might become "romantic" or might be identified as outward manifestations of romanticism. Wherever the concept came from and whatever it means, the notions of valorizing the past and whatever legendary, hazy, through rose-colored-glasses views of the past might prevail, implicitly suggest restoration or reconstruction of an imagined past. Such an amorphous but certainly related complex of ideas/sentiments might be seen as coexisting with another large nuclei of cultural/social beliefs and practices—more forward looking, less rooted in the past, in fact revolutionary: for change was in the air. Change had already happened to everyone, stimulating some individuals to turn backward. Some, however, looked to the future, were anxious to participate in the Age of Improvement and the philosophical articulation of that action movement, the Enlightenment, which privileged rationalism, taking control of the lived and experienced environment, and sparked agricultural and technological inventions. Such ideas were not for Scotland alone, but for all civilized humanity to grasp and reach for, to stimulate a new age, a new life for all. Such ideas naturally led, or should have led, to action, to doing something, especially in response to the multiple kinds of dislocations in process: urbanization, increasing heterogeneity and mobility, poverty, capitalism. Action, then, introduced revolutionary ideas about equality, about the dispossessed (both the urban and rural dislocated), and about representation (both secular and sacred) as means of expanding opportunity for all, of opening up the society to all.

Few individuals actually sat down and said, "I am a revolutionary" or "I am for the past" or "I am an 'enlightened' thinker." Even for those who in some ways were participants in affairs, I would suggest that life and feeling were more nuanced and contradictory. But these were some of the dominating and dominant ideas of the time and would necessarily have influenced the reflective and engaged; and even the dispossessed had responses, for the Radical risings of the West of Scotland and the later Disruption show multiple layers of discontent with the status quo.

This muddle of somewhat oppositional perceptual frameworks informed the world of William Motherwell. Yet he did not overtly lock horns with any of these issues until the last five years of his life, when, as editor of the *Glasgow Courier,* he was expected to represent a conservative Tory viewpoint that he must have shared—but that is little revealed, overtly, in what we can tease out of the extant private documents.

What Motherwell did, especially in his extraoccupational activities, reveals a close and affective world of men, sharing certain interests that can be seen to feed into the larger discourses but do not directly partake of those controversies. Motherwell accepts the political environment in which he lives; he values the monarchy; he has little anxiety it seems about whether he is Scot or Brit: he is a Scot and Scotland remains throughout his life his milieu—the given, not something that has to be theorized. And his Scotland was largely the middle, central belt—Edinburgh, Glasgow (Kilsyth, Paisley)—as his Glasgow was largely circumscribed, again geographically, by St. Mungo's Cathedral and the newly opened Necropolis, the Clyde, George Square, and the College Gardens.

As a young man, on the brink of adulthood and independence, he grappled with other more universal issues. The presentations he gave at the Literary Institution suggest some of the questions middle-class young men—between the ages of perhaps seventeen and twenty-one or twenty-two—were collectively considering: love, emulation, morality. And the commonplace notebooks and occasional travel diaries he kept, at approximately the same age, reveal a reflective young man grappling with his own identity, his preferences, his character. He reflects on knowledge, on contentment, on taste; he suggests that religion, philosophy, and literature are life's lasting pleasures; he writes that the government is necessary for keeping order; he refers to and quotes from works he is reading—to Alexander Barclay's *Ship of Fools;* he extracts from the life of Richard Watson, bishop of Landaff; he quotes Dryden and things overheard. He reflects on the decline of spoken and written Scots after the union when he refers to Jamieson's Scottish dictionary; he quotes Aldrovandus: "Beard. If thou wouldst have thy beard grow quickly anoint thy chin with the ashes of burnt Bees and Mice dung" (Robertson 28/1210)—does this entry reflect a lived anxiety? These last two topics, however, might be read as links to the general nationalistic-antiquarian axis of the times and hint at the side of the ideological struggle on which we can expect to find him as he moves through his life. In

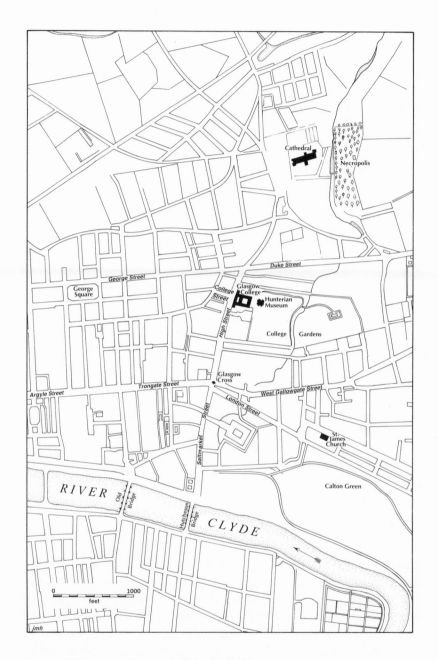

Map of Glasgow following M'Phun's *Guide*

general his random jottings suggest the kinds of things he was reading and considering: they give a tiny opening into his inner life.

Letters, too, reveal something about his character—his friendships and what they revolve around: publications and projects, ballads and song writing, and, in some, human feeling and concern and advice. Motherwell sends Peter Buchan's wife a Paisley shawl and offers advice about dealing with the materials Buchan has assembled; to R.A. Smith he expresses his frustrations with Paisley and his difficulty writing songs. Nowhere are there letters to family, but this probably does not mean he was a man adrift, without an extended family. We know his uncle John, an "extensive" ironmonger in Paisley, took him, and perhaps other siblings, in and provided for him at least until he became financially independent in 1818, at twenty-one. His mother had died in 1808, his father in 1827. His sister Amelia returned to Kilsyth in Stirlingshire together with their father in 1811. Either she or Elizabeth married an Ogilvie and their son was a major. Margaret, who probably lived as an adult in Glasgow, was said to have been the last of a depleted family when she died in 1849. A Stirlingshire uncle shared accounts of supernatural appearances with Motherwell. David, perhaps his brother, may have contributed to the *Paisley Magazine*. A nephew, David or John's son, C.A. Motherwell, was a pallbearer at his funeral. We must assume he wrote to and saw family members often during his lifetime. He did not marry. We can gather random comments on women: as a young man he wrote with enthusiasm about going with a friend to take two young ladies riding in the country; his poem refers to the gentlemen as two amorous knights. One of his first publications, anonymous, supported the Paisley assemblies as appropriate occasions for young women and men to meet without prior introductions. The Paisley Grammar School may well have been coeducational, providing him with at least some encounters with young women. He presented a motion that would have permitted women to hear the discussions of the Literary Institution. Yet there was a Paisley club, the Baron Club, that fined young men when they were married; I do not know whether he belonged. As late as 1832 in the *Day* an unsigned article's comments—perhaps his—call up the things a man must give up in marrying. His own creation, Baillie Pirnie, describes bachelors as men who could "gang hap-step-and jump through life without a licht burden upon their back." In some ways these articulations probably express his opinion: marriage would have meant giving up. His own world was a public and semiprivate world of men.

A variety of records exist that hint at this world: the clubs to which he belonged as a young man in Paisley, the Literary Institution and the Paisley Philosophical Institution, the Paisley Rifle Club, the collaborative publications in which he was engaged as editor or writer or contributor, even social gatherings (see appendix 4 for a suggestion of those involvements and some of their participants). Manuscripts, letters, and contemporary publications provide evidence. Motherwell's real world, between what social historians might identify as public and private, the world open to middle-class men with leisure to pursue avocational concerns and interests, was united by certain shared foci: getting published, creating publishing outlets, and acquiring books—a passion of his from before his days at Glasgow College. In the same letter in which he accepted Robert Walkinshaw's offer to serve as sheriff clerk depute, he described his search for a book for Walkinshaw in a letter that remains difficult to decipher fully:

> [L]et me say something anent Dan Chaucer. I have been thro'
> most of the auction rooms and booksellers in the town, but
> have been equally unsuccessful in them all. Not a ——— is to
> be found. With regard to an Edition by Godwin I find we
> ——— mistaken. Godwin only writes his life and the history
> of literature ——— age where in he flourished. Urrey or Urrie
> is the only one who edited a complete edition of this patriarch
> of English poets, and it sells according to the London cata-
> logues at some 26£. Tyrwhit only edites his ——— Tales,
> perhaps indeed the most amusing and cleverest part of his
> poetry but then you would prefer I daresay an edition which
> contained all his ——— and so would I. Few things are more
> provoking to sharp edge readers than to get but a single
> solitary bite of an Author, and not have it in their power to
> devour him altogether. Not withstanding I have lacked success
> in hunting one out as yet, nevertheless, I shall not give up the
> chase all at once, but continue my rambles in the Bibliothecal
> field. (Robertson 9/1207: 20)

This letter, written in his twenty-first year, reveals one of his strongest attachments: books and their acquisition. In fact, I can postulate that the real issue for him, had he been married, would have been the necessity of using the money he spent in acquiring an amazing library to provide for wife and family.

The men with whom he was connected belong to two related categories: poets, writers, journalists of sorts *and* people in the Scottish print trade, that is, a West of Scotland fraction of the larger Scottish literary field that has yet to be mapped. Such a field would consist of networks within the social world, sites of cultural production; the center would be Edinburgh. Motherwell's world was geographically confined by Scotland—Glasgow, the West, and contacts in the capital, Edinburgh. The poets, writers, and journalists with whom he associated were, for the most part, what we might call working men of letters: their writing activities were not professional; they did not live by writing, though, of course, their writing may well have provided supplemental income and probably provided the contexts for the most interesting parts of their lives—as it surely did for Motherwell. Analysis of his social world, including his fraction of the literary field, in as much as that is possible, also reveals contact with a smattering of other men: doctors, bankers, artists, lawyers, musicians, and government officials—a very middle-class assortment. Even before he left Paisley for Glasgow, he had become a member of Glasgow's Maitland Club: "The object of the Club shall be to print Works illustrative of the Antiquities, History, and Literature of Scotland" (*Catalogue of the Works*). Members during his lifetime include many of the important men of the day: Henry Cockburn, Walter Scott, John Gibson Lockhart, and various dukes and landed gentry. He served as member of the council for six years and was, in fact, the sixth member named before the establishment of election procedures. Clearly he was already known as a supporter of national and antiquarian literary endeavors—from his own publishing activities, not the least of which was the *Minstrelsy,* which had brought him to national literary attention and sparked his election as corresponding member of the Society of Antiquaries. Such involvements illustrate Motherwell's position in the conservative, past-oriented, antiquarian, romantic *habitus,* which in turn informed his position within the various fields.

Two early Paisley friends, somewhat older than he, helped launch his literary and publishing activities by introducing him to people, participating in his publishing activities, and encouraging his avocational interests. Both, interestingly, were musicians (for a list of some individuals with whom Motherwell associated and whatever biographical and connective information I have been able to ferret out, see appendix 5). Andrew Blaikie (1774–1841), who provided the musical illustrations for the *Minstrelsy,* was an engraver, a copperplate printer, and an early experimenter with lithography; he was also a musician. For a time he was precentor at Paisley's Abbey Church and served as the session clerk; in other words, he was a respectable and respected gentleman in the community. He also collected things antiquarian. He knew Motherwell through multiple channels: they were both members of the Paisley Burns Club and Philosophical Institution, and both were members of the Rifle Club, one of the local militia groups established in the wake of the French Revolution. In fact, Blaikie was one of the guard-room group about whom Motherwell wrote the humorous account, quoted earlier. And it may well have been Blaikie who introduced Motherwell to Scott and James Hogg. Here, then, was one of Motherwell's Paisley friends, middle class, antiquarian, and connected to similar persons elsewhere in Scotland.

One of the other early influences on Motherwell, richly captured in a correspondence that continued until his death in Edinburgh, was that of R.A. Smith (1780–1829). Smith's father had been a silk weaver and had apprenticed his son to weave muslin. Smith, however, abandoned weaving for his real love, music: he became a teacher of music, recognized composer, and leader of church choirs—this shift suggesting a degree of occupational and class mobility. In 1823 he became music director and choir master of St. George's in Edinburgh. Active in various publications such as the *Scottish Minstrel,* he was known for his settings of church songs and for writing tunes; and sometimes he imitated and passed on others as traditional, with Motherwell's knowledge. I have already mentioned the correspondence between the two men, particularly after Smith's move to Edinburgh. The letters reveal their close friendship and their collaborative activities and, like many letters, begin to provide a more intimate, private view of Motherwell. In one letter Smith importunes Motherwell to write a preface to one of his, Smith's, volumes; he suggests as well that Motherwell review another and pretend that it came from a London periodical rather than from his pen. Smith invites Motherwell to stay with him in Rose Street, Edinburgh, and was present at the signing of the rhyming testament (along with Peter Buchan of Aberdeen, another correspondent and boon companion—as the "fun" and obviously "spirited" testament suggests), attesting to Motherwell's singing, or rather non-, abilities. Between Smith and Motherwell there was obviously a shared appreciation and love of similar materials: old Scottish materials and an attachment to Paisley, where they had first met. Smith contributed to an early collaborative publication—*The Harp of Renfrewshire*—as well as to the *Paisley Magazine.* Motherwell wrote, or tried to, words to go with tunes Smith sent him. Smith had undoubtedly known the Paisley weaver-poet Robert Tannahill, and the materials concerning the poet's life that he gathered he gave to Motherwell, who intended to write of his life and poetry—a project subsequently completed by another lifelong friend, also an antiquarian enthusiast, P.A. Ramsay. Smith and Motherwell shared personal and antiquarian interests: there was a nice reciprocity in their friendship.

Motherwell's Paisley circle, a fraction of the literary field, is most fully revealed in his work as editor and initiator of the *Paisley Magazine.*

The magazine was a business as well as artistic venture, and various members of the community, Motherwell included, owned shares: John Neilson, the printer had three; David Dick, the publisher, had four. Other shareholders included P.A. Ramsay. Like Motherwell a member of the Burns Club, the Literary Institution, and the Paisley Philosophical Institution, as well as an obviously convivial group, the Hadgis Club, Ramsay became the editor of the Tannahill materials Motherwell had considered editing. Another shareholder, John Dunn, later became a lawyer. Robert Hay, a printer and lithographer and fourth editor of the *Paisley Advertiser,* of which Motherwell had been the second, subsequently became a partner of John Neilson's. These were middle-class men with some excess capital, joining together to support the establishment of a periodical focused on Paisley. Some of the shareholders also contributed to the magazine, in addition to Glasgow authors: Thomas Atkinson, J.D. Carrick, John Strang, James McConechy, members of his Glasgow circles.

The magazine brought together an array of men of letters, ran for thirteen issues, then closed. What the *Paisley Magazine* had sought to provide for Paisley and the West of Scotland was something very like the successful Edinburgh magazine known familiarly as Maga, *Blackwood's Edinburgh Magazine.* But Maga had significant support from Blackwood's, the publishers, a stable of known writers and pundits, and an audience outside the immediate locale. *Paisley Magazine* was a regional, even local in some ways, middle-class periodical without Maga's wider audience and appeal. Its failure to thrive was surely a disappointment, yet it provided Motherwell with a chance to try his hand at being editor, and that experience, together with the experience of editing the *Paisley Advertiser,* gave him the acknowledged know-how to become the editor of the *Glasgow Courier*—and move overtly into cultural politics.

Even while a resident of Paisley, Motherwell had Glasgow contacts, and, when he moved to the city to take over the editorship of the *Courier,* he joined a group of literati, perhaps minor men of letters, who seemed to cluster especially around the bookseller David Robertson, whose name has been repeated frequently in this work: it was Robertson who owned so many of the manuscripts of Motherwell's letters and holograph material now housed at Glasgow University Library, thus his name has become part of the manuscript identification. Apprenticed at fifteen, in 1810, thus almost an exact contemporary of Motherwell's, to William Turnbull, a Trongate bookseller, Robertson and another man (probably Thomas Atkinson) took over after Turnbull's death; eventually the business became Robertson's.

Booksellers were more than sellers of books: they stimulated and enabled publications and served as literary confidants and patrons to a variety of authors; their premises became centers for exchanges of ideas and brought together like-minded persons; often they served as conduits for exchange of information between individuals; and they might keep an eye out for rare and coveted volumes for friends. In other words, the bookseller might well be publisher, was even sometimes printer, and therefore could be at the very center of creative activity, certainly a central figure in the literary field. In the best of circumstances, the bookseller would guarantee support for the publication of a work by being linked to other publisher/printers in other towns or parts of the realm. The bookseller, then, did more than buy and sell books: "the bookseller could construct a version of literary culture"; "the book shops...were sites where literature became a social experience, where authors and readers and booksellers met"; "literature was read, pondered, discussed, planned, and at times written at the shop" (Boehm, "Poetics of Literary Commerce," xxiv, xxix). Certainly Robertson was one of the respected bibliophiles of Glasgow. He served in numerous capacities: he facilitated conversation and collaborative work and was conduit and catalyst for bringing people together. He had both economic and social capital and became a significant arbiter of taste. Economies of scale and publishing as a big business were clearly in the future. For the moment, however, the bookseller was important and often had clustered around him groups of individuals engaged in particular kinds of literary work. Robertson seemed keen on antiquarian, regional, Scottish materials. In fact, he was the Glasgow publisher of Andrew Henderson's *Scottish Proverbs,* for which Motherwell had written an introduction, and two works of poetic and anecdotal interest, *The Laird of Logan* and *Whistle-Binkie,* came out of his circle: Motherwell contributed to both.

Other members of the circle—that is, persons interested in local literature and vernacular history, members of the West of Scotland literary field—included J.D. Carrick, Andrew Henderson, Alexander Rodger, and John Strang. Rodger was politically active and assisted in editing the *Liberator,* a Radical weekly, and was later on the staff of Peter MacKenzie's *Reformer's Gazette.* In other words, his politics were the opposite of Motherwell's; but the two shared an interest in publishing, editing, and local humor and were reported to have frequented Mrs. Anderson's Sun Tavern, as did J.D. Carrick. Carrick had humble beginnings. Apprenticed to an architect, he ran away, worked two years at the Staffordshire Potteries, then returned to Glasgow and became a china and stoneware merchant. He was also clearly involved in writing, editing, and publishing: he was an author and poet, known for his tragedy or life of Wallace; he was the editor of *The*

Laird of Logan and the first series of *Whistle-Binkie;* he was on the staff of the *Scots Times*—perhaps author of the already-quoted squibbs referring to Motherwell; and he contributed to a number of periodicals of the day, including Motherwell's *Paisley Magazine.* He too was a liberal and for reform, yet he shared all sorts of activities with Motherwell: involvement in certain periodicals, the Maitland Club, the Sun Tavern rendezvous, and gatherings at the Saracen's Head. At the latter establishment, they were joined by Andrew Henderson, and accounts suggest they would share a bowl of punch—the ceremonious mixing and imbibing of a mysterious mix of rum, lemon, and sugar, *the* male convivial ritual about which writers are wont to wax eloquent: witness Cyril Thornton's (from Thomas Hamilton's *Youth and Manhood of Cyril Thornton* [1827]) description:

> To a native of Glasgow, there is, even in the sight of a punch
> bowl, something of exhilaration and excitement. It brings with
> it no mournful associations. It is linked to a thousand bright
> and pleasing remembrances, of youthful and joyous revelry,
> and of the graver intoxications of maturer years. Within its
> beautiful and hallowed sphere, are buried no "thoughts that do
> lie too deep for tears." In its very name there is delightful
> music. (417-18)

And "Nestor's" *Recollections of Old Glasgow* details aspects of the ceremony, so central to bachelor dinner parties:

> The proper manufacture of the concoction was deemed of no
> small importance. Several gentlemen were celebrated for their
> scientific skill in this art. Not unfrequently the artist, to ensure
> freedom of his arms, divested himself of his coat. The mixing
> of the proper quantities of rum and sugar, with cold water,
> seasoned with the juice of lemon or limes, was looked on with
> somewhat of veneration, and the operator became the object of
> envy amongst the uninitiated. (185)

Kilpatrick places Motherwell at the center of such male events: "There, at the head of them all, sat Motherwell, short, stout, and muscular of build, a man of fine poetic sympathies, full of stories about the Ettrick Shepherd, and never more animated in conversation than when engaging his hearers' interest in those old Norse legends which he loved so well. Motherwell was a very considerable personality in Glasgow" (*Literary Landmarks,* 212).

At the Saracen's Head over punch, Motherwell might have been joined by Andrew Henderson, the editor of *Scottish Proverbs,* but known most particularly as an artist—painter and portraitist: it was he who painted Motherwell's portrait. The portrait may well have been the result of the Hadgis Club's importuning Henderson to paint a collective portrait of the group, probably an idea generated by a punch bowl shared:

It being the wish of the Hadgis that Hadgis Henderson should undertake a Historical piece which shall contain the portraitures of the whole fraternity of Hadgis those who Subscribe this Document agree to pay each for his own ——— five guineas. The artist shall be left at perfect liberty in choosing his subject and grouping his figures. Happy that those who have passed & are passing thro the sandy deserts of this dreary world should at least reach the well springs of happiness promised by the prophet to the faithful the subscribers hereto affix their Signatures & Seals.

> W Motherwell Chief Molluk
> And the tin Helmets (?) and the Cast
> Robt Peacock
> John J Cowin
> P.A. Ramsay
> Alex Tennant. (Robertson 1208/10, 17)

Henderson was one of several gentlemen who attended a dinner given by Thomas Atkinson, whom Peter MacKenzie describes as a bastard and poet with political pretensions that laid him open to ridicule. He was also a bookseller, publisher, and editor of a local weekly, the *Ant,* and contributor to the *Day* and the *Paisley Magazine,* and thus involved in the literary, antiquarian milieu of the day. In his will he left money for the education of artisans. His dinner party was recorded because of an incident between Atkinson and his mother: she became sick, claiming that she had been poisoned when her son criticized the dinner; the "rescue squad" was called. But the general description, before the denouement, suggests the kind of social environment of which Motherwell and his friends partook: "The dinner itself went off with great hilarity. Proverbs and lines of Scottish poetry, and songs and sentiments went round; and aye the cold punch and claret and whisky toddy were getting better" (MacKenzie, *Old Reminiscences,* chap. 23).

Motherwell had found a semiprivate niche among a group of men with leisure to devote to the cultivation of the arts, including the arts of conversation and conviviality. The actual doing of the creative activity, however, would have been more solitary. In Motherwell's case, we can imagine him ensconced in his quarters in George Street, a fashionable address, surrounded by books and collectanea that must have spilled over into all his rooms: perhaps a large drawing room, an ample bed chamber, and service areas for a housekeeper/cook/general factotum, following the situation of Cyril Thornton's Glasgow uncle, the somewhat buffoonish but nonetheless solid human being David Spreull, or similar to the grander lodgings sold for four hundred pounds and advertised in the *Courier* early in 1834: "lodging at 134 George Street: dining room, parlour, 3 bedrooms, vestibule, street floor; kitchen, laundry, servants' room, scullery, water closet, and cellars in the sunk story." Motherwell's library and antiquarian collections were extensive, running to 1680 lots, with books and manuscripts dominating the twelve-day sale after his death. It is not surprising, then, to read that there were a number of painted book shelves in the sale as well as a mahogany book case and escritoire, a library table, and several plate chests, one antique—evidences of certain pretensions or values, outward manifestations of inner interests, signs of a certain status. We can picture a book-lined room, a fireplace, a centrally placed library table for writing and for piling up books, a comfortable chair by the window for reading. Spare wall space might be taken up with paintings and engravings: a painting of Sir Thomas More, a portrait of Shakespeare, an engraving of Chaucer, whose works he was searching in Glasgow early in his adult life. There was also a Nasmyth painting of the *View of Paisley Abbey* and a portrait of a Covenanter who was also a Motherwell (whose sentiments, atavistically, he may have shared, certainly on Catholicism), links to his own locale and past. An antique chest must have held some of his collection of armaments, the rest spilling over into the bookshelves, room corners, and available nooks and crannies: silver mounted pistols, a skene dhu, the shield of an Arab sheikh, an "African Assagaye and Seven Indian Arrows," a Turkish scymitar, "Two Indian Bows and Quiver, with Arrows," various swords, one said to have been used at the Battle of Bothwell Bridge, one from the castle of Sir John de Graeme, Fintry. All amply attest to his antiquarian and military enthusiasms as well as his economic capital.

His library, on the other hand, reflects his love of languages and literatures. It was filled with things Scottish, works on ballads and songs, on general Scottish traditions that reveal not only his own enthusiasms but suggest as well his Scottish identity and concerns. And there was poetry, much of it by local and regional poets, but canonical authors' works appear as well—certainly Chaucer, in two editions: a seven-volume Edinburgh edition of 1781 and a folio black-letter edition dated London, 1598. There were numerous dictionaries and works in classical languages, biblical works— and manuscripts of sermons in Swedish and Danish—critical works on literature, and works in a variety of languages: Latin, French, Italian, and German. There were autographs of authors; coins, mostly Scottish; and manuscripts—again with a Scottish and religious focus.

Imagine him at home on the rare evening when he was not with friends, taking down now this volume, then another, piling them around him at the library table as he prepared to write an article for one of his collaborative projects. His created, lived environment attests to his Scottish enthusiasms, his appreciation of the past. It also offers implicitly a comment on his economic status—his excess wealth turned into commodities to adorn and feed his interests.

A similar focus permeates his published, and thereby public, work as I suggested earlier. The Scottish interest, the past focus—not just Scottish, but Norse, as in the legends retold and imitated and in the poetry—suggest a longing and nostalgia for the past, a mental reconstituting of a milieu that seemed better, thus a personally restorative activity that makes his identification as a romantic possible. Clearly his literary activities, even implicitly, connect him with one of the prevailing perceptual frameworks of the day: antiquarian-national-romantic.

To that can be added Tory when his work for and sentiments in the *Courier* are considered. His vehement stand against the Reform Bill of 1832 illustrates his preference for the status quo, or the past, and an unwillingness to move into a future that would offer representation to more men, that would expand the opportunities of some of the working class, the dislocated, the other. The position he took in the *Courier* on the Irish question reveals his fear of the different—the Catholic. His subsequent membership in the Orange Society also suggests a fear of change—of the different, of the future, of changed arrangements. These public, printed expressions of politics and preference were felt by some of his contemporaries to have been aberrations, particularly his Orange Society involvements. Yet they are of a piece, albeit more political and public, with the motivating concerns of his life. If the Irish Catholics came and took over—and Catholicism was an international religion and "promised" papal intervention—this was clearly a threat to the Scottish and the national, which were both his experienced milieu and, in a way, his personal passion, expressed in almost everything he did and achieved. His public positions are not the muted articulations of a preference but, rather, proclaim a position. And I can imagine his delight in doing just that, in moving into the concrete, in having a forum for expressing in a very real way his political and cultural preferences. Dr. Charles Marshall's reminiscences of a meeting he witnessed between James Hogg and William Motherwell, shortly before Motherwell's death and on the subject of their collaborative edition of Burns's work, corroborates my surmise. Marshall suggests first that he had known Motherwell's poetry, which he characterizes as "Goethe-like gems of thoughtful, dreamy cast," and then describes the man he met: "Motherwell affected to care for neither literature, nor sentimentalism, nor song; his great ambition was to shine as a wit, and to talk politics—for he was at the time editor of the *Glasgow Courier.*" Yes, his political posturing and statements were an aberration from his earlier work in being extraliterary; but, still in the print medium, they articulate but another facet of the larger Scottish literary field. His choice, both implicit and explicit, was for the past and involved a romantic nostalgia for some possible organic community that exists only in human imagination, never in lived reality. He resisted change that would move his world even further away from his own ideal, however muted and unarticulated.

The fact of change, then, was the glue that held together Motherwell's involvements in various fields, especially the literary, as the Calder mobile, mentioned earlier, also has a central, uniting structure. And his response to change was derived from his *habitus* and his preference for an imagined past. He was against change, despite its ubiquity in his world. He was not, of course, the only person aware of it; John Galt's "theoretical histories" touch on change over and over again. Change was in the very air: the shift from an artisanal to a class-based society; the closer ties with England; the presumed Irish dilution of Scottish culture; the extension of male suffrage; the growing commodity fetishization of things, of books. Fear of change might be perceived then as the element, external, that unites all Motherwell's activities.

Man of his time he definitely was, more romantic than not, he represents one of the prevailing perceptual frameworks in the air in nineteenth-century Scotland. His life offers an avenue into the very human experiences that give life to the ideologies that history proclaims pervade one or another period of time and hints at the way those "ologies" and "isms" might have been articulated by those who experienced them. It would, however, be inaccurate to suggest that Motherwell was "everyman," for each individual, man and woman, experiences the world, then as now, in particular, from his or her own background and life trajectory. Yet the experience of Motherwell puts some flesh, some reality on a period normally thought of as being populated by individuals of note rather than by individuals of more ordinary experience and position. Here was a man richly involved in provincial life. He did not have an overt crisis over identity, national or otherwise; he did not look to the South to London or even to the East—Edinburgh. In that sense he was nicely rooted in the West, especially when he moved to Glasgow. Glasgow expanded his position and may more nearly have enabled a uniting of his public and private life, which had, in Paisley, been divided and separated. Maybe he was, in the best sense of the word, provincial. As a westerner, he saw his environment selectively and was undoubtedly governed in his political views more by feeling and sentiment, emanating from his own self and his lived experience, than by intellect and genuine awareness of others. He was the very model then, or a very model, of a romantic Scot.

Informants and Items

(*Indicates Motherwell wanted to get the tunes; †indicates he called them "old singing women.")

Margaret Bain
parish of Blackford
Perthshire

What's become of your hounds King
   Henrie my son

Mrs. James Baird, husband
forrester at Dalrymple

The Water o' Ganrie

Mrs. Bell, Paisley
Miss Montgomerie, Edinburgh

The Gay Gos hawk
The Gay Gos hawk

Margaret Black, wife of
Archie Black (sailor), Ayr

The Earl of Aboyne

Mr. Blaikie

I'll down to my dearest that now in the
   deep

Mrs. Blaikie

My father has seven plows and a mill
O Jeanie Douglas its but, he says
The Lass o' Aikengaw

Mrs. Brown, Linsark Parish
Lockwinnoch

Jamie Douglas

Brown, of Glasgow, sister of
Dr. Jas, learned from blind aunt,
Nancy; list of what know; Mrs.
Brown's sister is Mrs. Rule, Paisley

The Chronicle of Kings
The Turkish Galley
The low silver ee
Geordie
Gil Morice
Jamie Douglas
Johnie Faa
Young Tamlin
Andrew Lammie
Robin Hood and the Pedlar
Young Beichan

	Johnnie Armstrong Madam Guy
Robert Brown, Howwood	Lady Dundonald
Mrs Burns, late servant to Mr. Orr, 10 Oakshaw St	Broom blooms bonnie
Mr. John Cleland, Glasgow (marble cutter)	The French Galley/Turkish Galley
Mrs. Wm Craig	There's bread & cheese for Musqueteers
Marrhew/Matthew Crawford, Howwood (weaver)	Jamie Douglas
Mrs. Crum, Dumbarton	Montrose he had a poor Shepherd The Buss o' Bonnie Broom O fair maid and true maid Mary Myles
Mrs. Cunningham, Ayr	The Twa Brithers
Mrs. Charles Drain, Kilmarnock, husband low gelder	Jamie o' Lee
Mrs. Duff, Kilbirnie	Barbara Allan The Boy o' the Wood The Widow o' the West Down by yon bonnie bonnie gate Irish Dragoons The Maskin Rung The Black Waters of Dee Open the door love and let me in
Rebecca Dunse, Galloway	Jamie Douglas Little Sir Grove
Henry French, boy, Ayr	The High Banks o Yarrow
Mrs. John French, Irish wife of porter, quay of Ayr friend of Agnes Lyle Kilbarchan	Johnston Hey and Young Caldwell Lizie Wan

	Richard Storie
Mrs. Gentles, Abbey Street, Paisley[+]	Sir Patrick/Spens Mary Hamilton Sir James the Rose The Young Johnstone Isbel Child Norice The Elphin Knight Lord Ronald
Wm George, Cumbus Michael Perthshire	The Coble o' Cargill
J. Goldie	There were three sisters lived in a hall There were three sisters on a road
Miss Hamilton	I shall do for my true love
Miss Nancy Hamilton	Mary Hamilton (with Gentles)
Mr. Henderson, Glasgow (artist)	Turkish Galley
Janet Holmes, Kilbarchan[+] if Nancy—a singing woman	Fair Annie*
Mr. P. Jackson, Greenock	Paul Jones
Marjory Johnston (servant to W. Parker, manufr, Paisley)	Lord William Lady Margaret sits in her bow window Burd alone
Allan Ker, Greenock	King Edelbrode
Mrs . . . , Kilbarachan	Ritchie Storie
Edward King, Kilbarchan (weaver)	Lamerlin Kin
Mrs. King, Kilbarchan[+]	There were three Sisters lived in a bouir Hind horn It is talked, it is talked, the warld all over
Agnes Laird, Kilbarchan[+]	The Brown Bride and Lord Thomas

The Wee Wee Man
Johnnie Scot
Lord Robert & Mary Florence
There was a Knight in Jessamay*
The Cruel Mother
Willie of Winsberye/berry*
 "our king hath been a poor prisoner"/
 Lord Thomas of Winsbury
The King had only one daughter
There was a lady brisk and smart
Gay Goss hawk

John Lindsay
(cowfeeder) Wallace Street,
Paisley

There were three merry maids
Johnnie Scot

Agnes Lile/Lyle, Kilbarchan⁺
(c. 50, learned from father
customary weaver, Locherlip)
had two sisters⁺ M. also called
old singing women[1]

Lord Dunwaters
The Dowie Downs o' Yarrow
Mary Hamilton
The Eastmure King and the Westmure
 King
Lord Jamie Douglas
Young Patrick
Fair Janet and Sweet Willie
Sweet William's gone over seas
The Broom blooms bonnie &c
Geordie Lukely
Lord Barnabas' Lady
Four and twenty ladies fair (Barbara
 Livingston)
Earl Richard has a hunting gone
Davie Fla (Gipsy Lady)
The Bonny Bows o' London
There were three sisters lived in a bower
The Cruel Mother
The Turkish Galley
Johnie Scott
The Knight & Lady
Young Hyn Horn
The Gay Goss hawk
There was a lady liv'd in Luke
Fair Margaret of Craignargat
Johnie Armstrang
Slippings o yarn—a song

Mrs. McConechie, Kilmarnock	Wee Messgrove
Widow McCormick Dumbarton	Its hold your hand, dear judge, she says Lord Thomas & the Brown Girl
Widow McCormick[+] Westbrae, Paisley	Tamaline/Tam lin The Knight and the Shepherd's daughters Child Noryce/Child Norice The Cruel Brother Marjorie & William/Wm & Marjorie The Brown girl May Colean
Alex(r) Macdowald (coal-heaver, Harkis, parish of Dalry, from his mother, Irish)	Robin Hood
Mrs. Macindoe, washer woman[+]	
Mrs. McLean, Glasgow	Susie Cleland
Mrs. McNiccol	Love Johnnie Scot
Jean Macqueen, Largs	Queen's Mary
Mrs. Macqueen, Lochwinnoch	Mild Mary
John McWhinnie, Newtown Green, Ayr (collier)	The Deil's Courting
Miss Maxwell, Brediland	The bonnie Wee Croodlin dow
Widow Michael, Barhead[+]	The Jews Daughter Child Nourice Gill Morice
James Nicol, Stricken, via Peter Buchan	The Clerk's two sons of Oxenfoord
Jean Nicol	Jamie Douglas
Jeanie Nicol	Sweet William and the Young Colonel

Jenny Nicol	On the Buchan
Miss Nicol	Swift swims the swan on the high streams o Yarrow
Widow Nicol, Paisley[+] native parish of Houstoun, learned from parents, says "not of great value"	The Loyal Lovers The Young Laird o' Kelty Old Row Down a Derry The Trooper Somebody Robes of Brown Captain Kid The Bonnie Lass of Newport I'll tell thee the true reason Its braw sailing here one stanza: The Buss o' Bonnie Broom—Mrs. Nicol? Earl of Aboyne or Bonny Peggy Irvine Johnie Scot Kempy Kane Charcoal Jenny
Mrs. Nolman[+] (widow), Buchanan; also called Miss Birchanan, from Crofthead, Neilstoun	Sir Patrick Spens Willie the Widow's Son Jamie Douglas Lord Doughlas Tamlin Mary Hamilton Wallace My love he's young but he's growin yet Hynd Horne Lord Gregory Johnie the Valiant Scot Johnie Scot or McNachton
Mrs. Parkhill, Maxweltown	Lord Thomas
Margaret Paterson, Widow Michael, Covecoteha', Barhead	Gill Morice
Old Pedlar	Where will bonnie ann lie

May Richmond, Old Kirk of Loudon	The Burning o' Loudon Castle
Mrs. Rule, Paisley[+]	Fair Annie Geordie Lukelie The Turkish Galley Jamie Douglas I have a sister Lord Clifford says Young Tamlin
Old maid servant of Mr. Alex(r), Southbar	Lady Jane
Servant girl, Walkhead	Young Hyndhorn
Robert Sim, Paisley (weaver) (his father knew many heroick ballads)	In Borders bell in there did dwell
Thomas Risk Smith, Paisley (Thomas Rick, smith ?)	New Gown of Gray Variation of the Gaberlunzie There was a mouse lived in a mill Montrose he had a poor Shepherd Gilderoy McNachton When I was a servant into Aberdeen The Jolly Beggar
Widow Smith, George St. Paisley, Widow Nicol's sister	Clerk Saunders The Seven Bluidy Brithers
Mr. N. Steele, Greenock	Lamkin
Miss Stevenson, Glasgow	Earl Richard
Mrs. Storie, Lochwinnich	The Deil's Wowing Rosie Ann Bob Norice The Laird o' Ochiltres Wa's The Unco Knicht's Wowing The King's dochter Lady Jean

Mrs. Thomson, Kilbarchan[+]

Lady Marjory
Lambert-Linkin
Catherine Johnson[*]
King William going a hunting
Robs Bridal
Earl Robert[*]
Skipper Patrick
Chield Morice
There was a May and a bonnie May
Susie Cleland[*]
Lord Sanders
Johnnie Scott
Lord Brangwill
E down & oh Down[*]

Mrs. Trail, Paisley

The Mousie in thee Mill and the Froggie
   in the Well
Lord DunWaters
Mary Hamilton
Jamie Douglas

Malcolm Whyte, Moss-raw
of Paisley[2]

Lady Essie Dundonald[*]

Miss Ann Wilson, Tontine Inn,
Paisley

The Beggar Laddie

D. Wilson, Glasgow

Here's to you, an' yours

Mrs. Wilson
Renfrewshire Tontine

The Wee Wee Man
Hynd Horn

Old Woman, via Buchan

Sir William Wallace

Drafts on Variation

DRAFT 1

With this [existence of commonplaces] exception these versions may widely differ from each other. From these different versions one text is brought out better it may be allowed than any one of the individual versions, but like none of them. In truth it becomes a beautiful poem worthy the pen of Modern Genius. This collated version agrees with no recited copy and can never it is clear be appealed to as a fair standard of the state in which our ballad poetry has been preserved. This process of improvement tho' it may be considered the least heinous mode of changing Ancient Song is liable to much objection. It alters the distinctive character of the piece destroys its simplicity and produces very erroneous impressions regarding Traditionary poetry. Those canons of Criticism which regulate the Collation of Mss cannot be applied to the case of early poetical pieces which have only an Oral existence.

DRAFT 2

In both copies however the same story is narrated. Out of their conflicting texts the Editor of old ballads produces a third which contains the quintessence—the flower—or what alchemists would term the quintessence of all the authorities consulted for that purpose—by selecting the most beautiful and striking passages presented by one copy and making these cohere as they best can with similar extracts detached from other copies. In this manner a beautiful but a suspicious version is obtained having a faint resemblance it is true to the different copies from which it has sprung; but wholly without individuality. A collated version of this description becomes in fact a beautiful poem worthy the pen of Modern Genius. But it agrees with no recited copy and can never be confidently appealed to as a fair standard of the state in which out ballad poetry has been preserved. This mode then of refining Ancient Song though it be more conscientious and less liable to censure than another way shortly to be noticed it is obvious must still very objectionable on many accounts. These appear so obvious that it may perhaps suffice to dismiss this subject with merely observing that such a method of editing old Ballads as effectively mars the venerable simplicity of these early pieces, utterly destroys their distinctive characters and finally is the means of producing most erroneous impressions on the mind of the Reader regarding Traditionary poetry. The canons of criticism which regulate the collation of Mss do not apply to the case of early poetical pieces which have only an Oral existence.

PRINTED VERSION

It is perhaps unnecessary to mention, that of every old traditionary ballad known, there exists what may be called different versions. In other words, the same story is told after a different fashion in one district of the country, from what it is remembered in another. It therefore not unfrequently occurs, that no two copies obtained in parts of the country distant from each other, will be found completely to tally in their texts; perhaps they may not have a single stanza which is mutual property, except certain common-places which seem an integrant portion of the original mechanism, of all our ancient ballads, and the presence of which forms one of their most peculiar and distinctive characteristicks, as contrasted with the modern ballad. Both of these copies, however, narrate the same story. In that particular, their identity with each other cannot be disputed; but in many minute circumstances, as well as in the way by which the same catastrophe is brought out, sensible differences exist. By selecting the most beautiful and striking passages, which present themselves in the one copy, and making these cohere as they best may, with similar extracts detached from the other copy, the editor of oral poetry succeeds in producing from the conflicting texts of his various authorities, a tirdd [*sic*] version more perfect and ornate than any individual one as it originally stood. This improved version may contain the quintessence—the poetick elements of each copy consulted, but in this general resemblance to all, it loses its particular affinity to any one. Its individuality entirely disappears, and those features by which each separate copy proved its authenticity, in the collated version, become faint and dubious, confused and undistinguishable. Such copies, however, are those which find their way readiest into our every-day compilations of such things, as well on account of their superior poetical merit, as of the comparative distinctness and fulness of their narrative; and to readers not accustomed to enquire into the nature of traditionary poetry, they thus convey very inaccurate impressions of the state in which these compositions are actually extant among us.

This mode, then, of editing ancient ballads, by subjecting them to the process of refinement now described, though it be more conscientious and less liable to censure than another method also resorted to, is nevertheless highly objectionable, as effectually marring the venerable simplicity of early song, destroying in a great measure its characteristick peculiarities, and as being the means of introducing erroneous conceptions regarding our vernacular poetry, which has been recovered from tradition.

Memoirs of a Paisley Baillie

THE DAY

A Morning Journal of Literature, Fine Arts, Fashion, &c.

Glasgow, Wednesday, January 18, 1832

Memoirs of a Paisley Baillie

Portentous and lengthy is the title of a voluminous manuscript which came into our publisher's hands, two days ago, by one of Lyon's Paisley Coaches. We give that title in the same shape as it appears in the MS.:—

Sober Thoughts on Men and Things,
Conceived and Set Furth
In writt, by me, Peter Pirnie, Esq.
Late manufacturer (now retired
from business upon a sma'
Competency) umquhyle a
Baillie, &c. &c. &c.
Of Paisley,
For the manifest instruction
And
Delectation
Of Rational and Reflecting Public.

The packet was addressed "Mr. Every Day, Esq. Glasgow," and the stout wrapper of calendar paper in which it was carefully swaddled, had these precious directions:—"with care and dispatch" on one corner, "and be sure to deliver on arrival" on the other. The erudite Mr. Pirnie must have been grievously alarmed at our silence respecting his valuable labours; but the truth is, they could not be examined much sooner, though we had had as many eyes as Argus, and as many heads as we have fingers and toes, which, we believe are now only nineteen in number, having in our younger years lost a finger, volunteering.

Of Mr. Peter Pirnie's sober thoughts, (he surely is president of some Temperance Society) we cannot well, even yet, deliver an opinion, nor can we pledge ourselves further than from time to time to transfer such portions of his volume to our columns, as, in our opinion, have some claims upon the attention of a "Rational and Reflecting Public." He is, with grief we confess it, somewhat too prosy and circumlocutory for this smart age; but, in so essential a particular as style, we never like to take any very extraordinary liberties, more especially as our worthy and dignified contributor has, in a postscript to "a letter of directions," informed us that we are welcome to his "leeterary effusions, free gratis, for nothing," and having retired from business, he does not expect to realize any thing from the manufacturing of books.

We wish our one thousand and one sharp wits who write for the "DAY" were equally considerate and obliging. But no—if they possess the cleverness of eels in the use of their pens, they at same time possess the rapacity of sharks in their demands upon our exchequer. Let that pass however, and now for a concluding word to our Paisley Baillie, who, in the evening of his days, has devoted himself to the cultivation of polite letters. We cannot promise to our valued correspondent that we shall publish *all* his "Thoughts on Men and Things," nor even publish them in the order in which his wisdom has arranged them. From his work we shall select only what suits our own purpose, and pleases our own fancy. This to be the rule hereafter; but, for the present, we think it no more than an act of justice, as well as of common civility, to give Mr. Pirnie's opening chapter:—Our readers will perceive that he, like every other sensible man, has a very elevated opinion of himself.

CHAPTER I.

Some of the Reasons which induced me, Mr. Peter Pirnie,
Baillie, &c &c &c to commit my Thochts to Paper.

There will, no doubt, be an uncommon clatter amang the Corks of the Causeyside, as weel as upon the plainstanes at the Corse, and amang all the members of the *pap-in* clubs that forgather in the Water-Wynd, now called St. Mirren Street, or in the Towns-House, where the Baillies and other ostensible and sponsible persons meet at orra times to weet their whistle, when it is known and understood that I have the pen in hand to write my ain life, and to enlichten all and sindry anent my manifold experiences of men and things, seasoned with suitable reflections upon passing occurrents. I am sure, as I have a head on my twa shouthers, that though the Sneddon Brig had faun down like a rickle dyke intil the Cart, (and that's no that unlikely—for its sair bursten in the wame,) or the haill shipping of the toun, including the wee steamer and the big luggage-boat that plies between the Sklait quay and the water neb, had been wrecked past redemption; sic awfu' calamities could not mak' a greater stir, nor set mair idle feet a-ganging, or mair souple tongues a-wagging, than the fack of me writing a book with my ain individual hands, and getting it set furth in print for the behoof of a discerning public. But, stir here, or stir there, my mind is made up; and, like Earl Grey, I will noo declare, that I mean to stand or fall by my Bill. It's clean ayont the power of mortal man to change my resolution after it has been ance tane. The Cart may as weel think to ding doun the Hamel's Head in a spate, as for freend or foe to drive me out of my ain opingyon; for the fack is, it has ay been allowit, at the Quarter Sessions or in the Police Court, that when I was a Baillie, and a J.P. *ex officio,* I was as douce as I was dour, and would have a mind of my ain, come of the lave of the Court what likeit. And sic stubbornness in upricht thinking and honest action stands to pure reason; for it is a very remarkable, but certain fack, that in every plea where I was ower-ruled by numbers, as was no that unfrequent, yet, when it was appealed to another and superior tribunal—sic as the Lords of Session, the Barons of Exchequer, or, aiblins baith Houses of Parliament—it was commonly found by their judgments that Baillie Pirnie was straucht as a plumb-line in his notions, and the lave of the Justices as thrawn as a cow widdy. The whilk it would be the heicht of hypocrisy to conceal, was unco welcome for me to hear in the club whenever the thing became causey-talk; as the feck of things, whether great or small, are sure soon to be in our intellectual community. A hen winna break its leg in fleeing down fra its baulk; but we are sure to hear tell of the accident next morning at the Corse, as weel as whether it was a good layer or no. But I dinna mention thir things out of vanity, but just to make apparent, to the meanest understanding, that I am perfectly correck in my notions anent undertaking to write my ain life.

I ken that it will be objeckit by some of our wise folks in the West, that, for a man to speak of his ain havins, is naething better than stark vanity; but it must be allowit, on the other hand, that though it be vanity, it's natural for us to rooze oursells, and furthermore, it is to be observed, that the number is unco few that prefer to hide their candle aneth the bushel in place of sticking it abune it, where it may appear as a burning and a shining licht in the eyes of all men. From these observes it will be seen, that I am an outspoken and hamely free aff-hand kind of man, caring neither for good report nor bad report, sobeit that my conscience is satisfied of the richteousness of its motives, and the cleanness of the actions, whereby thir motives were brocht to bear upon the grand concernments of social life. Wherefore I can easily find an apology for now and then saying a good word for mysell when I deserve it, and my warst enemy, if I have an enemy at all in this world, I am sure will neither, afore my fact nor ahint my back, daur to say, or insinuate, that I ever took mair credit than I was fully enteetlit to tak for honest deeds done and performed, without fee or reward, as we Baillies say when we purge witnesses at a proof, and put them upon their great aith, whilk is a very solemn proceeding, and has a grand effeck in a court of justice.

But, to continue the threed of my argument, I am obligated further to remark, that naebody, man, woman, or wean, can say, or allege, that I ever socht, in the lang course of my useful and busy life, to rooze mysell and my actions at the expense of my neibours. Backbiters and sicklike garbage of humanity, I hold in great detestation. They think, puir born fules that they are, that, by pulling anither doun, they will rise themsells. They may be a illdeedy as a twa hornit deel, and yet, after all, they are but sumphs and gomerils. A backbiter or cat witted creature, that spends his time in picking out and railing against the faults and frailties of others, may jalouse that, by spitting upon their character, he is bigging up a bonny bield of goodly thochts for himsell in the minds of his hearers, but he is out of his reckoning as far as ever Captain Parry was when he thocht to tumble the wulcat at the North Pole. They will, no doubt, hear the body till an end, and some, nay I may say a good wheen, will relish his sklander, (for, after all, man's heart is desperately wicket and naturally a gayen black ill-faured concern, when it's no thoroughly purified thro' the soul-searching influence of religion and godly conversation,) but nevertheless, and not withstanding, they never can, nor will like the sklaunderer. He'll aye be suspecket and keepit at arms-length. Sweet is the treason, but foul is the traitor. The backbiter is like a leper, he has aye a clapper to warn others of his infection, and that is, his ain ill scrapit and venomous tongue. Now, we have just put down this bit cavaet for the good of the Ettercaps, that will be clishmaclavering and shooting out their tongue and winking with their ae e'e and scartin their nebs with their forefinger as if it youkit, and thrawin' their mouths as if they were gaun to tak' a dose of salts, when they behold that I have turned author in earnest, and in the course of the narrative of my moral campaign may have occasion to say, this *I* said, and this *I* did, and so it even fell out as *I* said it would do, and as every individual of sense must have foreseen, had he been similarly situated and enjoyed the same opportunities as me Mr. Peter Pirnie, Baillie and what not, had of judging correckly of the incomings and outgoings and ongoings of men and things in general, and particular, in public and private life. But one must lay his account with receiving very indifferent treatment at the hands of the unthinking and the malicious, and learn to put up with much injurious misconstruction, especially if like me or a Minister of State, he has had great public duties entrusted to his care and guidance. When I was in the Magistracy at a very troublous time, I was sair fashit with the dounricht lies that were told against me, but I had just to put a stout heart to a stey brae, and do my duty, in spite of man or deevil. Hech, Sirs, what an awsum weight of duty and dignity is sometimes laid upon the head and shouthers of ane efficient Magistrate in perilous times. But on this point I have a word or twa to say when in due course of time and of nature I was eleckit a Baillie, and took upon me the discharge of the duties thereunto effeiring, as the Town Clerk said when he clapt a cocked hat for the first time on my beld pow, and, shaking me by the neive, added, that I was the fountain of all justice and a ruler in the land, which was naething mair than a simple condescendence of facks.

Our friend, Mr. Pirnie, ex-baillie "and what not," as he would term it, has been very wroth with us for dividing his first chapter. We did so reluctantly; but we had no alternative, as our space was limited. Today we give the conclusion of his first chapter, containing his *reasons;* but, we promise him, that we will not bind ourselves to obey his injunctions, of publishing his MS. "Forefit forward." We must select as we like, and when we like; and, if the Baillie does not leave us uncontroulled in these particulars, we shall have nothing to do with the chronicles of Sees'tuland.

I will be so bauld as to say, that of good books there never can be a superfluity; and farther, as some auld-farrant and draughty author, lang afore my day and generation, has observed, there never was a book compiled so mean or worthless but a wise understanding could sook therefrom something good and wholesome in the samen way as the leetle, busy, hummil-brummil bees feed indifferently on fragrant flowers, wholesome herbs, or pushionous weeds; and yet, frae the last as weel as the first, they distil maist sweet hinnie for the savour of man's mouth, and the nourishment of his haill corporation and members. And may this no be the case with this book of my life, friends? I winna pretend to say that it is the very best of books, though a Baillie and a man of great and sickar observation and worldly knowledge has indytit it; but I'll uphauld this threip, that syne the days of Moses, the Prophets, and King Solomon, there has been mony waur given to the public, and mair sang made about their merits than I mean to mak about mine. Ae think will be apparent to the meanest capacity, tho it were that of a modiewort, quhilk is, that my book disna contain ony wicked allusions or profane ballatry—and that gif it does no good, it will, like the doctor's potion of cauld spring well water, flavoured with peppermint—do no harm to either beast or body, or sooking bairn—the whilk is a negative virtue of some consequence in this sin-laden and unregenerate age.

But Solomon, when he delivered his opingyon anent book-manufacturing, with some thing mair of bitterness than a body could expeck from ane that has written meikle and no leetle himsell, has not stated his balance-sheet fairly; for ye see he has lost sicht of the credit-side of the account a'thegether. He has forgot to balance the weariness of the flesh, with the pleasour whilk every sensible mind feels when, day by day, and page by page, it beholds the works of its individual hands prospering and increasing; and the images, and creations, and visions of the brain assuming a tangible shape, whereby they can influence and direck other minds, and be as eternal finger-posts in the paths of learning and virtue for generations after generations, to guide them in their search after the wells of divine truth and universal benevolence. It does not come well aff ane like me to differ with a greater and a better man than mysell—ane that was a crownit king, and ruled over a powerful and singular people; and ane whase name rang frae the outermost ends of Ethiopia to the farest bounds of Assyria, marching, as I would jalouse, with the Chinese dyke; as renowned for natural wisdom and acquired knowledge, while I, at the heichest pitch of my earthly dignity, was naething mair than the first Baillie of a great manufacturing and intelligent town, and wauked and sleeped for full twa yeirs with a gowd chain, significant of authority, about my neck—and my name and reputation was soundit nae farrer nor Glasgow or Embro, Manchester, or, aiblins, Lunun. I needna say, aiblins, regarding Lunun; for the late King kent me full weel, I having had the pleasour and honour to kiss his loof, and welcome him to his auld kingdom of Scotland, when he cam to Embro in the year twenty-twa, as will be seen in the papers and records of the day, and as is mair fully detailed in an ensuing chapter—weel, I was saying, it was na decent for me to differ with King Solomon on speculative points; but, nevertheless, I maun be honest aneuch to say, that his sentence anent the manufacture of books has an unco strong taste of the weariness and peevishness of auld age, and a mortified speerit. For the present, we shall insist upon this point nae farder, till I hear what my good friend Dr. Kittletext (of whose kirk I am an unworthy vessel, having been an elder thereof for ten years bygane, of the whilk office mair in its proper place hereafter) has to say, in his ain yedifying, and pleasing, and soul-refreshing manner. I may just hint, however, that I think the Doctor, honest man, will side with me; for he writes books and pamphlets himsell as fast as a mill shills groats; but they are all ower good, as he assures me, to sell weel in the market—which is undoubtedly a desperate pity.

Having couped the creels ower King Solomon and his glory, I may now shortly state the solid and substantious reasons which weighed with me in this great concern. And, first, ye must observe, that tho I am or have been a Baillie, a Councillor, a Commissioner of Police, a Director or Manager of various public establishments, and have kist the King's loof, and been muckle thocht of here and elsewhere; yet, at the outset of life, I was as puir and humble as my neibours, and had a weary and lang faucht to fecht afore I got my neb abune the water, and then as sair a strussle to soom to dry land, to beik upon the banks in the sunshine of prosperity. The fack is, and I take pride in telling it, I raise frae naething to something by the sweat of my brow and the lawbour of my twa hands. Step by step I muntit the ladder of fortune, till I speelit up to the heicht I now enjoy; for I may tell ye that I am neist bore to the Provostship. When that dignity is put to my offer, I dinna think I will accept it; for I feel myself growing downwards like hawkie's tail—cauld in the blude, and a wee thocht ower auld; an am really no quite sae gleg and whippy as I was sax years syne, quilk, nae doubt, is but pipper's news to the feck of the world: for, though I say it myself, Baillie Pirnie has been gayen kenspeckle in his day. Weel, ye see, getting on frae little to mair, and frae mair to muckler things, and instead of doing business in a wee way, but upon a graund scale with augents here, and there, and every where, and with correspondents and merchants ower the haill face of the country, it must be acknowledged that my progress thro life, with all its ups an downs, must serve as a good example to the young and an incentive to the thochtless, to try and tread in my footsteps. It will pruve a moral lesson to man in ilka station of life—high or low, rich or poor; which, if learned and pondered upon, must conduce to their weelfare and happiness in particular, and thereby contribute to the general good of society.

Secondly, it must be self-evident that one who has, like me, come thro' sundry vicissitudes of good and evil fortune, and has been reckoned by the public as a man of steady, moral, and religious habits, that in his ain person has filled many onerous offices of trust and dignity, and kept a sickar outlook upon all that was acting or transacting around him, far or near, here or beyond, for the better half of a century, cannot fail, in the natural coorse of things, and under the favour of Providence, to have gathered much useful and practical knowledge, and made many weel-grounded observations anent ocurrents, worthy of remembrance to all after times, as weel as of great good to the rising generation, which is unco uppish, and apt to sneer at the wisdom and calm ways of jogging through life, familiar to their elders.

And, thirdly, having jotted doun, in an old ledger, which was only half used when I gave up business and retired upon a competency, to enjoy, as my sin, Tummas, says, (wha is bred for the kirk, and is this year in the Hall,) my *otium cum dignitate,* every thing remarkable in my life, accompanied with moral reflections and precepts for after guidance, I thocht it would be a pity not to make all mankind welcome to the fruits of my matured experience, that they might be made better and wiser by scanning the omissions or commissions, and the errors of head or heart, of ane of themsells.

And, fourthly, and lastly, I will confess that my ain gratification has had no inconsiderable weight with me in becoming an authour. Books are a sort of passport to worldly immortality. Bairns may keep up a name, but they cannot maintain the fame of ane that has actit his pairt like a man of this theatre of the world. I have liked weel to hear poets and sang writers express themsells feelingly on this natural passion of man's heart. Really, without a sark to their back, a bite in their belly, or a saxpence in their pouch, I have heard, in my time, some o' them speak like emperors about the way they wud be idoleezed by after ages. Puir creatures, my heart bled for them and their dreams, and aften hae I stappit a sma trifle intil their loof, just that they micht not die of downright starvation. They aye received it as a lend, and lookit as proud as gin they had obleegit me by taking it; however, their term day never came roun, and I didna mind, as the sillar was never posted in ony ither way in my books, than as "incidents disbursed." But some of the words of these flichty creatures stuck in my memory; for, fou or sober, they had aye some glimpses of a deep-searching wisdom into human nature and feelings, very profitable for a man of my understanding to ponder upon after warehouse hours, and the cares of the day were bye. There is anither observe which I think I am enteetlit to mak, and that is, that it is an uncommon fine thing in itsell, for a man, in the fall of his days, to meditate upon his bypast life, and the uncos thereof, its lichts and its shadows, and all its turnings and windings. For my ain individual pairt, I may well repeat, as I have before observed, that meikle have I seen, and meikle have I learned, in this idle stramash, and that, being of an observing turn, my hope is, that every change in the crook of my lot has not owerslided without improvement.

It has been my constant endeavour to sook the marrow of reflection out of every circumstance and accident of life; and, as weel as I could, to preserve, above all, an even mind and a resigned speerit. Fiery tempered bodies get aye into a carfuffle about trifles; but I never saw ony good come of losing temper about what it was out of the power of man to mend or prevent. "To jouk and let the jaw gang by," is an old proverb, though it may not be in Davie Lindsay; and, "what cannot be mendit suld be sune endit," is anither. My puir faither, that's deid and gane, and laid in the mools mony a year syne, was a deacon at proverbs, and, saving some pickles of warldly wisdom of that sort, education I never had, till I wrocht to put mysell to the schule, when I got on like a house in fire, and ran thro' the wee spell like a lamplichter, which was an uncommon thing for a bairn of my years.

But, as I was saying, I aye keepit an easy turn of mind, and that, in my opingyon, is a great lengthener out of a bodie's days in this weary warld, and helps wonderfully to eik out the silly thrums of life. Were it not for this quiet contentment in ilka situation it pleased an owerseeing and divine Providence to place me, I will not say I would be living and life-like at this moment of time, pleasantly occupied in endyting my ain life, in my cozie back parlour, whilk looks into a pleasant bit garden, weel plenished wi' vegetables, sic as leeks, cabbage, green kail, turnips and carrots, forbye pinks, sweet Williams, roses and lillies, and other savoury herbs, and sax grosset busses as round as a bee's skep, and, without leeing, ilka ane the bouk of a rick of hay, wi' twa apple trees, a pear tree, a geen tree, and some ither bonnie things that needna be named, over and above a fine sun dial, standing in the centre of the middle walk, the whilk is nicely laid wi' gravel and white chuckey-stanes, and bordered with bachelor's buttons, daisies, boxwood, spearmint and rosemary, the smell whereof is very pleasant and refreshing in the callerness of morning, or the saftness of the gloaming.

Such are a few of the digested reasons which have promuved me to turn authour in my auld days; and, having told the public who I am and what I mean to do, I shall cease my labours for the present, and, in my second chapter, enter at ance into particulars, like a man of business habits.

MY FIRST ASSEMBLY.

There was a sound of revelry by night,
And Renfrew's capital had gathered then;

Her Beauty and her Baillies, good and bright,
Four hundred feet beat merrily.

MR. EVERY DAY,—As ye have a kind of body servant, named "Spentacles,"
that gangs till assemblies, and sic like fine splores, I wonder ye didna send the
lang-leggit cretur out our way, to write an account of the uncommon fine han'ling
that we had in Paisley, on Friday was aucht nichts. Me and the spouse of my
bosom, as weel as twa of my auldest weans, were there bodily present; and, to
be candid, and to tell the truth, we managed, atween dancing, claverin' and
taking a sup of het toddy, or aiblins, noo and then, a glass of port wine negus,
seasoned wi' cinnamon cloves and a bit sugar baik, ginger-bread snaps,
queenscake, or some sic snyster, to pass twa or three very pleasant hours. I had
my e'e upon ilka body that came doddin intil the room, and speerit ance or
twice, in my ain hamely, condescendin' way, at Willie Tamson, the toun's offisher,
gin ony gentleman of the name of Spentacles, frae Glasgow, or that airt, had
drappit in frae a noddy or Omnibus; for, ye see, our Lord Provost, to gar the ball
gang aff wi' greater effeck, and to strike the gentles that might arrive from far
awa pairts of the country with awe and wonderment, had set Willie at the outside of the Assembly door, in his single-breastit scarlet coat, edged with blue,
his white vest, blue plush breeks, and white silk stockins, and, wi' halbert in
hand, in great state, to act as usher to the company as they poured in thick and
three fauld, and to direck them whare to pay their sillar, gif they hadna providit
themsells with tickets aforehand. Willie, wha kent me for mony a year, as weel
as seeing that it was na sae mony years syne I had the wand of power as a
magistate mysell, naturally touched his hat, and, with a pleesant smile, said
jocularly, "Deed, Baillie, if the spentacles didna ride in on the brig o' your ain
nose, I'm no thinking they'll be here the nicht." With that Willie gied a bit
nicher o' a lauch, and I leuch too, for the thocht struck me at the time that I
might do waur than write a bit sma' narrative, anent our ain assembly, and the
ferlies that micht strike my individual een during the evening. Its really wonderful how a man of judgment can avail himself of ilka hint that falls out in the
coorse of conversation, tho' it were held with a born fule or bletherumskyte, no
to say that Willie Tamson is anither ane or ither; on the contrair, I will say for
him, that he is a weel behaved and sensible man as ony in his station, and good-
natured to the bargain. He was never nae boo-cow to the wee bairns when they
were playin' at the hand ball, the shinty, or dosing their peeries on the plainstanes,
like some ither offishers; but aye dealt furth the law of the land and the burgh, to
the puir things, with leniency and mercy; but amang big throuither neer-doweel
blackguards, he was as manful as they were maisterful and flegged them mair
nor a man of bigger bouk would do, or I'm mista'en for ance in my life, though
it ne'er may be again.

But, as Dr. Kittletext says, this is diverging from the main branch of the argument which was anent the ball, the whilk as ye couldna fail to observe from our newspaper, was to help the relief fund that was got up here when wark grew scarce, and a number of puir bodies were thown on their ain shifts to sink or soom as the law might direck in this christian land. I am no conneckit with the Board of Health, or the Relief Board, tho' as a man of substance and a christian brother, I've subscribed according to my means, not being greatly in the way of taking a charge in public affairs, having, as ye will see in my memoirs, had my ain share of thankless labour in my time; but I am creditably informed, and I tell it to you and the world with nae sma' pleasure, that wark is a wee thocht plentier, and that maist of the hands that can and are willing to work, can noo get on, no saw weel to be sure as ane could wiss them, but in a moderate way I think they might mak a fend.

Weel, as I was observing, this ball was proposed at some County meeting, and was patroneesed by all the principal folks in the toun, and there was an unco talk about this lord and that lady being sure to be there, till the hail place was in a perfect fizz, frae the East till the West toll—frae the head of the Causeyside till the Score. Its impossible to tell you the forenoon visits amang the leddies, and the bit quiet cracks amang the gentlemen ower an afternoon's glass anent it. As for me, I keepit a gayen quiet sough for a while, no wantin to take a lead in the matter; and, indeed, sic sichts were, in comparison, naething to me, that had rubbed shouthers with the first nobility in the land, forbye seen the king, as is written in my life; but it was quite different with my wife, that hadna seen ony sic grand adoes, and as for our son, Tummas, and my auldest dochter, Miss Jean, that had just got a finishing touch at a fashionable scule in Embro, and could sing like a linty, loup like a maukin, and play on the piano to the bargain, they were neither to hand nor bind. They insisted that they should be allowit to show aff their new steps, and they said it was expeckit by the hail respectable inhabitants of the toon, that Baillie Pirnie should countenance the assembly, seeing that the magistrates had sic a lang finger in the pie. Of coorse it was out of the power of flesh to stand against their chaunering, mair especilly as afore they spok I had coft four tickets, just for the credit of the thing, but no intending to gang—nor would I hae set mysell forrit on the occasion, had it no been looked for by the public. This is a positive fack, and my being there was no piece of ostentation; for sic a thing is no in my hail corporation, as ye may have observed frae first to last in my written buke. To me, as the faither of a family and the head of a house, it was the soorce of no small contentment to be the means, in an honest way, of adding to the innocent pleasures of my wife and bairns; and really, when I tauld them it was my final determination that the gudewife should hae her ain way in the matter, and that the family should appear in sic state and grandeur at the ball as effeired to their station in society, I was downright worried with kindness. The young things danced round me as gin they were clean gane gyte, and nearly grat for fainness, and the worthy and virtuous partner of my bosom and bedfellow said no a word, but just gave me ane o' the auld langsyne blinks of affection, when we first foregathered as lad and lass, and used to take a bit daiker to the country to see how the gowans and the gerss were growing, and the birds singing in the woods, in a simmer Saturday's afternoon. Hech, Sirs! its mony a year sinsyne; but the memories of these sweet days of youth never die in the heart that has truly and purely luved, as me and my wife have done.

Kenning fu' weel that our house would as a matter of course, be turned upside doun for a day or twa with mantua-makers, taylors, milliners, shoemakers, bonnetmakers and siclike clamjamfary, making new dresses and ither necessars for our domestic establishment, I thocht it behooved me to give mysell a day's recreation or twa by visiting a freend either in Greenock or Glasgow, till the house calmed again. Accordingly, I just daunered doun to the Bank and drew a bit five pund note, and with that in my pouch I thocht I need neither fear cauld no hunger, for the short time I was awa frae hame. Weel, as I was standing in the Bank chattering familiarly with the Teller, a nice sensible man, wha should step in a but a gomeril chield of a manufacturer, no that lang set up in business or he wudna hae sae lang a tongue in his head, and with less havins than harns in his pow, and, whanever, he clapt e'e on me, the toom cretur got up wi a guffaw of a lauch that might be heard at Dumbarton. Me and the Teller thocht the body had tint his senses, howsumever he got round again and then he said, "Gie's a shake of your paw, Baillie, and with that he leuch again louder than ever:" "What's the joke," quo' I—"Joke, nae joke at a' sees'tu," said he, "but I'm like to burst my twa sides when I see, Baillie, that ye have retired from busines just to write haverel books." "Did ye see The Day, the day, Mr. Sillerloof"? "I see't the now," said the Teller, turning up his e'en quite innocently to the sunshine that was playing upon the iron stenchers o' the window. "Touts that's no what I mean; did ye see the penny pamphlet call'd The Day, in which the Baillie cuts as fine a figure as gin he had mountit a new harness for a fancy web?" Od when I heard tell of this, I didna ken weel whare to look, howsumever I just buttoned my breeks pouch, and taking up my hat, said, with something mair than ordinar bitterness, "a strae will gar a fule cackle." "Atweel it will quo the menseless sumph," and with that, out I bangs, determined to see to the bottom of the concern. But, thinks I, to mysel, this is a fine fetch to put the Teller in good humour, I would lay my lugs that the body will be wanting a wind bill discounted.

Coming out of the bank, what should I come plump against but our Doctor, gaun in as I would jalouse to lodge a twenty pund note, for the Doctor is a tenty and thriving man, and has attended me and mine ever since he set up business on his ain *can*—and meeting with him, he took me all in his arms, "Ah, Baillie, Baillie, quo the Doctor, there's more wit yet in a beld pow than a hassock of hair. Yon's clever, really clever, but for gudesake avoid personalities.

Just proceed as ye have begun, and ye'll bewitch the town?" "Deed Doctor, to be plain with you, I dinna understand this daffin?" "Daffin! its no daffin, buy "The Day," Baillie, and become enlightened—Phoebus is a spunk to it. Bravo, Baillie, go on and prosper day after day, till Death and the Doctor"—"Houts fie, Doctor, quo I, ye're mad as a March hare. Gude mornin Sir, but mind to send round your laddie wi' the healing saw for wee Johnnie's cuttit finger, it's fashing him sair."

Parting with the Doctor, discreet man, up I gade thro' the town, booing to this ane and to that ane, for there was an unco wheen of my auld acquaintancees afit, and every ane of them had, in my opingyon, a pawkie smile on his lips; and I soon came to ken the cause for just as I was stumpin by the Deil's Elbow, (that's the auld fashioned name for the neuk at the Smiddiehills, but aiblins ye'll no ken the town, and maybe its no worth while drawing a sketch the noo, there being already a very good plan of Paisley, drawn and engraved by Mr. Knox of Embro,' in which the streets and the properties of every feuar are fairly set down, and amang the lave, I'll no say but ye may see my ain name prentit on twa or three gayen big steadings, as weel as vacant ground;) I passed a knot of clavering weavers, haflins callants I may call them, and when they observed me—they got up with a screigh of a lauch that might have deaved Satan himsel, and the tane gieing the ither a dunch in the side, cries "Gordon's Lone! Willock, that's the Baillie o' The Day." "It's no possible," says anither; "as sure as death it's the bit body. Losh, man, how pensy he bangs bye as if he wudna ca' the king his cousin, or thocht there wasna as gude men on the crown o' the causey as himsell?" "What is he? Was he no a weaver like oursells? Seest'u, my freend, he was ance a drawboy to my faither."

This is a swatch of their idle conversation, howsumever it didna muve my gall the least scent, and sae I just steppit up to David Dick, the bookseller, at the auld brig, and on purpose bent to fley him a wee about The Day. Intil his shop I gade accordingly, and whenever he got his ee upon me, I saw the colour come ower his chaft blades at nae allowance. "Mr. Dick," quo' I, in my maist serious tone, "this is a bonny plisky ye have been playing with the respectables of the towns. Leeberties of an unwarrantable kind have been taken with me and mine, in a bit pamphlet that ye sell, and I am determined to howk out wha has ventured to satyreese me, as I understand it does, though I have not yet seen it. Sae confess this moment of time, so that the innocent may not be poonished with the guilty? Mak' a clean breast, sir, speak the truth and shame the Deil."

Od, Mr. Day, had ye seen how the other Mr. D. looked, ye would have pitied him from the very bottom of your heart. His face grew as white as paper and his fingers and lips trembled as if ye had been standing before a Justiciary lord, with his black cocked hat on, when he is about to pronounce the awful sentence of death. I'm thinking I looked as serious, and spak as stour as the best of them, and kent weel enough how to put on an awsum countenance, having had practice, as ye may weel ken, when I was a Police Magistrate, and struck terror into the heart of mony a hardened thief and brazen-faced limmer. Having keepit him in this unco funk a minute or mair, I unscrewed my face, and, with my usual smile said, "dinna think ony mair on't. Baillies and siclike public characters are public property and maun put up with these leebirties. But let me see what the paper says anent me." With that I took up the twa numbers and read them ower in the back shop, and after that I called Mr. Dick ben, telling him that the "Diel's no as ill as he's ca'd," and that, for my part, I saw na that muckle wrang with what the feckless fule had written about me, and that he might put down my name as a subscriber, for I'll no say but our ain Tummas, or some ither wag that's in the Divinity hall will have had a hand in the concern. With that Mr. Dick's face brichtened up like sunshine, and, as he was muttering something about "uncommon magnanimity, unparalleled generosity worthy of all laud and reverence," some fine blawflaun that he maybe heard at Political Unions, Burns' meetings, or siclike gatherings, I slippit out of the shop, bookit myself for an inside with Lyons' three o'clock coach, where I foregathered with some queer folks, but it's no necessar for me to speak anent them in this letter.

Having spent a day or twa with my auld friend Mungo M'Wattie, ye'll ablins ken him, a retired bachelor in the Stockwall—he was ance in the fleecy hosiery line—and very bien in his circumstances, I returned hame, just in time to see my wife's and my lassie's braws come hame, forbye a braw new blue coat with yellow buttons, a silk vest bonnily spraingit with various colours, and tight pantaloons, made to fit like a glove, for Tummas. Sic an unco wastry in the way of claiths, great feck o' whilk coudna look decent a second day, made me a thocht donsy, I must confess: but, when I began to refleck on the matter with a mair philosophical speerit, I saw there was even in this prodigality and vanity, the workings out of a beautiful providence. For, ye'll please to observe, Mr. Every Day, that this was a charity ball, and operated as such in a twa-fald sense or degree. First, the sale of the tickets created a fund for real sufferers under the sair pinch of want and starvation: And, second, a lively impulse was given to the industry of ithers, wha were necessarily employed in the decorement and gar-nishing furth of them that bocht the tickets. Manufacturers of broad cloth, mus-lin, shawls, tailors, mantua-makers, milliners, bonnet-makers, hat-makers, shoe-makers, glove-makers, haberdashers and shop-keepers; even the sellers o' needles and preens, and sic sma' wares, had either frae this soorce a direck or indireck gude. And, when I saw that the ball was devised, not for the mere bodily recreation of them that attended it, but to supply food and raiment to the necessitous and hungry, and that, when it did this to a certain extent, it moreover added a spur to the industry of mony a hard-working, weel-meaning and indus-trious body, that lives by the lawbour and skill of their ten fingers, I could not but admire the twa-handed way in whilk the milk of charity was squeezed frae the human heart, and made, like a refreshing shower, to fall ower a far wider surface than the wee clud in the sky would at first betoken.

(*The remainder of the Baillie's Letter we must postpone till tomorrow.*)

MY FIRST ASSEMBLY—THE DANCE ITSELL.

> Was neer in Scotland heard nor seen
> Sic dancin or deray;
> Neither at Christis Kirk on the Green,
> Or Peblis at the Play.

The eventful day of the ball at last came round in due order of nature, and an unco ganging up stairs and doun stairs there was in our bit self-conteened house. Wife and dochter were putting on and putting aff this and the other thing, Tummas was like to drive doun the roof of the parlour trying his new steps in the toom garret abune, and, when unwittingly I turned up my face to consider where the din could come frae, a lump of plaister, as big as the croun of my hat, fell right in my face, and dung the fire frae my een like sparks in a smiddy. Sic things in a weel regulated family, canna be tolerated in ordinar cases, but as this was a day expressly set apairt for enjoyment, I owerlooked the faut, and took a turn twice round my garden, to cool my blude, and see gif ony robin redbreasts were hirplin' and chitterin' about; for ever since the melancholy death of the babes in the wood, one has an uncommon sympathy for thay wee considerate creatures, on account of them theeking the perishing innocents with leaves, as is set furth at length in the auld ballat.

As ye may jalouse, there was few in our house could tak ony denner that day, but for my pairt, I may say I took my ordinar pick; mair be token, we had singed sheep's head, trotters conform, and a very sponsible looking chuckie, as tender as could be, the whilk fare is no to be despised as times gang. After denner, I comforted my stamack with a leetle brandy toddy, and sooked it off hooly and fairly, being nowise concerned, like the rest of the household, anent either dress or looks, on the approaching grand occasion. The fack is I had made up my mind frae the first, to appear in the samen dress as that in whilk I had the honour to visit his late gracious Majesty, at his palace of Holyrood, where I can assure you I was a civilly entreated as the first of the land, no excluding the Lord Provost of Glasgow, tho' he and his touns folk tried to put themselves desperately far forrit; but the King saw thro' them brawly, and kent a spoon frae a stots horn, as weel as the maist of his liege subjects.

Tummas, in the course of the forenoon, being doun the toun trysting a pair of new dancing pumps, his auld anes being a wee thocht bauchlet about the heel, as weel as worn clean thro' at the neb, where the big tae presses, forgathered with Mr. Frazer of the Town's-house, and was on the eve of striking a bargain with him anent the hire of a noddy, when wha should drap in as luck would have it, but the individual secretar of the Stewards of the ball, really a weel favoured young gentlemen as needs be, and he set things to right at ance by mentioning, that if ony leddies were of our party, that a noddy would call for them at a proper hour. Noo this is what I call really genteel, and particularly obleeging, and ere mony days gang ower, I maun hae the secretar to denner, as sure as my name's Peter.

Preceesely as the clock chappit ten, a noddy and a pair of horses drew up at our door, and out came the hail byke of us as clean and trig as gin we had been falded by in a bandbox. Its a fack, my heart lap in my mouth when I saw our gudewife buskit and bedinkt in a real fashionable new silk goun, and with a beautiful spreading umbrella, shaped cap, transparent as a butterflies wings, and ornamented with gumflowers and other conceits, as natural as the life. I was just about to take her all up in my arms, and gie her a bit smack on the cheek, she looked saw bonny, but na—away she spouted into the noddy, with her good-natured "hout awa' gudeman," "behave yoursell before folk," as the sang says, "do you ken that you would birze my balloon sleeves out of a' shape." Dochter Jess was very modestly attired in a nice pink-coloured robe, the fashion of which I cannot weel describe, and her hair was done up in the most approved London style, by Mr. Moore the perfumer, whose fingers no to mention his legs, running about frae morn till e'en, I'm guessing were gayen sair. It did me good to look on Tummas, he was sae straucht, slim and perjink, tho' I thocht quietly to mysell the lad was looking mair like a sodger than a saint, but let that flee stick to the wa', seeing that his auld faither was in fack drum major at this march to Vanity fair.

Into the noddy we got at last, bag and baggage, and up streets and doun streets, dunting and jingling we brattled like mad. Shooting out my neb at the window, I could see chaises and noddies fleeing about in a' directions like sae mony fiery comets, which was a very enterteening and enlivening sicht; howsumever, some wandeidy weans cried "whip behind! whip behind!" and quick as thocht, scringe cam the driver's whip alangside the noddy, and in its waganging gave me a skelp athort the chaftblade, that was smarter than it was welcomer, and keeped me from poking out my head again, till the steps were let doun. Without further misadventure we drave up in graund style to the Inns' door, and, lang or we cam there, we could hear distinctly the sounds of music, dancing and gilravitching of all kinds, and baith my bairns were just beside themsells for fear they had lost all the fun. But I quieted their apprehensions on that score, by remarking, that it was not likely that anything very particular would take place till *we* arrived, seeing that the stewards had expressly sent a carriage for the accommodation of our party. And tho' I wasna eleckit a steward, they kent fu' weel that it couldna be in my nature to tak umbrage at unintentional negleck, and bide awa frae the ploy like some conceity bodies, that bizz, and fiz, and spit fire like a peeoy, in spite and vexation whenever they are no made the tung o' the trump, and happen in ony way to be owerlooked in the making up of the lists. About the door there was an uncommon crowd of men, women and weans, curious to see us alicht, and for a time, I could not see a spot where to pit a foot, unless I made a straucht step forrit, and making a virtue of necessity used the first head in my way for a stepping stane. Seeing our dilemma, a police offisheer at the outer door, wha had recognized me, immediately cleared the road, right and left, in a twinkling, with his baton, crying all the time, "Mak way for the Baillie, ye born deevils ye—mak way can ye no for the Baillie?" and by his exertions we all got safe and sound within the porch, and without any of the women folk getting their braws the least soiled or crumpled.

It's needless to tell you ony mair about Willie Tamson the town-offisher, standing at the ball-room door, in his new stand of scarlet claes with halbert in hand. Whenever he got wit of me, wide open flees the muckle door as if by magic, and in I gangs gallantly supporting my wife on my arm, while Tummas cleekit with his sister. No having been in the room for this many a year, in fack, to be plain, no since the Pitt dinners and Waterloo dinners were given up, there cam a stound to my heart, to be shooled in as it were all of a sudden into a most spacious hall, and amang a perfect hatter of unkent faces. But just as I was in a kind of swither whether to march forrit to the head of the room, or slip quietly doun upon an empty furm near the door, up comes ane of the stewards, and taking my loof in baith his, shook me heartily, saying with a very kindly laugh,

"Oh! But ye're lang o' coming,
  Lang, lang, lang o' coming;
Oh! But ye're lang o' coming.
  Right welcome, Bailie Pirnie."

And then the Lord Provost and other gentlemen gathered round me, and in the twinkling of a bed-post, I see mysell after all amang kent friends and no frem faces, cracked as a crouse as if I had been in my ain house, laying doun the law anent domestic obedience, ower my third tumbler of double nappy.

A scene of greater splendour, beauty and magnificence, saving and excepting, always, the royal doings at Embro,' I never witnessed in my life. I am sure there was full twa hundred gentlemen and leddies, and every ane seemed happier than anither. Then there was a perfect sea of waving plumes and sashes, and ribbands, and artificial flowers, and sic a variety and tasty combination of brilliant colours, I'll be bound to say, I never saw equalled in the best India shawl pattern, that ever came thro' my hands, and that's no few, as the feck of my friends ken. When I was in a bewilderment of delight, looking at the fine swanlike shapes of the young leddies that were gliding up and down the room, like sae many beautifu' intelligences, or speerits from a higher world with e'en glancing like diamonds, and feet sae wee and genty, that when they touched the floor the sound of them was nae mair heard than if it had been a feather lichting in the water, all at once there burst furth, just abune my individual head, a particular fine concert of big fiddles and wee fiddles, horns, trumble-bumbles,* ("We suspect the Baillie means Trombones.—Ed. of *Day*.) trumpets and what not, which was quite soul stirring to hear. At first, I thocht this might be out of compliment to me, and, not to be unceevil, I graciously bowed to the company; but I fund I was mistane, for it was naething mair than the music striking up for a quadrille, and, as I live, wha did I see standing up in a set, but baith my childer, son and dochter, as prejink and genteel, or I'm far out of my reckoning, as the best born that was there! The pride of a faither's heart, on sic an occasion, naebody but a paurent, that likes his offspring weel, can possibly conceive.

Fashions in music and dancing have suffered great changes since my young days, Mr. Day. I cannot say that I understood either the figure of the dance or its music; but they were pleesant eneuch. The quadrilles are graceful and dreamy-like motions, but they dinna bring the colour to ane's cheek, and gar the heart's blood gush, like a mill dam, frae head till heel, like the Scotch reel or Strathspey. And then there's nae clapping of hands, and whirling round, and crying "heuch, heuch," when the dance warms, and the fidler's arms are fleeing faster than a weaver's shuttle, and they, themselves, lay down their lugs to the work in dead earnest. Being a gay noticing kind of body, I may observe that, in general, the leddies had the heels of the beaux in the matter of dancing. A good wheen of the latter, though they might slide backwards and forwards, and gee awa to this side and that side, with a bit trintle and a step weel eneuch, seemed often in a kippage to ken what to do with their shouthers and their arms, and their heads. The upper and the douner man did not move in accordance, something like a bad rider that gange wigglety wagglety, clean contrary to the motion of the beast he is on the back of. But the feck of the leddies carried themselves like queens; frae head to heel they moved as a graceful and complete unity; and oh! Mr. Day, had ye seen as I saw, their bonny modest faces glancing past ye, radiant with the sweetest natured smiles, and their countenances presenting every variety of fine outline and expression, ye wuld have exclaimed with me, and Burns the poet:

> "All nature swears the lovely dears,
> Her noblest work she classes, O
> Her prentice haund, she tried on man,
> And then she made the lasses."

It's no for me, ye'll be saying, Mr. Day, an auld man and a married, to be speaking in sic a strain of young ledies, and all the fligmaleeries of a ball room, so I'll try to contain my feelings and proceed in a calm course, like a patient historian.

After the quadrilles we had country dances; but, so far as I observed, neither the Haymakers nor the Soldier's Joy formed a part of the entertainment, though there were a good number of gentlemen connected with the agricultural interests of the country present, and a fine show of strapping officers from the barracks, under the command of that excellent gentleman and good soldier Major Robertson, of the gallant 25th. The scarlet coats of the officers, with the great bobs of gowd on their shouthers, had a fine effeck, and contrasted nicely with the silks, and sattins, and muslins of the leddies, and the blue and black coats of the gentlemen civilians. Unless ye had seen the sight yoursel', it is out of the power of language to describe the liveliness that a sprinkling of red coats gives to a dance. Some of the officers danced with their lang swords at their side, and I was looking every minute for ane or twa couping heels ower head, but they keeped their feet unco weel considering all things: nevertheless I shall be bauld to mak this observe, that it is desperate difficult to gang, let abee dancing, with an ironspit hinging at ane's side. But, abune a', I thocht I could see the swords sometimes come deg against the tender shanks of the leddies, and a lick across the shins fae cauld iron is sair to bide. Our yeomanry cavalry never dance with their swords on, and the foot soldiers should tak a pattern and example from them there-anent, from this time henceforward, and for ever.

The country dances blawn by, then cam waltzes, and the leddies and their partners gade round and round about like teetotums, at sic a frichtsum rate, that, really, I lost my presence of mind for a time on seeing our Miss Jess as forward as the lave, and twirling and sooming about like a balloon on fire. She was driving doun the room with a tall grenadier officer, and, seeing her whirling round him and better round him, I cried, at the highest pitch of my voice, "For Gudesake, Jess, haud fast by sash or shouther, else ye'll for a certainty flee out at the winnock bole like a witch, and break your harn pan on the hard causey!" There was an unco titter amang the leddies, and my wife sidling up to me, telt me to hauld my whisht and no to mak' a fule o' the lassie, for she was just under the protection of a mercifu' providence like the lave. Be that as it may, I confess I was glad to see the waltzing at an end, and our Jess again anchored on a form, peching and blawing, but safe and sound, lith and limb, and as red in the cheek as a peony rose.

About this time some of the principal gentry made up parties for playing at cards, and ithers gade to the adjacent to weet their thrapples, for the stour kicked up by the dancers was like to mak' the maist of us, onlookers, a wee hue hearse. Some of us had brandy toddy, ithers scaudit wine—while anither class contented themsells with sma' stell whisky, made intil toddy. When I appeared in the adjacent every ane was louder than anither in praise of my fine family, and, with faitherly pride, I told my friends that I spared na expense in giving my bairns a good education, for which I received an approving nod from some gayen influential quarters that shall be nameless.

No having served an apprenticeship either to the tailoring or millinery line, I'll no pretend to give an account of the leddies' dresses, or the gentlemen's costume. In general, I may say, baith were very becoming. Some leddies were tastily, but plainly put on, others were gorgeously bedecked, looking like Indian Empresses, or Princesses of the Blood Royal at least; some had caps and others had naething but their bare heads with a bit simple flower, or sic like chaste ornament stuck among their clustering ringlets. The newspapers give but a faint idea of the Toutin Assembly,* (*QUERY, *Tout ensemble.*—Printer's Devil.) but, tak' my word for it, it was in every respect uncommon pretty and creditable to the toun, beating, by far and awa ony thing seen in the kingdom since the King's ball at Embro'. Anent the music, I shall say, Kinnikame played his pairt with great birr. In fack, I fand my auld timmers like to dance in despite of mysell, and noos and tans I cracked my thooms like a whip, for a gush of pleesant rememberances conneckit with the scenes of early life, when I mysell figured at "penny reels, bottlings" and "washing o' aprons" came ower my heart with a fullness that even amounted to pain. I wasna then as I am now; but circumstances have nothing altered the naturality of my heart, or gart me feel ashamed of the pourtith of my younger days, or turn up my neb in scorn at the innocent recreations and pastimes, whilk were then within my reach. I would be weel for the hail tot of our prosperous men of the world, did they think and feel like me, on this and many other important subjects.

But I'm spinning out the thread of my discourse, I fear ower sma, and least it should break, I'll just wind up my pirn, and hae done with a remark or sae. And first, I will say, that frae beginning till end, frae the A to the Zed of this uncommon splendid concern, it was every thing that a good and charitable heart desired. Gaiety, elegance, good humour, and unsophistocated taste, went hand in hand throughout the night. Every one seemed anxious to please, and bent upon being pleased. There was nae upsetting, nae unpleasing distinctions keepit up farder than what correck feeling, and a due regard to the conventionalities of good society required. We were in short, Mr. Day, as it were, all chicks of ae cleckin, cuddlin close and cozily under the expansive wings of kindliest sympathy and godlike charity.

All human enjoyments have an end, and sae had our assembly. About three o'clock in the mornin', the company began to lift, and the room to get thinner and thinner. In a wee while afterwards, a flunkey cam up to me and my wife, and telt us that our carriage was waiting at the door; whereupon we bundled up our things like douce sober folks, and gade our ways doun the stairs, thro' the lobby and intil the chaise; but there being only three insides, Tummas had to take an outside, on the box alang with the driver; but he was weel wrapped up in a camlet cloak, with a red comforter about his neck, besides, his mother insisted that he should row her shawl ower his head, just to keep his teeth frae chitterin', but whether he did sae or not I cannot say.

Hame we got a last without ony mischanter. My wife was quite delighted with the entertainment—she is a real feeling and sensible woman, and when we were in the coach and began talking about our twa bairns, their first appearance in public, she could scarsely speak, for her motherly affection and pride were gratified to the full, but just tenderly squeezing my hand, she said, "Oh, Peter, this was a nicht!" and I had just time to reply "Deed's I, my doo," when the coach drew up, and the hail lot of us alighted at our ain bourock.—Your's, till the morn.

PETER PIRNIE.

ANENT ME AND THE ANTIQUARY.

Hear, Land o' Cakes, and brither Scots,
Frae Maiden Kirk to Johnnie Groats';
If there's a hole in a' your coats,
I rede you tent it:
A chield's amang you taking notes,
And, faith, he'll prent it.

In a man's pilgrimage through the weary faucht and thoroughfare of life, he meets with mony queer customers, as weel as sindry adventures, the remembrance whereof is very pleesant recreation to a contemplative spirit like mine. One of these incidents in the variegated web of my existence I mean to endyte; but, first and foremost, I maun set forth, in due order, how and in what manner I first foregathered with the oddity, it shall be my endeavour to describe.

It is weel kent to ilka body that has a muckle harns as will be contained in the doup of a nit, or a steely point of a woman's thimble—for, as to tailors' thimbles, they had nae doup whatsumever—that a married man has a hantle of things till fash him, that bachelors and single-living individuals are exempted from. In fack, they that are no joined in the bands of holy wedlock are a kind of land-loupers, and can gang hap-stap-and-jump through life with a licht burden upon their back, in comparison with us that are married men, having wife and weans, and their manifold concernments and adoes hinging at the tail of our coats, and sometimes clawing our lugs, if it durst be mentioned. Howsumever, as is very weel observed by an eminent writer, no to be found in Scot's or Barry's collection of the Beauties of Eminent Writers, that we married folks are the sponsible and landbiding individuals, who give hostages to society for our gude behaviour; and it stands to reason that a man who has a family, that he loves, should like to see them all put in a way to do for themselves creditably; and that, every one must see, canna be brought about, unless he, in his ain person, pruves that he is enteetlit to the consideration and support of his neibours, by conforming to that mode of thinking and of acting quhilk, by long experience, is found to be most conducible to the peace, happiness, and weel-doing of society at large. On this point it is needless for me to expatiate, having already treated it at great length in my moral digression anent "the single married and the double happy," which forms the subject of a chapter before the ane that speaks of my ain marriage, and settlement for better for waur in this transitory scene.

Nevertheless, I maun repeat, that we married men hae an awfu' hurl-come-gush of wee things to tout us, baith within doors, and without, that nane but a married man can form ony conception of, though he were to think from this day till the morn-come-never, and that is a gay lang and dreich spell, or I am aff my eggs. In this argument I scorn to mention the graver polities and bounden duties of the faither of a family, sic as the needcessity of providing, from day to day, their daily bread, of cleeding them, and sculing them, and keeping them ticht, thack and rape, as we say, in every thing conform to their station; and as little will I mention the local stents and public taxes that, like sae mony condies, sook the sap and substance out of ane's purse, be it ever sae weighty; but I'll just instance ane or twa of the bit sma' things that put us aff our ordinar, and mak a man like me no that easy to be guided, unless he be cuiterit up by some canny hand and oily tongue. In the catalogue of domestic grievances, I will particulareeze, in the first place, the painting of the house ance a-year, commonly about the Whitsunday term, whilk is sure to keep ane in a coat of het water, and a' the house asteer, for the space of a fortnicht, or aiblins three owks; for the painter chields are latherin bodies when they get a job in hand, as weel as desperate claverers wi' they idle hizzies of servant lasses. Neist in order comes the general lum soopin, whilk, in my establishment, takes place regularly every month, enduring the winter season, and, with the scraichin o' the wee black modiewarts o' bairns, that gang creeping and speeling up the lums, besom in hand, and the breingin, rampaugin and yellochin of the servant lasses in ilka corner of the house, it is clearly manifest, that they kind of monthly purgations of the lums and chimleys, of a weel ordered self-conteened dwelling house, are unco drawbacks upon a man's comforts; howbeit, they may add to the security of his ain person and property, from danger by fire, as weel as help to keep the minds of all agents for the Fire Insurance offices tolerably composed. After painting and lum sooping and sicklike gentle airts comes washing, and, Gude forgie me, gin my teeth dinna chatter in my heid, whensomever the apparition of a general washing traverses the chambers of my brain. Every person must have seen and beheld with fear and wonderment the ghost of Prince Hamlet's faither, but it's not half so gruesome as the spectral eemage of the washing day. But least I faint, I will forbear for the present from narrating my first acquaintance with the uneirdly eemage of "Sheet synd and Blanket fauld," and the wonderful twa-handed crack we had thegither ae afternoon, a wee while after I had come out of a raging fever, though, I can assure you, I was then in my sober and collecked senses, as ever man was. The laird of Coul's Ghaist was a fleabite to my concern with the aparition. Passing frae spiritual unto material matters, for the meantime, I may sum up my invective against washing days very briefly, by just observing, that the rippetting hurly burly din and confusion, are quite unbearable by a quiet minded man like me. In fack, to be plain, on these occasions, and that in our house is ance a fortnight, I feel quite frae hame in my ainhouse: I feel as a stranger in the land, dowie and forsaken, quhilk is queer eneuch, considering that I am the laird of the hail tenement mysell, high and laigh, back and fore, with its outshots and inshots, back jambs, wings, offices and hail pertinents whatsumever; and therefore, in a fair different situation from one that is merely a tenant, and liable to be furth put and ejeckit by the strong arm of the law, whenever he disna cash up byganes, and settle scores at the term day. Hech, sirs, it takes an unco scartin now to get in a body's rents! It is a sair trail to ane's patience to have them come dreepin in shilling by shilling, or pound by pound, instead of being paid in the slump, as was the case lang syne. What it is to come of this new and orra state of things, and mair especially of puir landlords, that have all our weel-gathered and weel-tented gear, sunk in stane and lime, and improvements for the benefit of society and the kingdom at large, is mair than I can foresee. It's a black look forrit at the best.

Our Janet (that's my wife's name), a real good hearted creature as needs to be, kenning my trim, and sensible til the last, that it is ayont the power of woman or the face of clay to mak me John Tamson's man, or to be less than a Magistrate holding authority in my ain house, maks it always a point of her duty to straik me with the hair, asweel as to give me timeous warning and premonition whenever ony of the stramashes to the whilk I have alluded, are about to tak place. Of course, when I receive warning of a washing, a lum soopin, or a regular cleaning in our domestic establishment, I just make up my noble mind to tak a day's play, and to refresh body and speerit with a bit stravaig into the country, and then to tak my chance of pat luck with some freend that disna stand on ceremony, and kens like mysell a hawk frae a handsaw. If the day be uncommon fine, and the sun a wee thocht our het, instead of walking, I prefer taking a sail down to the water neb, and there one can get aboard a steamer, or else they may tak their foot in their hand, and bundle owerby to Kilpatrick, or up the gate to Arinthrow, where ane is aye sure of getting a cauld chack of meat, a bit cauler salmon, or something comfortable. In thir excursions, I aye ettle to be hame about gloamin, or afore the ten hours' bell at the very fardest, for there is an absolute needcessity for a paurent like me, in thir sliddery times, to set a pattern and example of good manners and early hours till a young and numbersome family as mine by the blessing of providence happens to be.

Aweel, as I was saying, the worthy partner of my bed and bosom, ae nicht, in the year 1828, when we were sitting thegither by the ingle cheek, in the parlour, after the weans were put to bed, says to me, in her ain couthy way, "Baillie, ye maun trintle aff to the country the morn, for I hae an unco big washing, and me and the twa servants, as weel as an extra hand, will be busy as bumbees amang blankets and washing boyns. Aiblins ye can gang doun and see the provost of Arinthrow, the auld toun clark, or some ither respectable freend and acquaintance." "What maun be maun be, quo' I, my bonny doo; but really ye should have let me ken o' this hurry afore the now, for the fack is, I dinna weel ken where to show my neb. Arinthrow is out of the question; for ye ken the last time I was there, I got mair drink than was good for me, and there is nae need for a man just to throw himsell in the way of temptation and mischief. "Atweel, Baillie, and that is true," said my wife, honest woman; "but maybe ye can rax your shanks up the length o' the Parish,* (*We believe this to be the parish of Neilston; but this is not the only obscurity that occurs in the Baillie's autobiography.—ED) or tak a sail to the Brig o' Johnstone in the canal boat." "We shall see," rejoined I, "the morn's morning; for, if I maun be an alien and wanderer frae my ain being house and clean fireside, I maun make the best I can of my lot. Sufficient for the day is the evil thereof;" and, afore I settle where I will gang the morn, I'll tak counsel of my pillow, like a considerate man.

The morning, as a matter of course, came round; and, after swallowing my breakfast, consisting of tea, eggs and ham, two penny pan-soled baps, forbye a farl of cake-bread and a thimbleful of brandy in the last cup, by way of a lacer, I sallied furth, staff in hand, to "puss" my fortune, as the fairy tale says. First and foremost, I gade up to the Bowling Green, and took a turn round it, just to make up my mind anent the airt I should direck my steps. It was a particular fine halesome simmer morning, and the Kilpatrick Braes, and, indeed, the hail country round looked beautiful, and I thocht to mysell that it was scarcely possible to see a finer landscape in nature. The Cart was skinkling like silver in the sun, and the woods doun about Blackstoun, Erskine, and Renfield, were looking so fresh and green that I could almost make mysell believe that I heard the blackbirds and linties whistling in them; and, with perfect fainness, I couldna weel contain my feelings and was just on the point of uttering some haver or anither anent the beautifulness of the day, when I got a dunch on the elbuck frae an auld freend, who asked me if I would take a hand at the bools, or pree a glass of herb ale in Sandy Sandy's; but no being inclined for either the ane or the ither, I slipped my ways doun the Hie Kirk Brae, then intil the New Street, to get a new shod on my stick at Mr. Findlay's chop, and to speir what clavers he had got either about shooting, or fishing, or tulip beds; but he not being at hame, I then proceeded to the Causeyside, to hear what was doing in the manufacturing line, and if ony good stroke of business had been done in the Spring or any thing worth mentioning expeckit at the Fall.

Here, of course, I forgathered with an uncommon number of *Corks,* for they were all standing at their warehouse doors, watching for the Glasgow customers, for it was the market day, and every one was glegger nor his neibour in looking after the main chance. Not being in business, I was perfectly easy in my mind, and sticking my twa thoombs in my waistcoat, at the oxter, chatted with this one or the other, just as it might happen, while taking a turn on the sunny side of the street, frae the head of Plunkin till the Water Wynd. Me, and some six mair had made a sort of pause opposite the Cumberland Well, when lo and behold a figure turns the corner of the Wynd, and makes straucht up the Causeyside, casting a blink, now and then, up till the sign brods on every hand. He is a merchant, says one, I'm no thinking that says anither. He is a perfect stranger, says a third; and in a jiffey, the hail tot left me, and to my astonishment, they, one by one accosted the stranger, but he seemed to be desperate short with them, for every man and mother's son of them bundled aff into their warehouses, as if they had touched a nettle. Losh preserve us a', says I to mysell, this maun be a queer shaver that ventures up the Causeyside on a market day, and neither means to buy, nor sell, nor pick, nor dab with our manufacturers. It's a desperate tempting of providence to say the least of it; howsumever, we shall see the upshot of sic a reckless course. But, having come till the boddam of my page, here I shall pause for the present; my next chapter shall detail the curious passages that happened between me and this strange-looking niebour, and how we grew as thick thegither as horses' heads.

"Printed books he contemnes as a novelty of this latter age, but a manuscript he pores in everlastingly, if the cover be all moth eaten, and the dust make a parenthesis between every syllable."
—*Miscrosmographie, or a Piece of the World Discovered.*

MORE ANENT ME AND THE ANTIQUARY

Weel, as I was saying, this figure of a man cam saunterin up the street at his ain leisure, and my curiosity was naturally roused to an uncommon degree, to get an inkling of what he was, what he wanted, and where he came frae. It was clear and manifest in the licht of my understanding, that he was not a buyer of muslins or shawls, nor a seller of silks or cottons, from the way in which my friends, sae soon as they spoke to him, snooled into their warehouses with their tails atween their feet, and their hands in their pouches, as if they had strampit on a taed or mistane a docken for a daisy, whilk would be foolish eneuch even tho they had been born stane blin', or had lost their precious eesight blastin rocks in a quarry, or by ony sic pitiful accident.

Seeing him bent upon making good his passage thro the Causeyside, whether for profit or for pleasure it was hard to say from his manner, I determined to keep a sickar look out on his motions, and if possible to discover what his motives were in coming to pry into the iniquities and abominations of the land. Of course, I continued to stand fornent the Cumberland Well, keeping the tail of my ae ee upon him, while with the other I was pretending to overlook the

erection of a new sign that some painter lads were fixing aboon a spirit chop
that had opened there the day before, and whilk, as ye may weel jalouse, was
very conveniently situated for the commodity of water, the pump well being
just at the step of the door, and quite as handy as the bool of the pint stoup on the
compter. Standing in this easy-osy way, and giving my stick a bit authoritative
flourish noos and tans, who should make straucht up to me but the very individual that I was quietly watching, who enquired very politely if I would have
the goodness to inform him whereabouts in the city Mr. Pirnie resided.

Hearing my ain name mentioned, I felt a bit flitter at my heart, but, as he
was ceevil spoken, and in the quality of his cleading as weel put on as mysel, I
immediately replied, that there were twa or three of that name in our gate end,
but if he would condescend on the business or profession of his freend, I thocht
it might probably be within the compass of my power and ability, to put him
upon the right scent, and thereby keep him frae ony mair bell-wavering or wan-
dering up and down the streets. And with that, I gied my watch seals a bit jingle,
satisfied that it was not very likely that ony ither of the Pirnies of our town was
ever kent in far-awa' pairts sae weel as mysel.

Of Mr. Pirnie's profession or business, says the stranger gentleman, in a
very solemn and discreet tone, I am profoundly ignorant; but the gentleman
from whom I received a letter of introduction, to Mr. Pirnie informed me, that
he was the Lord Provost, head baillie, or some such other municipal dignitary,
and an individual of great respectability and notoriety in this city—and indeed
the only gentleman who could be of service to me in my peculiar pursuits,
connected as these are, at the present moment, with Local History and Antiquities.

Ye're a sma' thocht wrang freend says I, but I'm thinking the person ye
want is now standing bodily present afore your een. Whenever I had said this,
the thin chafted and thochtful looking gentleman brichtened up wonderfully,
and, after blessing his stars, that he had met with me so readily, he claps a letter
intil my loof, written by my Embro man of business, which begged me to pay
all the attention in my power to the very learned Reginald Roustythrappil, Es-
quire, of Deafnut Hall, he having come to Paisley for the purpose of making
some antiquarian researches into the nature of its pearl fisheries and shipping
during the time of the Romans, forbye a hundred other odds and ends that were
set furth in such lang nebbit words that I really found it diffeecult to spell them,
let alane understand them.

However, I shook hands quite frankly with Mr. Roustythrappil, and said I
was glad for to see him in Paisley, and that I was sure he would get muckle and
no little to please him in looking at the Abbey Kirk, the Sounding Aisle, the
Grave Stanes in the Quier, the Roman Camps at the Bouling green, Castlehead
and Woodside, and concluded by declaring, that in my humble opingyon, there
could not be a better bonnyfeedy panorama, than frae the buttlins of the Hie

Kirk to tak a vizy of the hail town, including the suburbs, sic as the Corslatts, Douzland, Charleston, Maxwelltoun, Ferguslie and the new houses bigging or to be bigged on the Arinthrow, the Greenock, or the Nethercommon road. And here I just had mind of twa or three lines by Sandy Tait, touching the Hie Kirk, quhilk I repeated as follows:—

> Paisley High Kirk's like a temple,
> Craigans, Duchal, Castlesemple;
> So tightly co'ert wi' slate,
> The Abbey Kirk sounds like a horn;
> There bury'd is Lord Abercorn;
> Embalm'd he lies in state.

Ods, my life! It was diverting to hear what a keckle of a laugh Mr. Roustythrappil set up when I had finished, and then with water gushing frae his e'e, as if he had squeezed an ingan peeling intil't, he complimented me in the maist condign terms for my uncommon delicate taste in poetical description. This naturally led me to explain to him how I liked to read every thing that clinked harmoniously, as weel as had a curn of good rough and round common sense in it. And, as was to be expeckit, my new friend said the same, or as our Town clerk used to say at the tail of a deposition when it jumped till a hair with the ane before it, he concurred *idem in omnibus* with the preceding deponent.

Folks may say that they like anent not giving way to first impressions when they get a visy of the pheesug of a stranger; but I will be caution, that let a man of understanding do all he can to resist these impressions, they nevertheless, exert a great influence over his mind in forming its judgments. For my pairt, I will candidly admit, that the first sicht of a man's face and figure, decides for him or against him in my affections. The harmonies and sympathies, the discords and antipathies of nature, are as apparent in the moral, as they are in the physical world. "Like, draws to like, as the Deil to the fail dyke," and aiblins it was for this reason, that me and Mr. Roustythrappil cottened sae well frae the first even until the last of our learned correspondence. We hadna exchanged twa words—we hadna heard the sound of ilk other's tongue and seen the twinkle of our e'en, and the smile about the lip, till a mutual liking began. Considering the manifest oddity of his look and manner, this was mair remarkable on my pairt; for it is the effeek of all departures from established modes in dress, to engender repugnancy in the minds of those who hold by the orthodox fashions of the day.

My new freend and acquaintance, the laird of Deafnit Ha' was a tall, thin, wiry man, standing on his stocking soles I would guess him about 5 feet ll, or 5 feet 11¾. His complexion was a sort of iron-grey, shaded off with a clearish yellow about the chafts. In the matter of a nose he was like mysell, ordinar weel gifted, but his was a scent langer, as weel as heicher in the brig, and not sae braid in the neb as mine. His forehead was heich and cone shaped, and, I may add, that though he had a gay tate of hair on his e'ebrow, his locks were thin about the haffets. From his looks I would have guessed him to be about forty, mair or less, but ane can never guess within aucht or ten years, the real age of bany and skranky bodies. Anent his cleading, I will say this for him, that in the quality of the claith it was good eneuch, for I got an opportunity of drawing my finger over his coat sleeve quietly and unnoticed, and it was the best superfine black, 36s. or 40s. at the least, per yard. But it was apparent to any one that had the sense of a sooking turkey, and kent what was what, that the adorning of the outward man didna form ilka morn, after leaving his nest, an essential part of his moral duty. There is an observe in an auld writer anent the wearing of our garments, which is worth rehearsing for its excellence:—"Two things in my apparel I will onely aim at, commodiousness, decency; beyond these I know not how ought may be commendable; yet I hate an *effeminate sprucenesse* as much as *a phantasticke disorder.* A neglective *comeliness* is a man's *ornament.*"* (*We wish our friend the Baillie, when he quotes his old authors, would tell us their names. It cost us some hours' labour to discover, that his reference here is to a passage in the "Resolves, Moral and Political, of Owen Feltham," a quaint and epigrammatic writer of great esteem in his own Day as we hope to be in ours.—ED. Day.) Now, the *neglective comeliness* was carried rather to an extreme, and his coat pouches were sair bumphlet out with books and papers and ither trashery. Every bit queer thing that came first to his hand plump it went into the pouch, and in this way it led nae better a life than a Gaberlunzie's meal pock, or a Tinkler's budget. One of the pouches was sae stuffed and panged, that to secure it the flap was steeked down with a fardin prin, that really, I must confess, didna look very becoming in the coat of a landed gentleman, and I almost brocht myself to believe, that at the douner end of the pouch, claith and canvass were made sure in the same way. This I thocht at the time when he was speeling up the ladder before me in the Hie Kirk steeple; but good breeding, at that particular time, kept me from taking ony correck view of how things stood in that quarter.

Anither thing I observed with the tail of my e'e, for the whilk I was sorry, as it looked liker the *fantastic disorder,* than the *neglective comeliness* mentioned above, and that was that, in his hurry in the mornin, he had forgot to shave ae side of his cheek, and the black stibble left didna look weel, considering that the ither chaft was as bare as the how of my loof and just a pleasure to look upon: it was so uncommon weel scrapit that auld Peter Gordon, though he was as sober as a judge, couldna have made a better job. But all these wee overlooks were, doubtless, occasioned by him living a single life. Had he been a married man, his better half would have naturally tane a pride and a pleasure in snoodin and toshin him up in the morning, and setting him furth to business nicely brushed frae head to foot, and as clean as a new prin, all which is a part of the affectionate wife's duty, the mair especially if her marrow be of a thochtful turn and careless anent the vanities and pernickities of dress. To conclude my description of the laird of Deaf-nit-ha', I have just to observe, that his e'en were grey, and, at times, unco heavy, drumly and dreamy like, but when he was struck suddenly with any special, sensible remark of mine, up they lichted, with a desperate flashiness, and gade bleeze awa like a pluff of gunpouther, and then gradually sunk doun into more than ordinar dullness. A man like me that notes every thing, be it great or small, soon perceived that my Antiquarian friend was a wee thocht short sichted, as will be explained hereafter, when we were copying Abbot Shaw's inscription at the Walneuk, and nae wonder, for it maun have worn out the very strongest and best e'en that ever were set in a man's pow, had they been stented as my Embro man of business alleged, to look for pearl mussells amang sand, and mud, frae the time of the Romans till the present day. Howsumever, I fund this to be a mistake, for my agent didna ken the main object of Mr. Roustythrappils visit to the West country; for it referred allenarly to ancient evidents anent Kirk property in Papistical times, the deciphering of auld inscriptions up and doun the country, visying of dilapidated Kirks sic as our Abbey, and taking draughts with his keelavyne of monumental crosses and siclike eemages erected in the Heathen times of darkness and sinfulness.

All this I discovered in due course of post, as a body might say, and that was just after denner, when we twa got upon the crack about auld-fashioned ferlies, and occasionaly dipped intil poetry, music, and pearl-fishing in the Cart, upon the which last I was quite a Don, and shewed him that there was life in a mussell yet, having picked up mony a thumpin horse mussell, with my ain hands, when a hafflins callant I used to gang a-fishing for brazes, flukes, flounders and eels, and such like inhabiters of the great deep alang the towing path; and who that has done that, said I to Mr. Roustythrappil, must ken that there is a desperate big bed of pearl mussels near the place that was called the Wee Island, but is now nae mair an island than a tea-pot, since the recent improvements were executed on our river, for the purpose of rendering it navigable to veshells of 300 or 400 tons burden, or even ships of war, as was the case, no doubt, in the time of the Romans and the Pechts.

In handling of these divers subjects, ilka ane was mair deep than his neibour: and, as we sat comfortably over our glass of port wine, the langer we drank, the deeper, of course, grew our observes. The fack of the matter is this the Antiquary saw that I was a perfect dungeon of knowledge, and, to do him justice, I will be candid eneuch to say, that I dinna think he was far ahint me in some points. He might, I make no doubt, have a little mair book lair nor me, as weel as understand mair languages, which is a wonderful help to a person of but ordinar gumption; but, on the other hand, I had a natural far-sightedness and practical wisdom, worldly experience and observation anent things in general, that enabled me to whummle him ower upon his hinder end in argument, in a way that was perfectly surprising. It's no to be concealed, that Mr. Roustythrappil learned a lesson frae me that he'll no forget in a hurry. He tell't me that philosophy was learned amang the shepherds on the hills, as Cervantes says in his excellent history of the Laird of La Mancha, Mr. Don Quixote; but I let him ken on the deafest side of his head, that the marrow of common sense and philosophy could be obtained just as weel in a twa-handed crack with a Paisley Baillie; and, no to "blink the question," as Dr. Chalmers says, that was my ain individual self. Egotism is disagreeable; but truth is a pearl to be prized, though found in a grumphie's snout.

All this took place, however, after dinner. Indeed, through the hail of the forenoon, I could only play second fiddle to my learned friend, he speerit sic a number of questions at me anent places I had never heard wit of before; and besides, there was anither thing I sall explain presently, that hung heavy on my heart, and keeped me frae wagging my tongue sae glibly as I would, in other circumstances, have done. But, man is born to sorrow; and there is often much to pine the heart, that the tongue daurna weel tell, even amang them that, in the world's e'e, have least to fash them. Naething is a greater pain than to be obleeged to feign happiness, and to wear a sweet and contented face, when the heart is just torn to rags with consuming passion, or is the prey of moody thocht, despondency, or stark despair. To ordinar minds, it would seem perfect nonsense that I should be noyed as I was, when squiring Mr. Roustythraple through the toun, and pointing out to him all its ferlies; but, to a sensitive man like me as sma' matters will occasionally look as big as mountains. The sum total of my vexation rested in the fack that, I coudna invite the friend that was commended to my care and hospitality till dinner at my ain house, on account of our gudewife's big washing; and how to get aff from the suspicion of being inhospitable, without frankly telling the hail outs and ins of the story, was what I could not bring my mind to. With an auld freend it was naething; but, to a distinguished man of letters, a stranger and an estated country gentleman, it was out of the question. Weel, I was just worrying mysell to death with the thochts of this dilemma, and the day was drawing nearer and nearer the dinner hour, and, what with walking backwards and forwards, I was getting quite clung, and as yaup as a greyhound, that I determined to run all risks, and tak my chane of Mr. Roustythrappil having a prior engagement on his hands. Never venture, never win, thinks I; so, out I whups my goud watch, (a very nice jewelled and capped concern it is, as weel as being correck as a dial. It's unnecessar to mention that I coft it frae Mr. Rait, that has a fine jewellery chop in Argyle Street, Glasgow, and who is a very tasty, pleesant and genteel man as ever I did business with; and a gay bit clatch o' my sillar he has gotten, one way and anither, for toddy laddles, silver forks, silver spoons, forbye the grand silver equipage that I got the year I was made a Baillie,) and twirling the chain and seals round my finger, says quite easily, as it were, I'm thinking, Mr. Roustythrapple, it's drawing near dinner time; sae, I hope ye'll find it convenient to take a step down our length, and tak a bite of what's gaun. No expecking company, ye maun content yoursell with pat luck. It'll be quite a family party I'se assure you.

"How unfortunate, that I precipitated myself into an engagement," exclaimed Mr. Roustythrapple; "I really must—"

Na, Sir, I can tak nae excuse, quoth I, getting as brisk as a bee; I maun positively insist on your dining with me. Denials are out of the question. It's no every day the like of us twa foregather; and, forbye, I have a claim upon you—a warrant for your apprehension—whupping out my Embro' augent Sandy Seisin's letter of introduction.

"Nothing do I regret more, than my inability to avail myself of your kindness and hospitality; but, indeed, I am pre-ingaged to another friend, or rather, we agreed to dine together in a tavern, before I had the happiness of falling into your delightful society—I must throw myself on your mercy—you must excuse me."

Weel, weel, says I, that is too bad. I am sure ye would have been as welcome as flowers in May, to my house; and the fack is, Mr. Roustythrapple, as ye are an antiquary, I was gaun to gust your gab with some particular good auld wine, that I never sport, except on occasions, when ane is needcessitated to give a grand spread to the Town's Council, or when, as now, I fall in with a real friend, and have resolved to be happy "for ae nicht in our life."

Poor Mr. Roustythrapple looked quite dumfoundered and vexed, for the mair he pled his engagement, the mair I insisted that he should come, and even hinted (but that was certainly taking a step beyond common prudence,) that his freend would be as welcome as himsell. This argle-bargling lasted for sometime, at last I thocht it wudna be safe to prolong it much farther, sae winded up the concern, by remarking that since I couldna enjoy the pleasure of his company to dinner, I hoped he would look in upon me in the evening, and enjoy a bit claver ower a cup of tea.

Here there was a shade cam ower Mr. Roustythrappil's brow, and, with some hesitation he at length said, "My dear Baillie, it is really taking too much liberty with you; but, can you not make it convenient to dine with my friend and me to-day. You'll like his company much: he is an old acquaintance." Pleased with the blateness of my freend, and seeing that he evidently manifested, from his manner, that he kent it was doing him a favour for me to comply, I tell't him I would put mysell aff my ordinar to obleege him, whilk was bit white lie, by the way, but it disna signify. And with that, seeing a laddie gaun by that kent our house, I gies him a penny, desiring him to rin every fit of the road, and tell Mrs. Pirnie that the Baillie wudna be hame to dinner, and that she needna expeck him afore the ringing of the ten hours bell.

This arrangment relieved Mr. Roustythrapple, as well as it did me, and awa we gade, antiquity-hunting brisker than ever. In the way I cuitlit up things, I am thinking I preserved baith the good character of the town, as well my ain for kindness and hospitality. A Baillie learns lots of policy in the course of his official duties, and he would need; for let an ill-speaking public say what it likes against Close corporations, Self-election, and Town Councils, I will maintain my threep that their pains owergang their profits, and, that the wearing of a cockit hat and a gowd chain for the uphalding of dignity and order in a community, is at best, an honour barren of all praise in a thankless and wilful age. Nobody envies the King upon the throne; for the crown he wears is but a circle, and significant of never-ending cares; and as little need they envy a Baillie; for his cockit hat is but a type of toil and tribulation, and the chain about his neck, though it be of gowd, is still the symbol of bondage, the fetter that binds him hand and foot to the oar of public duty.

But talking of these magisterial cares, aye makes me sad, and unfit for writing in my usual lively strain, so I must postpone till anither day, my confab with Mr. Reginald Roustythrapple in the "Three Tuns," at the end of the Auld Brig, where we dined together with his friend, after seeing the feck of the auld ferlies that our town presents to the curiosity of intelligent travellers and antiquaries.

> Oh! Paisley is a pretty place,
> It shines where it stands.
> —Street Ballad.

THOUGHTS ON SIGN BOARDS—
THE ANTIQUARY GANE WOUF.

According to the esteemed fashion of real *bony-feedy* book manufacturers, I ay like to stick a wee bit morsel of verse or prose at the head of ilka chapter, just to let the reader get an inkling of the nature and speerit of its contents. This device serves the same purpose as a Change-house sign. If the entertainment disna offer to be such as ane could naturally hae expeckit, we can look about for something better elsewhere. But, anent change-house signs, there hae been wonderful revolutions of late. My son alleges, that the improvements in this branch of the fine arts have been very marked and quite in harmony and keeping with the speerits of the age. So full is he of this conceit, that, whenever he is admitted a member of the Daffin down dilly* (*Query, Dilletanti?—*Printer's devil.*) Society, he intends reading to the members a grand treatise on "Signboards in general, and ale-house signs in particular, from the earliest times down to the present day, accompanied with suitable reflections, as to the manner in which these illustrate the progress of civilization, the customs, habits and tastes of a people." Some chapters, here and there, Tummas has, occasionally, read ower to me, for the purpose of improving his diction, and gathering a few hints frae his faither on different topics, which, of course, I am no sweir to do, taking a natural pride in seeing him employ his leisure hours in cultivating polite letters like a very tiger. Reading a passage or twa to me the ither day, Tummas expressed his regret that ane disna observe the words "Entertainment for Man and Horse" sae rife now as they were lang syne on the door lintels of village inns; nor the winnock broads covered ower, as thick as they could pang, wi' representations of bottles, bowls, gill stoups, tankards, glasses, caps, quaighs and cans, pipes, buns, baps, bawbee farls of cake-bread and shugar baiks, forbye ither eatables. "It's maybe all the better," says I, "that this change has occurred, for seestu, Tummas, my opingyon is, that they flesh baits—they painted eemages of things pleesant to the mouth of man are, in fair weather, or foul desperate, temptsum to the wayfarer. Ane needs nae extra inducement to drink. In this cauld climate, we are, naturally, prone to lay our hands on the bool of a pint-stoup and to steep our nebs intil a deep bicker. If ye hae studied history, to ony purpose, ye will find that the Scots and English, as weel as the wild Irishers, have all, every man and mother's son of them come of a hard drinking and hard fechting race. In fack, the twa gang hand in hand, or rather, the latter is the consequent of the first. Had ye been a Police magistrate like me, in my day, ye would have seen the truth of this remark made visible to the darkest understanding, every morning that ye sat in judgment. Now, Tummas, quo' I, this being the state of the case, it may be considered a great blessing to the country that eemages, reminding daidlin' bodies of their tipple, have become unfashionable. To my certain knowledge and experience, sic sign-boards haetystit on mony a feckless creature, to the very brink of ruination. Witness the heart-breaking story o' "Will and Jean, or the Waes o' War," where it is clear, that a new painted sign-board was the first thing that led puir Willie aff his feet, and I have nae doubt that Mungo Blew, that is mentioned in the ballad o' "Watty and Meg," had a particular braw scroll of iniquity flourishing ower his door. I will even gang a point furder, and maintain, that decent men have mislippened themsells in the same way—and, when glowering up at these devices (aiblins trying to find out what they were meant to represent, whether fish, flesh, or fowl,) by some unaccountable fatality, have found themsells sitting in the ben end before they wist, and slockening their drouth oftner than was at all necessar for their ain good, or that of their wives and weans at hame. Now, when this failing occurs in discreet and prudent men, how much oftener must it overtake them that have, night and day, an unquenchable spark in their weasen. It's out of their power to flee frae temptations, and therefore, it is, really, a good turn done to them when sic temptations are removed. Flesh is frail, Tummas—flesh is frail, and man's heart is desperately wicked. See, for instance, how in very different circumstances, ane aye finds a ready excuse for an auld sin. Gif it be a het simmer day, the roads stoury and the sweat pouring down a body's chafts like rain aff the sklates of a house, intil the change-house we maun trintle to rest our shanks, to cule our blood and to synd down the spider's webs that we hae swallowed on the road. Then gif it be cauld, blirty, or weet weather, the same excuse is quite as ready. We maun skug oursells frae the shower, and we maun tak' a thimblefu' of whiskey, or a tass of brandy, to warm the heart and make the blood circulate. And this is the way that man is ever busy deceiving his ain better judgement, and trying to complouther his scruples of conscience about right and wrang. But I have anither objection to these wicked sign-boards, Tummas, and that is, the desperate greening they excite in a body that may not hae a plack in his pouch, or a bawbee to birl ower the counter in the wide world. Conceive the cruelty of picturing before his e'en the reaming yill caup in a burning day, or the big bellied bottle of real stingo, and a farl of cake bread, when he has been droukit to the skin in an even-doun pour of rain, or has been plashing knee deep for twa or three hours thro' snaw broo? Tummas, this is the very perfection and refinement of the most deevilitch cruelty, and gif I were up in Parliament, I would bring in a bill to regulate ale-house signs in a jiffy, or my name's no Peter Pirnie. For, the safety of the State and the preservation of peace and order in society, in a sense, hinges upon these daubings, though nane but a far-sichty man like mysell can weel see how. But I will explain. Ye'll observe, that, when a man's desires are roused, and his mouth waters, and he has nae sillar nor means whereby to gratify the ane or gust the ither, then he gets ill pleased with himsell, waur pleased with his neibour, and, what is mair to be deplored, entirely dissatisfied with his lot and condition in life, and, when this comes to be the case to ony extent, then the back-bane of society is in a fair way to break in twa."

Here I ran mysell out of breath being a wee thocht short winded, which allowed Tummas an opportunity of edging in a word to the effeck, that he would cast my observes through his mind afore he concluded his essay, and that he hoped to see me a Member of Parliament before I died.

Tummas said this sae slyly, that I couldna help laughing to mysell at the naturality of the feeling which prompted him to make use of this expression of admiration for my taulents; howsumever, I took nae notice of it furder than merely hitching mysell a bit heicher in my arm chair, laying my right leg ower my left, sorting my white cambrick neckcloth, looking a little graver, and then giving a significant dirl on the broads of the auld ledger, containing my life, I replied, "Tummas, Tummas, for Gude's sake let abee your claverin. It's stark folly to even me, at my time of life, to the bodily fatigues of a Parliament man. It's clean ayont my fit noo to intermeddle with affairs of State; but I've seen the day, nae doubt, when if I could nae clatter with the best in the way of making speeches, I might have shined particularly weel as a Committee man. There's a difference, ye ken, between a lang head and a lang tongue, and the twa seldom foregather in the same corporation." And with that the conversation dropped.

All this while, I have lost sight of my worthy friend, Mr. Reginald Roustythrappil, with whom I got on uncommon weel, particularly after the arrangement anent the dinner. Frae the hour we forgathered, till that at which we sat down to feed, we were not off our feet for a single minute. He being younger and lichter nor me, couldna feel the fatigue sae sair; however, I dare say, baith were fain eneuch to cruik their hough and handle knive and fork. Inspecking antiquities is wonderfully appeteesing, and that, honest Hugh Fletcher's beefsteaks can weel tell, could they rise like ghaists frae the grave, and find a tongue to speak their woes. Me and my friend were mair than ordinar witty, on the occasion of their rapid demolition. He likened me to Time, that spared nothing, and I compared him to Death, that swallowed up every thing, stump and rump. I may here observe, that on every occasion, ane should be particularly cautious with their jokes, for, wi' the tail of my e'e, I could see, that my jest didna gang very pleasantly ower with the laird o' Deafnitha'. Being a thin spare man, he didna like to be compared to an Atomy, just because there was ower close a resemblance, in point o' fack, between them. Painters of faces ken fu' weel, when they are whisking aff a leddy's cheek, or touching aff her neb, no to copy nature, anent plooks, pimples, wens, wrats, or siclike oddities, that may come in their way, in due course of providence.

Afore dinner, however, we had seen every thing worth seeing in the town, that was ony way curious. He was particularly weel pleased with the auld fashioned houses about the Cross and there awa, that had their gavel-ends to the street, and which, he said gave a fine air of picturesqueness, melancholy grandeur, and antiquity to the town. He lamented, very much, the spirit of improvement that was going on here, as well as in Glasgow, Edinburgh, and other towns, that he had passed through, and which, in its reckless course, was removing these great landmarks by which historians were enabled to trace, with precision, the progress of society and civilization. If I was a Baillie, said Mr. Routsythrappil, I would hang, on the next tree, the first uncircumcised knave, that defaced an ancient monument, cut up an old manuscript for tailors' measures, or tore down any venerable edifice.

"'Deed, Mr. Roustythrappil," quo I, putting in my word, "I have been a Baillie for years, and I never durst lay a finger on the bodies that drive doun auld biggings, and put up decent substantial tenements, three or four stories heich, with chops for merchandise in the ground floor, forbye garrets wi' nice skylights, for the accommodation of nitties, and sic like tradesmen, that needs to hae an e'e in their head, as weel as in their needle! And, really, Sir, when ye look upon the matter as a mercantile man—

"As a mercantile man," roared out Mr. Roustythrappil, at the top of his voice, and faith that was nae mouse's cheip—"I cannot think, sir, as a mercantile man, on any subject. What have antiquities to do with a mercantile man? He has no more taste than a toadstool—Sir, he has no more sympathy for the elevated contemplations to which the study of antiquity leads the scholar and the gentleman, than that dog has for Algebra."

"Wheesht, wheesht, Mr. Roustythrappil, we'll talk of thir things ower a tumbler. You are speaking sae loud, and making sic awsum faces, that, I declare, every body on the plainstanes has his e'e upon us."

"Whist—I'll not whist, Sir. One must lift up his voice, fearlessly, against the rank and crying corruptions of these degenerate days. Think as a mercantile man! lack a mercy! No, Sir, I will not think like any such ideot. He who asks me to do so, insults me as much as if he called me liar and coward. Answer me this question, Sir—What have your mercantile-point-of-view men been doing, are doing, and may yet do? Why, Sir, there, in Edinburgh, they are making an ass of the castle—they are, besides, disfiguring every natural object which the finger of Divinity has fashioned with most exquisite skill and endowed with eternal beauty of form. The same destructive spirit rages elsewhere, with equal impudence and tastelessness. Sir, the taste of the present day is on a par with that of a ginger-bread baker, or a French milliner. In Glasgow, the Bishop's Castle was tumbled down—hundreds of quaint looking edifices have shared the same ruthless fate. Whole battalions of these standard bearers of glorious antiquity have been swept down by this battering train of utility, and heartless blundering. It mads me to think of it. To come home to your own bosom and business, Sir, why did your mercantile-minded men destroy your magnificent Abbey Wall? why root up the noble fruit trees of that princely orchard? why eradicate the gigantic plane tree which stood at the chancel window, and under which mitred Abbot, and hooded Monk have knelt, murmuring orisons to the blessed confessor, St. Miren, and St. James, the apostle? Sir, do the words, *Posce Mirene Christum pro famulis tuis* not ring in your ears? I hear them chaunted yet, by a choir, which has been resolved into dust four centuries ago. Are the dirty buts and bens you have, subsequently, built, with the ashler square stones of Abbot Shaw's wall, and styled the New Town, to satisfy me, or any man that has the slightest sympathy with past ages, for its demolition? No, Sir, they never can. Then, again, you stole the stones of the church choir, to build your Abbey Bridge—the transaction is scandalous and infamous, to a degree. Where is Gundy's cross, I ask, (Gowan Dhu or the Black Smiths' Cross, I believe,) but so abbreviated in pretty ancient writs. What did you do with the market cross of the Burgh itself? How dared ye let the great stone chamber at the place of Paisley, to fall into decay, which princes and peers, yea, lords, spiritual and temporal, have honoured with their presence? Why did ye demolish the balcony at the north side of the Abbey? Barbarians, scoundrels, dregs, and scum of the earth, what infatuation induced you to demolish St. Roque's Chapel, and eradicate the stump of St. Roque's Cross? Lastly, what the devil induced you to make away with the Wee Steeple, and silence forever, the pensive harmony of its bell, ycleped Yaummer Yowls!"

Hearing sic a spate o' clatter, I was clean dumbfoundered for the feck of five minutes, mair or less, at last I mustered up courage to say, "preserve us a,' what's the need of being in siccan a kippage about they auld concerns. Really Mr. Roustythrappil ye're quite gane wouf about they antiquities. What does it signify now to either of us, whether the Wee Steeple is till the fore or not? I mind it fu' weel, it was but a stumpy clumsy nidderd like thing, no unlike the Renfrew ane, but considerably laicher, and that in the way o' steeples is no to be borne—Never fash your thumb—its a' toom sound they havers about a bit rickle o' stanes—I am surprised to see a man of your sense and mense worrying himsell to death about sic sma trifles."

Trifles, Mr. Pirnie, and Mr. Roustythrappil looked as ashey pale as a weel whitened door cheek, while his een were positively lowing in his head—"Trifles! Good heavens, Sir, do you know with whom and about what you have been talking?"

I confess, that I felt unco queer, when I saw by his manner that his corruption was really up about something, but what that was, naebody could weel see, and no wantin to anger him mair, I mildly said, "Losh pity me Mr. Roustythrapple, your surely no meaning to ding my head aff in braid day-licht, in my ain toun, and afore my ain kith kin and kindly neighbours, and against all law and conscience, at the very market corse?"

"No! No Mr. Pirnie, you mistake me, or I have mistaken you. We have been both too warm I daresay. All enquirers after truth are somewhat irascible. "Fools and knaves conspire to murder truth and to cheat the world of her sunshine."

"Warm!" quo I, trying to laugh, "na, na, Mr. Roustythrappil, ye've kept me this five minutes in a nice cauld bath of a sweat, and considering the uncommon heat of the sun, I cannot but say I'm obligated to you."

> But nearer see yon hill with tall spire crown'd
> Studded with many a mansion, school and church,
> Whilst round its base a thronging town is wound,
> A town, upon whose merits we would wish to touch,
> But which, so great they are, we cannot say too much.
> —Renfrewshire Characters and Scenery.

A STEEPLE CHASE AFTER ANTIQUITIES

(A continuation of last chapter)

Having got things toshed up in this way, I was anxious to get our Antiquary harled up to the High Kirk, for his strange figure, violent gestures, and the way that he wapped about his hands, had by this time gathered a gay pickle folk about us. What faschit me maist, was some of my ain freends in daikering backwards and forwards in the square, with their hands in their breek pouches, or stuck in their oxters, coming within earshot, and saying till ane anither, loud eneuch for Mr. Roustythrappil to hear, "Whatten a queer neighbour is that the Baillie's got in tow with? Surely they winna cast out—I declare they'll fecht. Weel it's a pity, the Baillie, puir bodie, demeans himsell wi taking ony sic chat aff the hands of that dour doun-lookin, sneck-drawer. Od, if it was me, I would hand him ower to Captain Jamffray of the Police in the dooble of nae time." This was really a tempting of Providence on their part, as weel as an affront to mysell, that I didna pass ower neist time we foregathered in the Baillie's club, for I gied them their ditty—het and heavy; but, after they had apologeesed, I telt them, as in duty bound, all I kent, and a wee scent mair, about Mr. Roustythrappil. It was really a mercy, however, that that gentleman being a thocht deaf in his near lug, owing to his having catched a cauld while sitting at the sea side ae stormy afternoon, listening like a seamaw or kittywake to the sough of the wind and the jaupin' of the waves. He assured me, that the thundering waves of the ocean, as they dashed themselves belly-flaucht against the caverned rocks, made far grander music to his ears, than all the orchestras in the world heaped together, could produce. No being particularly weel skilled in musical science, never having advanced farder therein than to croon ower the "Auld Hundred," of the "Martyrs," I could not contradict him, howsumever, I closed the business by observing, that if it wasna that good, it was at least dirt cheap, which in a mercantile point of view, was a great objeck. Now, this sensible observe of mine, brought on another brulzie between us, that was out of a' character; but I may keep that to speak about in due season; all that I wish to have explained here, is, that my fiery freend had that great conveniency and positive advantage till a man in his progress through life, called a deaf lug.

Off we set at last for the High Kirk, and after warsling up the brae as weel as could be, we got into the steeple, and up the stair we scrambled like twa cats after a cushy-doo or a mealy mouse. I never had ony great liking to speel up to the heichest buttlings, for a body's head is apt to get licht at that extraordinar altitude. Then the ladder is aye shoughy-shouing, and the idea is perfectly frichtsome, least it break, and a body be tumbled doun headlang and brained without mercy upon the muckle bell. It really gars a' my flesh grue to think upon sic a catastrophe. It is weel kent that I am as bauld as my neibours, having been enrolled in the Gentle Corps of Volunteers, and having marched doun to Greenock with knapsack on back, cartridge box at my hinderlets, musquet shouldered and bayonet fixed, determined to face and to fecht the bloody French, if they ever daured to land at the shore; but for a' that, there is nae needcessity for ony man, by way of a boast, to put himsell in unnecessar peril. Thir were my reflections, I candidly confess, when I was climbing the ladder after Mr. Roustythrappil. The twa sides of it were so thin and shachly, in fack they looked nae gritter than a fishing wand, and they geed and sweyed hither and thither, at sic a rate, that I looked for the hail concern breaking thro' the middle, and baith of us losing our precious lives for a piece of idle daurin.

Weel, we were baith creepin up the ladder like twa monkey beasts or jackey tars, and I was beginning to look and mak my observes upon my neibour's bumphlit pouches, to see whether they had a steek as I jaloused to keep a' tight, when the ladder gie such a creak and heisy up and doun, that I thocht it was all up, and that baith of us were on the eve of spinning heads ower heels frae tap to boddum, getting a dunch here, a clour there, and a jundie every where, till we came clash doun, twa disfigured masses of broken banes and lifeless flesh. A man of ordinar courage would have swarfed. But for me, I held a death grip of the ladder, and jamming my head between twa of the steps, to be out of the way, in case my freend had lost his futting, I laid mysell as flat as possible, to let him trintle ower me in his douncome as easily as possible. In this posture I clung for some time with my een steekit; for the fack is, I couldna bide the sicht of seeing ony body, far less a freend, cutting flourishes in the air, and posting aff till eternity, as a body might say, in a coach and four, with the diel himsell for an outrider. The sensible heart may conceive the horror of that awsome moment. There was me, the head of a house, a married man and a faither, swinging midway between earth and heaven—the ladder creaking and jigging under my weight, and threatening to snap richt thro the middle, and then labouring under the apprehension, that poor Mr. Roustythrappil wouldna hae the benefit of a clean fall, but come bang against the back of my neck wi' a thud, that might either break it or the ladder—in ony case a fatal issue—or that he in his mortal desperation, (drowning men catch at straes) might mak' a claucht at me in passing, and harl me after him to the pit of destruction. Abune me I heard a sair strusslin', fitterin', pechin', and grainin', though I saw naething, on account of my een been steekit, as aforesaid, but it immediately came intil my head, that this breingin and stramash must needs be atweesht my puir unfortunate freend and the Bethral, as ilk ane was strivin' to save himsell frae distruction, at the expense of his neibour, according to law. Ane was eneuch, but baith to tumble down upon my tap, was naething short o' dounricht murder. I roared out to them no to get intil grips, but, if they bood to come hurtling ower me, to tak' time and do it, ane after the ither, and wi' that I steekit my een closer and closer thegither— jammed my head farrer and farrer through the steps, and made up my mind to die, like a Roman or a real game cock. To look doun was impossible—a body's head would hae spun round like a peerie, to contemplate a tumble of a least twa hunder feet. About half way doun, ane was sure to come whack against the bell, and there be clean knocked to shivers, afore reaching anes sad and feenal landing place, in the session house, at the boddum of the steeple. Then, in the middle o' the meantime, it came to my recollection that I had seen that the wood of the ladder was sairly wormed through, which, added to its desperate thinness, greatly increased my confloption, and with pure reasoning, on my imminent danger, I was just dissolved into a lump of geil. Were it a case of fire, and ane up even four stairs, and even haflins smuired wi' reik, I wouldna hae been nearly sae sair distressed, for then, a body might get blankets and sheets, and swing themselves ower intil the feather beds, that, nae doubt, gude neibours would be spreading out, to kepp our fall, or the leeries and sklaiters, and firemen would set to their ladders, and carry a body doun on their backs, just like—aye, just like ony thing, as Dr. Kittletext says, when he comes to a dead pause, in a string of lively similitudes. But, in my case, there was nae kind friend or neibour, nae bauld sklaiter to lend me a lift in my needcessity and peril. I was a prisoner in a dreary steeple, far out of the hearing or help of man, and in momentary expectation of dreein' a death, waur ten thousand times waur than that of a common malefactor, that gets naething mair than a bit insignificant fall of a foot or sae, and has nae precious bane broken in his body, excepting an ugly twist in the vertebrae of his neck. All they thochts and considerations galloped through my head like lightening, and then a deadly cauld shiver gae through my heart, when I reflecked on the distress of my puir wife and bairns—when she cried upon her husband and they cried upon their faither, and the voice, forever dumb, that could have meized their sorrows, and put an end to their woeful lamentings.

Further I needna endeavour to describe my precarious and frichtsome situation, but at ae time I was in sic a fever wi the thocht of what might happen, that I positively cried out, "for Gude sake, Mr. Roustythrappil, dinna lay hands on me, if ye hae tint your futting. There's nae fun in twa Christians perishing by a miserable death if ane can serve. Catch rather at the jeists or the tackling o' the bell, grip till ony thing, but haud aff me, the faither and bread winner of a family of small innocents."

Weel, I was in siccan a state, that I lost all count of time, and having my een steekit, didna perceive that Mr. Roustythrappil, and the Bethral that led the way, had got landed safe and sound on the gallery that leads out to the buttlins, and there the twa had been cracking like pen guns, no missing me at all, till they commenced their descent, which, of course, was arreisted when they saw the dreadful situation and agony of suffering that I was in. "What's come owre ye, Baillie"! cried the Betheral. "Are ye unwell," shouted the Antiquary. "Either come up, or gang down," continued the impertinent body of a Bethral, "for Ise assure ye the timmer winna carry three, its as souple as a rash, and would scarce do for steps and stairs to a hen's bauk, let abee three ordinar-sized men."

Seeing now, how the land lay, and that nae mishanter was likely to occur, saving what might arise through unnecessar apprehension, I opened my een at ance, and cried, courageously, "Ou aye, talking's easy, but how am I to get my head out frae between the twa steps that it's jammed in? I'm nearly throttled— ye maun lend a hand quickly, twa three minutes mair would have finished me." With that, I heard my friend laughing, as if he had found a mear's nest, whilk was ony thing but kind or considerate, considering the jeopardy I put mysell into, entirely to obleege him. "I declare, Baillie, it is the first time I ever saw a magistrate in a pillory, and I hope it shall be the last." "Sae do I mysell," quo I, rather sharply; "but if ye canna help a friend at a dead lift, wi' naething better than a bitter mock, I'm no thinking ye'll ever be axed twice, or thanked ance."

This brocht them baith to their senses, and seeing me to be really jammed atween the twa spars, and held tight and fast, without the power of thawing my head to ae side or the ither, (a fack, I was nae mysell aware of, at first, but thocht to play it aff as a good guise, to keep them frae laughing at the posture they found me in) Mr. Roustythrapple turned himsell round, like a lamplighter, and descending on the ither side of the ladder, hinging by his hands in a wonderful way, wrenched out the step, at once relieved my head, and swung himsell down to the floor, before you could say Jack Robinson. I was really thankful to him for his good offices, but I didna think it worth while to tell him how I had mysell to thank for that plisky and causeless tribulation of soul and body.

Coming out of the steeple, we then proceeded alang Oakshaw Street till the Bowling Green, at the Hutheid, and there we twa had a desperate argle-bargling about the probable extent of the Roman camp. Of course, as in duty bound, out of respect to my native town, I threipit that it occupied fully mair ground than the present town stood upon; and, that in these far awa times, there was really a superior harbour at the Sneddoun, as weel as het and cauld baths, of the most sumptuous description, forbye ither luxuries and arts, introduced by these uncommon clever people. Anither point I insisted upon, and Mr. Roustythrappil either could not, or would not contradict me in, quhilk was, that the Romans never conquered Paisley, but were invited to winter there, for a year or twa, and to mak themsells quite at hame, till they could be better provided for, in some ither pairt of the kingdom. In remembrance too, of this great historic truth, regarding the concord and amity subsisting between the natives of Paisley and Rome, I proved, to my ain satisfaction, that the name of the town was altered from Vanduaria to *Pax et Lex* and softened down, afterwards, by elision and otherwise to Paselet, Passelay, and now as it is written Paisley.* (*This notion I had frae our Tummas, in his Lecture, delivered before the Paisley Philosophical Institution, in the Abbey close, upon Local Etymologies, and Lingual Transmogrifications.) Mr. Roustythrappil couldna contravene a single bit of my argument in this engaging subject, and did naething, all the time I was haulding furth, but laugh and rub his twa hands thegither, and girn in my face, like a thief through a widdy. The fack is, I jaloused the deil's buckie might be meaning to write a bit history of our antiquities, and, for the credit of the place, it was necessar that a few new thochts on the subject, forbye them that are to be met with in books, should be driven intill him; and I handled they matters with sic an aff-hand kind of fluency of speech, that I am sure Mr. Roustythrappil thought me nae sma' shakes in history and antiquities; and the farrer back I gade, I universally found mysell mair at hame, which I look upon as a very fine discovery in the philosophy of the human mind. Facts and dates are just anither term for falsehoods and errors, and a perfect down-draught to clever thinking. But upon this head, we got into a sad tirrivee. Mr. Roustythrappil was neither to haud nor to bind, and had the impudence and wickedness to say that it was just owing to the fanciful speculations of sheer and conceited ignorance that the inquisition of truth was rendered so painful in its progress, and so dubious and unsatisfactory in its results. Now, this was a bit spitefulness in him, that I couldna have looked for at the hands of ane that was born and bred a gentleman. However, I gied him up his fit in my ain way, and at my ain time and convenience, according to law, as the following chapters will declare.

THE POLITICAL METAMORPHOSIS—A SAIR
MISCHANTER AT A REFORM MEETING

A man of rummilgumption like me, mair especially after he has retired from official duties and the concernments of active life, is no often in the way of burning his finger nebs in the lowe of party politics; however, it sometimes occurs with the maist prudent and discreet, that they occasionally get themsells scoutherit in that way when they least expeck it, as was my ain case nae farrer gane than last year. As an impartial historian I sall make it a point of duty to give the hail outs and ins of my case, just as they happened, neither concealing nor colouring, in a flichty fashion, any particular, that either made for or against my exemplar character for sagacity, prudence or political consistency.

When my freend, Mr. Andrew Touchy, was out painting the grand family piece of mysell, my wife, and the bairns that is hung ower the mantel piece of our chimley in the dining room, and is finished aff in a very grand gilt frame by Mr. Finlay, carver and gilder in Glagow, that cost me mair sillar than I would like to mention, for fear the world would set doun the ransom I paid to the score of personal vanity and pridefu' upsetting, a thing no possible in my case, he was accustomed to observe, that the great art baith in painting and writing, was, to copy nature faithfully, and then a body had a chance of getting on either as an artist or an author, before the morn-come-never. No having any far-fetched principles in either painting or writing mysell, I have tried to keep my e'e, in the course of this book, pretty sickarly on the advice of my freend. However, I'll be candid eneuch to say, that I think Mr. Touchy, when he painted me, might, without departing unco far frae nature, have given me a wee hue mair red in the cheek to mak' me look youthier like, as weel as brocht out a link or twa mair of my gowd chain, than he has done in my picture. The fack it, I thought he might have drawn the gowd medal, that hings at the end of the chain instead of hiding it from the public a'thegither, as if I was ashamed to wear the insignia of civic rule. However, he argued me out of this conceit; for he is "no to be done," I find, in argument, alleging, that it was modester to hide the badge of authority, and hinting, that the chrome yellow might nae stand unco weel the test of time, and might grew blackish, in whilk case it would be viewed by a censorious and undiscerning public as naething but a ticket porter's pewter badge, which, in a historic piece, that was to tell a true bill till all posterity, was not to be thocht of for a minute.

My object in thir few introductory observes, is, to forewarn the reader, that that whilk is set furth in the ensuing pages is a perfect picture from nature, and as true as any thing that ever was acted or written on this side of time. I daursay it winna be quite sae entertaining as some of the chapters; but a man cannot be aye brichter and brichter the langer he writes and endytes, ony mair than it can be perpetual sunshine.

Being needcessitated to gang intil Glasgow for a day or twa at the time mentioned in the first paragraph, upon some particular business about ane of my wife's far awa freends that was jaloused to have died in foreign lands, and to have willed to her or her bairns a gay bit scartle o' sillar, as weel as some blackamoors in the woods, I thocht I might as weel kill twa dogs wi' a'e stane, and lift my dividends in the Canal Company, the Gas Company, the Water Company and ither concerns where I had invested some property, like a thrifty man that has an e'e till profit in the lang run. Weel, I booked mysell, without delay, in a nine o'clock coach, taking an inside, as I had a bit snifter of cauld upon me at the time, and, preceesely as the clock chappit ten, I was landed at the Tron Steeple of Glasgow. As good luck ordained it, there was the laddie of my Glasgow man of business waiting at the steps of the coach to tell me, that his maister was last night obligated to bang off in the Mail for London, in full hue and cry after my wife's sillar, and that he was determined to houk out the truth, or as he expressed it, till expiscate the hail facks of the case, and wishing me to keep mysell in readiness to follow him gif that circumstances rendered that step necessar. Seeing that better couldna be, in the middle of the meantime, I thocht I might trintle up the length of Port-Dundas, to draw my dividends at the Canal Office, as money would be serviceable at any rate, and was pleesant to receive at all times. But first and foremost, I slipt a brent new saxpence intill the laddie's hand, telling him to put it by, in a pinner pig, and it might grow a shilling ere he kend what was what. However, my present might hae been as weel cast in the strand, for the proud bit elf turned up his neb as gif he had been affronted, and marched aff like a feathery shankit bantam cock, without even offering me thanks. My lad, thinks I, when I was like you, they Lucifer-like notions were nae sae rife. A saxpence was a saxpence then and is still, and ye may come to ken the want of ane when its ower late, as your betters hae done afore ye. Really it's no to be born to see 'prentices acting the pairt of maisters, and looking as big as grey-bairded men as soon as they has cuisten aff their wyliecoats.

But let me on with my story. To Port-Dundas I walked, and there got my business toshed up, finished and perfected, in a particular handsome manner, and then just stepped down till the edge of the canal, to see a new passage boat that was on the point of starting for Lock Number Sixteen. Weel, I was standing making my observes in my ain mind, upon the leddies and gentlemen that were pouring intill the boat, as weel as the puirer bodies with bundles in their hands, that had to put up with the cheap end, thinking that I might foregather with some kent face or anither; but no, every ane was greater stranger to me than his neebour. Seeing me stand hinging on, as it were, till the last minute, the man that blaws the horn asked me if I was gaun to tak a trip in the Volcano (or Worrikow, I forget the name, but that's of nae consequence), and indeed the man had some reason to think I was bent upon a journey, as I was very genteelly dressed, from top to boddum, in a stand of new superfine claes, namely, a beautiful blue coat, with velvet neck and treble gilt buttons, silk vest, light drab trowsers, with straps under my boots, a thing I never had before, and ne'er will have again, as to a man of my years they are rather an impediment to cleverness of motion, and create some misgivings lest the pantaloons screed up at the knee or some gate else when a body loots doun to pick up needles or prins, or ony other thing that lies at their foot. My wife, however, approved highly of the shape of my coat when it came frae Glasgow, it being the first I ever had made in that town, and said it fitted my shape as nicely as a pea hool did a pea, which I'll no deny was the fact. Howbeit it was a wee thocht ower tight about the sleeves, and when buttoned I couldna say but I felt mysell like a leddy screwed up in corsets. But as weel out of the world as out of the fashion at times; and sae it was my bounden duty as a good christian to submit to the law as it is laid down by Caesar or the Pope, providing a body is landbiding in their dominions.

Being in a sort of swither whether or no I would not gang as far as Kirkintilloch, to look after a dubious debt that was owing to me in that place, five shillings, or even 2s. 6d. in the pound no being to be sneezed at in these fearful times of commercial distress, I didna just answer the man at the moment; and in fack the answer was tane out of my mouth by a sprush young gentleman, that quite familiarly thrust his arm intil mine—and pushing the horn-blower out of the way says, "to be sure, you fool, the Baillie unquestionably will honour your boat with the transportation of his learned corporation as far as Auchinsterry, where he dines with our friend the laird of Auchinvole, and returns in the evening." On saying this, my new friend and familiar lilts up this verse of an auld sang:—

> Hame again e'en,
> Hame again e'en,
> And can ilka bodie
> Come hame again e'en.

And before I weel kent where I was, I found mysell oxtered forward upon the deck by this impudent birkie. I was on the point of asking him what was the meaning of this manoeuvre, but couldna get the words out of my mouth before he set up a blyth skirl again to this effeck:

> Oh, as the haggis glowred,
> Oh, as the haggis glowred,
> Oh, as the haggis glowred,
>   Out amang the bree!

> For I suppit a' my ain kail,
> I suppit a' my ain kail,
> I suppit a' my ain kail,
>   And my neebour's too.

Such foolery was intolerable; so putting on a stern face, I plainly told my young man that I was not accustomed to any such liberties or insolence, and it was quite unbecoming any gentleman to behave in siccan a fashion to a perfect stranger. "Bless me, Baillie," said he, "with a face of brass, do you really not know me—I thought you were as well acquainted with Rob the Ranter as ye were with Gordon's Loan or Prussia Street. The truth is, your man of business turned you over upon my hands for dinner, and as I was to dine abroad, I determined to make you a partner of my fare, whatever that may be. Depend upon it old nunks hath good victuals; and then we shall go to a Reform Meeting in the evening, and have a little fun making patriotic speeches to the intelligent population of the burgh of Kilsyth, situated in the northern division of the island called Scotland, in the shire of Stirling, bounded on the east by the Barwood and Dullater Bog, on the west by the Strone, on the north by the hills of Tamtane and Tack-me-down, and on the south by the great canal of the Kelvin, or both, it does not signify much in either case. Baillie, you shall hear my speech, written and composed by myself, and a more elaborated specimen of dulcet eloquence never stormed the stony fortresses of the human heart."

"Blethers, Sir," retorted I, "ye aiblins are not aware that I am none of the sort to be trifled with in this manner;" and with that I was in the act of bidding the captain stop the horses, for the boat had gone off, without me observing it, whenever I got on board; but seeing that I was really in a desperate passion, Mr. Robert, as he called himself, apologeesed in the most humble manner, and pulled out a letter addressed to him, wherein I saw that my man of business had positively requested him to invite me to dinner, as weel as to give me some inkling anent the discoveries that had been made about the sillar, that was likely to come like a windfall into my wife's lap. Of course this reconciled matters atween us, and, after all, I fund that he could crack sensible eneuch when he was brocht till his marrow-bones, though, as it may be surmised from the foregoing scene, that he was a thocht ower flichty and forward in his manner for his years. About twal hours we adjourned till the Steward's room, and there he would insist that I should take a draught of good London Porter, a cauld chack of meat, or a hair of brandy, to keep my stamach; for that we wudna, in all likelihood, be enabled to get our denner before four or five in the afternoon at the soonest. There being naething morally wrang in the proposition, we of course sat down, and had a very comfortable meridian, as weel as an edifying, twa-handed crack, and a particular good sang anent whale-fishing, a copy of which he was to give me. This refreshment was, of course, afore the Temperance regulations were passed, forbidding the use of spirits on board, and this I think necessar to state, in order to exonerate the Captain, a very civil and obliging gentleman as needs to be.

It's unnecessar to tell all the uncos that occurred in this voyage on the Great Canal. In due course of time we arrived at Auchinsterry, where we landed, and in a few minutes found oursells in his friend's house, a nice, auld-fashioned place it was, with four wee tourocks at ilka corner, like pepper-boxes, for nae earthly purpose that I could mak out, except to accommodate the rookety-coo-doos. Looking at the thickness of the walls I couldna help remarking to the Laird, a very sensible man, and, like mysell, on the ither side of forty, that his house hadna been biggit by contrack, for there was as muckle stane and lime in his auld tenement as might bigg a hail street of modern weavers' shops and their dwellings. "Aye, aye," quo' the laird, "houses in auld times, if they were not showy, they at least were substantial, and that is more than can be said for modern mansions." After this he favoured me with a lang history of the antiquity of his tower, and its curiosities, and how a grand room in it was haunted at one time with a ghaist; and I, in return, gave to him a full, true, and circumstantial account how I purchased my ain self-contained house, and the improvements I made upon it, and what I meant to make; as weel as gave him a hearty invitation to make my house his hame whenever he came to the west country. "As for the matter of ghaists," quo' I, "I never seed ony waur than my ain shadow on a wall;" but the laird shook his head very grimly and said naething, and sae I drappit the ghaist argument no wantin' to tramp on ony body's sair taes.

In this way time wore away, and my young friend, Mr. Robert, keeped a reasonable quiet tongue in his head, nae doubt sooking in a fund of information from our converse, on a great variety of interesting subjects. Happening to look at my watch, I fund it was, before I kent it, on the chap of eight, and up I banged, observing, really this was dreadfu'—that the time had slipped awa like a knotless thread—and that if we didna mak a clever pair of heels we might lose our passage.

"Passage," said the laird, "ye'll not budge from this mansion to-night—besides, the boat passed two hours ago, so if you will condescend to accept a bed for the night, the best in the house is at your service, and, in the meanwhile, I will send a note to the Manse and invite the Minister to supper, and another friend or two—a literary gentleman, as my nephew informs me you are 'is a sicht good for sair e'en' in these parts." With some reluctance I complied, and still more unluckily I consented to gang up to see the toun of Kilsyth with my young neibour, to pass the time till the laird's freends could be colleckit, or the errocks for supper could be dressed.

About eight o'clock then I buttoned my coat, and taking the youngster by the arm, daikered up to the toun. It is an ancient say and a true ane, that auld men are twice bairns, and that there is nae fule like an auld fule, otherwise I canna conceive how I lippened mysell to the leading of that mad callant. I make nae doubt the refection in the boat—the gude news about my wife's sillar and the blackamoors in the wood, as weel as the wine and toddy afer dinner, all helped to elevate me something abune my ordinar on that night. We may shape our bairn's wyliecoat, but we canna shape their weird, says the proverb, and, as little can man, come to the years of understanding, at all times calculate the propriety of their footsteps. Hech! If I had foreseen what was about to befall me on that occasion, it wudna hae been in the power of a fifty-horse steam engine to gar me rax a tae that night. But man proposes and God disposes—and it was ordained that I should witness fules, and be a fule for a'e time in my life—sae it is needless to channer ony mair on what cannot be helped.

With this Diels' buckie, as I said, I took my way, and, before I weel kent where we were, intil the court-house of the burgh of Kilsyth, we found oursels stewing, like potatoes, in the heart of a batch of weavers, and siclike clamjamffery, all gabbling and smoking or chewing tobacco, and trying to look as wise as Solomon or the twelve Judges of Israel. The room was wee in size, laich in the roof, and desperately ill lighted up with twa penny candles and a cruisy, and a sconce at the back of the chair that was set apart for the preses. My young freend seemed to enjoy the company wonderfully weel, and was straiking and turning up his whiskers, and clavering wi this ane and that ane, speiring when the chairman was expected to come forward with a statement of his mission to Glasgow, on the bill, the whole bill, and nothing but the bill—the new charter of the people's liberties. Hearing that this was about Reform, my heart just began to grue, having, for the reasons advanced, determined to steer clear of politics, and keening weel that meetings of this sort were not countenanced by government, when I was in office as a magistrate. Howsomever, I thought naebody would ken me, and just snooled as far back intil a corner as I could weel do, without whitening my good coat on the wall. My pouches, I took special care to button up, as weel as to see if the safety chain of my watch was quite right and tight. Having eased my fears on these points, I determined to haud my wheisht, and hear how matters went on.

Weel, in due process of nature, in comes a man with a Kilmarnock cap upon his pow, a cutty pipe in his mouth, an apron tucked up around his waist, without a coat, but with stocking sleeves on his twa arms, and takes the chair, while cries of order, order, raised a din in the house that was quite unbearable. Some of the company, too, who had been wearying for the appearance of their directing spirit, were not slack in expressing displeasure at the slowness of his movements. Calm at last occurred, and then the chairman snuffled out, like a Cameronian precentor—Mr. Secretar, ye will read, to the members of the union, the minutes of the last congress, which being done, the chairman rose, and spoke as follows, in their individual words; for I had all my lugs about me, and can keep mind, baith of speeches and sermons, when I like:—

"Gentlemen,—Members of the Kilsyth Union, and freends of ceevil and religious leeberty all over the world, ye have heard Mr. Secretar read the minutes of our last congress, at which I was appointed delegate till proceed to Glasgow, for to attend the grand assembly of delegates that sat there, in the Trades' Hall, upon the bill, the whole bill, and nothing but the bill, which secures to us, for ever and ever, amen, our inalienable rights, and overthrows despotic oligarchists and corrupt boroughmongers. My freends and constituents, depend upon't, I will tell you every thing concerning my mission, depend upont. [Jack Blooter, mak less din, blawin your nose, and I'll thank you, Edie Morrison, no to hoast as if a meally taty had gane doun your wrang hause.]

Blooter.—Haud your snash, Rab Tamson, I'm as gude as yoursell, ony day, and can blaw my nose as loud and lang as I like.

Secretary.—Seelence, gentlemen—seelence, confound ye, and let business purceed. The preses is in possession of the house, the whole house, and nothing but the house.

Eddie Morrison.—Aye, and a gill besides, that we'll hae to pay for—but I'll vote for nae supplies.

Many Voices.—Order—order—quastion—quastion.

Tam Blooter.—We wad understan' him better if he cleared his ain snotty nose, instead o' scartin at mine.

President.—If I am to be assulted and interrupted in this way, the house must be adjourned.

Many Voices.—No—no—no—go on—go on—quastion—quastion.

President.—In continuation—After this unpleasant interruption till the business of the evening, depend upon it, me that has laboured morn and een, late and early, in the glorious cause of freedom, and the elective French cheese can have little pleasure in laying before my constituents, the tremendous and prolific result of the Glasgow Senate. It was an assembly, worthy of the palmy days of Greek and Roman liberty. The saviours of their country, the delegates from the various Unions, scattered over the face of this wretched and enslaved country, sat there, clothed with the burning aspirations of unconquered and unconquerable liberty. Depend upon it, in the bosom of your delegat, the sacred spark lost none of its brightness. I felt myself one of the chosen Spartan bands that left their bones and blood to manure the glorious field of Thermopylae.

Depend upon it, gentlemen. You saw me take my departure from Kilsyth—you saw me ascend the sides of the trackboat, you heard my adieus, and you marked the form of your delegate melting away in the azure distance of cerulean indistinctness. You now see me amongst you, depend upon it, once more with the same feelings, but more exalted hopes than those, which were mine, when I departed for Glasgow, to advance the cause of freedom, and carry the suffrages of a united and determined people, in favour of the Bill, the whole Bill, and nothing but the Bill. Here you know nothing of poleetics; but I have learned poleetics since I went to Glasgow—oh, we are blind, you are blind depend upon it, but the scales have fallen from my eyes, and I will teach you the divine study of poleetics. The day of the bloody sabreing boroughmongers is at hand—the knell of corruption is rung out. We shall be free to do as we like, when the people are represented in a reformed House of Commons, depend upon it. There shall be no taxes, nor greedy tax gatherers then. Meat and maut, gentlemen, we'll have them, depend upon't, and nothing to pay. Every man for his own hand then, according to the imperscriptible laws of nature and natural reason."

A good deal more of such unconnected discourse was blethered, the only pairt of which that was intelligible, was when the chairman gave his account anent being desired at the meeting in Glasgow, to cash up the subscription from Kilsyth, and his admission that there was not a rap in their exchequer. But this afforded to the secretary a handle for proposing, that a subscription should be set on foot for the exigencies of the Union, which being carried by acclamation, a greasy hat made its devious progress through the meeting. To my astonishment, Mr. Robert flung intil it half a crown with the air of a nobleman, but when it came to me I said naething, though the coppers were jingled in my face twa three minutes, in fack, as if it had been an elder's ladle in a landward kirk. I, however, muttered something about having nae loose change, thinking to mysell that my saxpence would be better waured niest Sunday upon my ain parish puir, than at ony sic gatherings. For this, however, I got some unco fierce girns,and ae dirty thin chafted hauflins callant had the impudence to blaw some pluffs o' tobacco reek direckly in my een.

Weel, the meeting was nae like to skail, and me being anxious to get out to the cauler air, was making my way to the door, when the cry got up—"He's a Tory—he's a boroughmongering spy," and I felt my coat tails pookit, and a gude wheen of the lovers of freedom dunching me with their elbucks in the ribs sae devilitsch hard that my corruption began to rise; but ye may guess what kind of a tirravee I was in, when a lump of a chield came ahint me, and with ae dunkle on the crown of my split-new thirty-shilling hat, drave it clean ower my face, and shaved the skin aff my unoffending nose at the same time. Seeing my dilemma and confloption, and that the bloody rabeatours were set upon insulting and abusing me, up springs my young friend on the table, kicking ower ane of the twa penny candles, which brought its lowe richt into the peery e'ed secretary, and burned half a thin whisker that the creature had on its chafts, and then putting himsell in a grand attitude like a playactor, to my utter astonishment roared out: "Mr. President and gentlemen, I am grieved and mortified at the conduct of my countrymen this evening. Some ruffians have dared to lift their unhallowed butcherly fists against my illustrious friend, the great Attwood of Birmingham—the father of the Unions, the friend of Earl Grey, and the instrument in the hand of providence that is to effect a regeneration in our system of Parliamentary representation."

Scarcely were these words said, when there got up a wonderful rampaugin, huzzaing and confusion. The chap that nearly foundered me was kicked out of the room—and a cry got up for a speech from Mr. Attwood, and here again my Deils' buckie got in a word to the effeck, that, considering the manner in which Mr. Attwood had been insulted, he would not consent that Mr. A. fatigued with his long journey, and irritated in his feelings by those whom he regarded as his own children should do any such thing, but he would beg of him to address them publickly next day on the Barwood.

Here deafening cheers got up—and a still louder cry that Mr. Attwood should be chaired home. With that, before I knew where I was, I found myself stuck into an arm chair. The arm chair was placed upon a hand barrow, and its spokes elevated upon the shoulders of four stout fellows, and in this guise was I parauded like a show after nightfall through the hail toun, with a band of women and weans and men rampaging about me like wild cats or hyaenas of the wilderness. For a while I was in a state of perfect bewilderment, and was not sure whether the savages meant to head, hang or burn me, but at length when I gradually came to my senses I could distinguish the sounds of a base drum, a wee drum and twa cracked flutes or fifes bumming and skirling before me, and twa cotton shawls stuck upon rake shafts, with some devices painted on them with red ochre and lamp black, flapping at ilka side. Sic a bizz I am sure was never heard in the village in a moonlight night, and cries of Attwood for ever, and the sovereignity of the people were clean dumbfoundering. I was sure some judgment was to light on me for my innocent pairt in this wicked affair, and sure eneuch my apprehensions were fully realized. Just as we were in the middle of our parade, it came to pass, that some horned nout, great big Angusshire stots, unfortunately met us full in the teeth, being on their way to the South in some cattle tryst, and the brute beasts, half in fricht and half in desperation, charged us right in front. Ane carried the base drum off on its horns, and dang the bowleggit drummer ower a feal dike. My body guard, with the twa flags, roared lustily, "stand fast in the cause of freedom—they're no bills, only stots," but at that moment, anither shaggy deevil that had been maddened with a poke in its ee, and wi a tail swirling about like a flail, came roaring against us like a bull of Bashan, that rather than stand the shock, my body bearers flung me, chair, barrow and all down, and magnanimously, like reasoning animals, betook themsells to flight. For me, I lighted something saftly in a sappy midden, that in the mercy of providence was near at hand, but mair dead nor alive. In fack, the beast contented itself with demolishing the flag, and as for the ensigns, they had run like leeries, leaving neither hilt nor hair ahint them. Having sank in this bed, no certainly ane of down, something abune the shoe mouth, it was five minutes or mair before I got mysell fairly gathered thegither, nor did I like to budge till I heard the rumours of war dying away far down the town. With a heavy heart and sair soiled raiment, I hirplit on to the laird's, where I found his freends waiting on me for supper, but his neer-do-weel nevoy, or whatever he was, that brought me into sic awsome peril of life and limb, didna show his impudent face that nicht. I am thinking he had fancied I was murdered, and no wanting to face the Lords of Justiciary, got into hidings, for he was not heard tell of for a fortnight or mair; but I was sae desperately mischieved, that it took sair prigging on the part of his repectable and afflicted parents and freends, to prevent me frae publishing an advertisement in the papers, offering a reward for his apprehension and punishment. What befell me in the auld castle after this bluidy mischanter, will afford matter for my next chapter.

BEING THAT PORTION OF HIS SUBLIME AND INSTRUCTIVE AUTOBIOGRAPHY, ENTITLED "THE TALES OF THE TOWER."

> Call up him that left half-told,
> The story of Cambuscan bold;
> Of Camball and of Algarsife,
> And who had Canace to wife,
> That owned the virtuous ring and glass;
> And of the wond'rous horse of brass,
> On which the Tartar King did ride:
> And if aught else great bards beside,
> In sage and solemn tunes, have sung,
> Of turneys, and of trophies hung;
> Of forests and enchantments drear,
> Where more is meant than meets the ear.
> —Il Penseroso.

Having by a special providence escaped, as stated in a foregoing chapter, out of the bluidy hands of the satans, men and brute beasts, that had frichtit me to the extremity of death, and whumlit me head ower heels intil a saft midden, it may weel be jaloused by the reflecting reader, that it took me sometime afore I recovered my wind, and still mair before I gathered as muckle breath as enabled me to wauchle on till the castle. With a sair strussil, however, and a heavy heart,

I managed to hirple on that length, the feck of a quarter of a mile or aiblins mair as I would guess, and sometime atween nine and ten hours at e'en I landed at the door step, to the admiration of the laird, who was unco anxious anent my lang tarrying in that wicked Jericho. When that douce discreet gentleman saw me belaigered with glaur and other commodities up to the very een holes, and in a state of abomination that needna be described, he was like to jump out of his skin with perfect rage. And when I tauld him the hail facks, and how his harum-scarum nevoy had behaved, he misca'ed him up hill and down dale at a wonder-ful refreshing rate to my injured feelings; however, I put in a word or twa for the widdyfou o' mischief, saying that he would mend as he grew aulder, and aiblins grow wiser after the black ox had strampit on his tae.

Seeing me sair scomfisht in spirits and abused in body, the laird sympathised with my misfortunes in the kindliest manner that ae christian brother could do to anither, and as all flesh is grass, and like it liable to corruption, he rappit out twa or three hearty malisons against the authors of my perilous douncome. Indeed, Baillie, quo the laird, had I not recognised your voice, it would have been past the power of my een to have recognised your person, in sic a pitiful and clarty pickle. Ye're like as if ye had been drawn thro a clay hole or something worse—and then Baillie, ye'll excuse me for observing, that your garments are not freighted with "Sabean odours." My man John, however, will assist you in your ablutions. Truly it is fearful to think how this world is running upon wheels to destruction, when respectable individuals of your years' stand-ing in society, intelligence and property are left at the mercy of the ill-deidy bodies, that have set up in this day and generation for politicians and parliament men.

In these sensible observes, me and the laird nicely mooled in thegither, and when I tauld him, furthermore, that the horned beasts that were travelling to the south to be slaughtered, to line the fat penches of the pluffy Englishers, were as far gane gyte wi processions and politics, as ony body that had a soul to be saved, he nearly rave up his vest wi' dounright guffawing, swearing that that conceit cowed everything and beat cock fechtin hollow.

Hech, quo I, getting up my spirits a bit, I am thinking, that if some of the four-legged and twa-horned diels that drave through our ranks this nicht, and smote us hip and thigh with the edge of the sword of destruction, get into St. Stephen's they'll rout there as weel as in a lang loan ony day. It wudna be hoastin, shuffling, blawing o' nebs and cries of order, order, hear, hear, that wud take the shine out of their trumpet throats. If they were not understood, they would at least make themselves heard, and that is a main point of parliamentary eloquence now a-days. It would literally Bull-y the house, and *cow* the hail tot. The laird leuch, and confessed that calamity had sharpened my wit—necessity being in most cases the mother of invention.

With siclike sma clavers, we continued to pass the time agreeably eneuch, considering my waesum plicht, while the laird's servant man was busy clawting, scartin, spunging and brushing me down to mak me look a wee thocht snod, clean and respectable like at supper. When undergoing this process of renovation, I learned to my great grief, frae John's sensible exclamations, the full extent of my losses in the way of wearing gear.

Save us, quo John, this superfine blue coat, lined with brimstone coloured taffety, is dished and done for ever. It's gude for naething after this nicht, but to turn and make down for calshes to a three year auld bairn.

That is a pity, replied I, and it only twa days auld, made fashioned, sewed and perfected, and coft with the hard cash frae that skeely and fashionable tradesman, Lockhart in Buchanan Street. That's £4, 10s. thrown to the dogs ony way.

That's been a bonnie hat, continued John, in its day; but noo it is sae dunklet and bedeevilled out of a' shape, that it will neither do to export to the wild Ieerishers or put on the tap of a potatoe bogle. What a waistry! Here the sympatheesing flunkey groaned heavily, and as he may be supposed, an echo thereto came from the inmost recesses of my afflicted bosom.

Turning aside the skirts of my coat, John after a short inspection let fall the brush, and raising his hands, cried out, worse remains behind. Here is a screed Baillie! Oh the vanity of wearing ticht pantaloons and straps under the boot. Humphrey Clinker's frail buckskins were naething in comparison to the woeful wreck of your double-milled kerseymere.

This new misfortune nearly put me frantic, howsumever, as time was short and the laird's freends impatient to fall tooth and nail on the vivers, John, honest man, proposed to rin a bit steek up my torn nether "integuments," to keep them frae flapping about in an unseemly manner, for neither the laird's nor his man's wardrobe could supply me with that article of dress, our personal dimensions not agreeing.

Being bred, originally, to the tailouring business, the laird's man did the job in a jiffey without putting me to ony unnecesssary fash, altho' I must say he gied me a jagg or twa in the hurry that gart me draw mysell thegither like a clew on ae occasion, and at anither to loup like a twa-year auld colt with perfect pain.—John, however, had an oily tongue and apologeesed sae handsomely for the nervishness of his hand, that I couldna find in my heart to say an angry word to him. In fack, he was a deacon at needle and thread, and I complimented him on his handiness; whereupon he observed with a smile, that ance in a day he could handle a goose with a face of clay, as weel as thread a needle without a styme of light.

After finishing this delicate job, John set to give me a finishing touch of the brush, and began to whisk me down, blawing and peching like an ostler, when rubbing down a horse, all the while telling me a lang story about himsell, and how he had ran awa frae his 'prenticeship, tane arles of the king, listed for a sodger, and gane aff the country, gilravishing, fechting, storming and starving, in foreign lands, for mony a weary and lang year; and all that kind of thing—which certainly was very curious and entertaining. Hearing him sae conversible, I advised John to write a book of his adventures, but John shook his pow, and said that he was nae hauf sae whippy at his pen as he was at the needle or the bayonet; nor had he the airt and cunning like me to indyte in black and white the naturalities of life in pleasant discourse. "Admitting, friend," says I, "that this be true, which no doubt to a certain extent it is, dinna for all that be down-hearted, for the gift of tongues as weel as of pens may come upon you when ye least think of it. Mind the proverb—that may happen in a minute what winna cast up in a towmond. I was auld mysell afore I thocht of making books for the edification of the public," and with that I stappit intil John's wauket loof a bonny sillar saxpence, thanking him cordially at the same time for his pains, in toshing up and cleansing my poor spoiled duds.

John said he was not allowed to take any vails by the Laird, but if I would allow him, he would just bore a hole through it, and hang it, by way of remem-brance, at his watch chain, beside his Queen Anne crooky that he got frae his sweetheart Mysie M'Gie, afore he embarked for Portugal to the wars. "She died, Baillie, o' a broken heart, for me forsaking her, and I canna say that since I came hame, and heard how the puir lassie peaked and dwynit awa, day after day, for a graceless neer-do-weel like mysell, till death relieved her of all earthly sorrow, that I have had a sound nicht's sleep. I think about her thro' the day, and I dream about her thro' the nicht; and in my dreams she speaks sae kindly and forgivingly, that I wauken in the wild belief that she canna be dead."

Here a heavy tear gathered in John's ee, and I'll no say but there was some sma' moistness in my ain; but at this moment the supper bell rang, and up I marched an auld-fashioned staircase. The balustrades were of black oak, as thick as an ordinar man's thigh, and wonderfully curiously carved—John leading the way with the cleverness of a whitterock. When we reached the supper-room, John threw open the door, and with a respectful obeysance announced me as Baillie Pirnie; on which the Laird and the assembled company saluted me with all imaginable civility, and ane and all condoled with me on my mishanter.

Having got by the formalities of introduction, such as shaking hands, booing and scraping, and a' that sort of conventional havers, I was glad to see that supper was to be forthcoming in the twinkling of a bed-post—and it must be owned that it being some hours ayont the ordinar time of taking my sleeping pick, I felt yaup enouch, and weel inclined to do full justice to the hospitality of my new friend's table.

Of the company it's unnecessar to be very particular. Right forenent me there was a thin faced, pale complexioned man, wi' a desperate bricht e'e, and wi' a queer foreign like name that my lugs couldna pick up, and, just at my left hand, was a buirdly rough muirland laird called the laird o' Doups, that evi-dently liked a skinfu' of good drink far better than a ladleful of moss water, as

the feck o' men will do if put upon their bible aith. We twa were gayen coothy
the hail nicht, for he was great in discourse about black cattle, and, considering
my fricht and stramash, that subject naturally came abune board. As it said in
the book of Ecclesiasticus, he was one of those "that holdeth the plough, and
that glorieth in the goad; that driveth oxen and is occupied in their labours, and
whose talk is of bullocks."

The laird apologeesed for having sae few guests; for, besides the twa
mentioned, mysell and some other three that had little to say for themsells, and
needna be individualeezed, that was the hail tot, sum and substance of the company. As they three gade awa after sippling twa or three glasses o' wine immediately when the covers were removed, they have still less need to be
commemorated in my pages. In fack it appeared to me that they were what my
son calls intellectual nonentities, whose absence is good company, when men's
wits begin to wauken and their tongues become just like soople jacks to whip up
ane anither with knowledge and pleesant inventions.

When I had satisfied the cravings of nature and managed to take my een
off my plate to glour frae me and examine the room, I was struck with its auld-
fashioned appearance. It was wainscotted with black oak, and, in the heavy
compartments, there were stuck a great wheen of auld pictures o' gentlemen
and leddies in the queerest dresses that could weel be conceived. The roof was
heich, and though we had nae fewer than sax moulded candles, three to the
pund on the table, forbye twa on the big mantel piece, the room looked desperate dysmal and solemn, and I coudna help drawing a comparison between its
chill grandeur and the cozie, snug comfortableness of my ain parlour. However,
I made nae reflexions, as the master of the house might not like to hear ony
opinions derogatory to his taste at his ain table; but I determined, that should he
ever dauner west to Paisley, to tak' pat luck with me, I would convince him of
the superior accommodations in my tenement, for every bird thinks its ain bower
brightest.

Motherwell's Affiliations and Associates

GRAMMAR SCHOOL CLASS

Auchencloss
Blair, William
Craig, Robert
Knight, Peter
Macalester, Robert
Menzies, John
Muir, John
Synburn, Mr
Walkinshaw, Alexander

LITERARY INSTITUTION (BEFORE 1818)

Auchincloss, William
Auld, John
Buchanan, Robert
Burns, James
Calderwood, Robert
Carlile, John
Carlile, Warrand
Cochrane, Robert
Crichton, Thomas
Danaldson, James
Dunn, John
Findlay, John
He(a)nning, Samuel
Hodgert, Ninian
Howie, William
Lamb, Robert
Lawson, Peter
Lennox, John B.
MacArthur, Charles
Maclean, Alexander

McEwen, John
McGavin, Samuel
McIntyre, Peter
McReath, Thomas
McShan, Alexander
Masson, Archibald
Masson, William
Muir, Robert
Nairne, James
Ogilvie, Archibald
Park, John
Paterson, Andrew
Ramsay, P.A.
Ritchie, Charles
Rule, Thomas
Sim(s), John
Sinclair, Andrew
Smith, John
Smith, William
Spalding, John
Stevenson, John
Walkinshaw, Alexander
Whyte, John
Wilson, James
Winning, Robert

PAISLEY PHILOSOPHICAL INSTITUTION (AFTER 1818)

Blaikie, Andrew
Neilson, John
Ramsay, P.A.

BLUE BANNET BATCH (GLASGOW)

Brown, William
Davie, William
Duncan, James
Ferguson, Robert
Kemp, Johan
Macelvane, James
Mckinlay, Johan
Peddie, William

RIFLE CLUB (1820)

Blaikie, Andrew
Buchanan, William
Craig, David
Crawford
Gemmill
Haldane
Henderson, Thomas
Lang
Lawson, Peter
Macalister, Robert
Macalpine
Macgibbon, John
McLeod
Maxwell, Robert (corporal)
Stevenson, Robert
Stewart
Sunn
Taylor, James
Thomson, George
Wylie

BROCK'S CLUB

Goldie, John
Jepsey
Kennedy, William
McLeod, "Cat" Joseph?
Ramsay, P.A.
Tait
Torbet

BOUGHT GIG WITH

Goldie, John
Kennedy, William
McLeod, "Cat" Joseph?

THE HARP OF RENFREWSHIRE (1819–20)

Allan, Robert
Lawrence, John
Smith, R.A.

MINSTRELSY: ANCIENT AND MODERN (1824–7)

Blaikie, Andrew
Crawford, Andrew

PAISLEY ADVERTISER (c. 1826–29 [BEGUN 1824])

Goldie, John
Hay, Robert
Kennedy, William
Neilson, John

RHYMING TESTAMENT (20 OCTOBER 1828)

Buchan, Peter
Ramsay, Alexander "Sandie"
Smith, R.A.
Stevenson, John

PAISLEY MAGAZINE (1828)

Carlile, Alexander
Dick, David
Dunn, John
Finlay, W.
Hay, Robert
Neilson, John
Paterson, A.
Ramsay, P.A.
Wylie, Dr. G.

Contributors

Bennet
Colquholm, Alex
Crawford, Andrew
Crichton, Thomas
Dunn, John
Fullerton
Hay, Robert
Kennedy, William
Lindas
Motherwell, David
Peacock, Robert
Pollock
Smith, R.A.

Glasgow authors

Atkinson, Thomas (a.k.a. Percy York)
Carrick, J.D.
McConechy, James
Strang, John

FRIENDS IN MAITLAND CLUB

Carrick, J.D.
Kinlock, G.R.
Laing, David
Ramsay, P.A.
Strang, John

HADGIS CLUB (1830)

Henderson, Andrew
Howie, John
Peacock, Robert
Ramsay, P.A.
Tennant, Alex

COURIER

Hutchison
McConechy
McNish

ROBERTSON'S BOOKSHOP

Carrick, J.D.
Henderson, Andrew
MacKay, Charles
Robertson, David
Rodger, Alexander
Strang, John

The Laird of Logan

Carrick, J.D.
Crawford, Andrew
Henderson, Andrew

Whistle-Binkie

Carrick, J.D.

Crawford, Andrew
Neilson, J.

THE DAY (1832)

Aitken, J.H.
Atkinson, Thomas
Buchanan, Walter
Carrick, J.D.
Couper, Dr. John
Craigie, L.W.
Crum, Walter
Davidson, Thomas
Dobie, James of Beith
Fullarton, Allan
Fullarton, Captain
Graham, Alexander
Hall, Richard
Henderson, Andrew
Hutcheson, Charles
Jamieson, R.W., W.S.
Lang, William
Lawrence, Craigie
Leighton, J.M.
Lumsden, Dr.
M'Conechy, Dr. James
Maxwell, C.W.
Maxwell, J.H.
Maxwell, Robert
Miller, William
Noble, James the Orientalist
Ramsay, Philip A., W.S.
Strang, John

MRS. ANDERSON'S SUN TAVERN

Carrick, J.D.
Rodger, Alexander

SARACEN'S HEAD

Carrick, J.D.
Henderson, Andrew

MACKENZIE DINNER

Atkinson, Thomas
Baxter, Isaac
Craig, William
Henderson, Andrew
Watson, James

MEMORIALS (1835)

Crawford, John
Hutcheson, Charles
MacKenzie, R. Shelton
Paterson, A.

PALLBEARERS

Campbell, (Sir) G.
Campbell, Sheriff
Hamilton, Capt. Andrew
McArthur, Mr
M'Laren
Motherwell, C.A.
Ramsay, P.A.
Whyte, Mr

SUBSCRIBERS TO MONUMENT

Davidson, Thomas
Howie, James
Hutcheson, Charles
Miller, George
Rait, D.C.
Robertson, David
from Boston, Montreal, New Orleans, New York

Annotations Relating to Motherwell's Associates

Allan, Robert: 1774–1841. Kilbarchan poet; contributed to *Harp of Renfrewshire;* father flax-dresser, he muslin weaver. Wrote songs at loom. Encouraged by Tannahill. R.A. Smith set his songs for *The Scottish Minstrel;* published by subscription in 1836, unsuccessfully. Died shortly after arriving in New York to take up life with his youngest son, a portrait painter.

Atkinson, Thomas (a.k.a. Percy York): 1801–1833. Publisher/editor of the *Ant,* a local weekly; contributed poetry and sketches to *Western Luminary* and *Emmet;* Glasgow bookseller; provided for education of artisans in his will; contributor to *Paisley Magazine,* the *Day;* corresponded with Motherwell about G.R. Kinloch's proofs; host of social event. Illegitimate, poet, had political pretensions that led to his being ridiculed; stood for liberal representative for Stirling burghs.

Auld, John: Writer, 16 Moss Street, house in Garthland Place, Paisley.

Baxter, Isaac: Social event.

Blaikie, Andrew: 1774–1841. Engraver, copperplate printer, musician, for a time precentor at Abbey Church and session clerk; called on to do music (notate tunes for *Minstrelsy*); collected antiquarian things; also did early lithography. May have introduced Motherwell to Scott, Tannahill's work, and Hogg. Belonged to Paisley Philosophical Institution, Guard Room group, Burns Club.

Blair, William: Advocate, said to have been Dux boy with Motherwell at Paisley Grammar School.

Buchan, Peter: 1790–1854. Corresponded with Motherwell, signer of rhyming testament; ballad and song collector and editor. Was poet, engraver, and printer in Peterhead.

Carlile, A: One share in *Paisley Magazine.* Probably Alexander, who was a thread manufacturer.

Carlile, John and Warrand: Father owned one of the largest thread factories;

members of Literary Institution. Warrand began as a thread manufacturer, then became a missionary to Jamaica.

Carrick, J.D.: 1787–1837. Contributor to *Paisley Magazine,* the *Day;* editor of *Laird of Logan* (Scottish tales and witticisms), editor of first series of *Whistle-Binkie* (humorous songs); on staff of *Scots Times* (perhaps wrote squibs on Motherwell); author and poet—especially "Tragedy/or Life of Sir William Wallace of Elderslie." Humble beginnings: apprenticed to architect but ran away. Worked two years at Staffordshire Potteries, returned and became china and stoneware merchant. Worked as well on Kilmarnock paper (Motherwell helped him get this position); was songwriter and journalist. Attended social event; member of Robertson's circle; at the Sun Tavern and Saracen's Head; member of Maitland Club. Was liberal and for reform.

Colquholm, Alex: Teacher of French and Italian.

Craig, William: Glasgow city councillor; attended social event.

Craigie, L.W.: Contributor to the *Day.*

Crawford/Crawford, Andrew: Disabled doctor; ballad and song collector. Contributor to *Minstrelsy, Paisley Magazine, Laird of Logan, Whistle-Binkie.*

Crawford, John: Wrote memorial.

Crichton, Thomas: 1761–1844. With Motherwell in Literary Institution. Schoolmaster and clerk, Paisley Managers of the Poor, then governor of the Hospital for the Poor. Wrote a memoir of Alexander Wilson and others. Best-known poem is "The Library."

Davie, William: Writer.

Dick, David: Publisher, had four shares in *Paisley Magazine;* published M'Alpie materials in thirty copies, which was advertised in the *Paisley Advertiser* in June 1827.

Duncan, James: bookseller.

Dunn, John: 1798–1869. Contributed to *Paisley Magazine,* later lawyer and man of letters; two shares in *Paisley Magazine;* belonged to Literary Institution, Burns Club.

Findlay, John: Gunsmith.

Finlay, W: Two shares in *Paisley Magazine.*

Gardner, Alexander: Printer, bookseller, stationer at 14 Moss Street, Paisley (1828–30), 5 Moss Street (1830), 3 Moss Street (1837). Began publishing religious tracts, then works with moral value before branching out. Printed Motherwell's poems and perhaps *Harp of Renfrewshire.*

Goldie, John: 1798–1826. First editor of *Paisley Advertiser,* member of Burns Club, poet.

Hay, Robert: Fourth editor of *Paisley Advertiser;* was printer and lithographer; joined John Neilson's firm; bought Blaikie's business; contributed to *Paisley Magazine* and held two shares. Called "amateur" journalist.

Henderson, Andrew: 1783–1835. Said to have been an original character, large, ungainly, impetuous, and loved by friends; full of humor. Father was a gardener and he was so apprenticed. Not suited to outdoor work. Studied in London at Royal Academy and became a portrait painter with success, exhibitions at Royal Scottish Academy. Painted Motherwell's portrait. Contributor to *Laird of Logan,* the *Day;* edited Proverb book; helped with *Minstrelsy;* attended social event; member of Robertson's circle; member of Hadgis Club; frequented Saracen's Head.

Henning, Samuel: Surgeon; brother John was sculptor who restored the Elgin Marbles; belonged to Literary Institution.

Hodgert, Ninian: Teller in Union Bank; at one point agent for North British Fire Insurance; member of Burns Club.

Hogg, James: 1770–1835. The Ettrick Shepherd, poet, songwriter, friend, and collaborator of/with Scott. In 1810 went to Edinburgh to try a literary career and received notice for parodies of known authors. Wrote for *Blackwood's,* one of the authors of the Chaldee MSS. Collaborating with Motherwell on edition of Burns.

Howie, John: Hadgis Club.

Hutcheson, Charles: Contributed to the *Day;* may be the Charles who wrote a memorial.

Kennedy, William: 1799–1871. Poet, writer, journalist born in Ireland to Scottish father. Went to London and published poems in 1827; went to Canada as secretary to the earl of Durham; served as British consul in Galveston, Texas; interested in local government. Contributor to *Paisley Magazine;* second editor of *Paisley Advertiser.* Wrote memorial poem to/on Motherwell; Motherwell's *Poems* dedicated to him; had works in *Whistle-Binkie.*

Kinloch, George Ritchie: 1796–1877. Editor and collector of ballads, became lawyer, philanthropist, register of deeds at Register House, Edinburgh. Edited numerous volumes for Maitland Club. Corresponded with Motherwell.

Laing, David: 1793–1878. Scottish antiquary who dealt with foreign as well as domestic books. Known as bibliofile. Edited ballads and romances; member of Bannatyne Club, which printed old, unavailable material on Scottish history and literature. Edited lots for Bannatyne and other clubs. Fellow of the Society of Antiquaries of Scotland. Became Librarian for Signet Library and center of literary circle. On his death, the sale of his books/possessions lasted thirty-one days (compare with Motherwell's twelve) in 1879–80. Known to Motherwell as Edinburgh bookseller, presumably initially in business with his father William at premises in 49 South Bridge, East Side; corresponded with Motherwell; member of Maitland Club.

Lawrence, John: Colorful personality, called "Tiddy Doll." Willing to do all sorts of things to get money. Published *Harp of Renfrewshire,* corresponded with Motherwell, stationer.

Lawson, Peter: Writer.

Lucas, William: Physician; "Poetic Underwoods" dedicated to him, presumably a Paisley figure.

Maacelvane, James: Merchant.

Mackay, Charles: Physician; member of Robertson's circle.

MacKenzie, R. Shelton: Wrote a memorial.

McConechy, James: Surgeon; contributor to *Paisley Magazine,* the *Day;* biographer of Motherwell, followed him as editor of the *Glasgow Courier.*

Macgibbon, John: Ironmonger or wright.

McIntyre, Peter: Shoemaker.

McReath, Thomas: Wright.

McLeod, "Cat" Joseph?: Medicine.

Mason/Masson, Archibald: Manufacturer.

Miller, William: 1810–1872. Wood-turner, known as "laureate of the nursery," especially for "Wee Willie Winkie"; contributor to the *Day* and *Whistle-Binkie.*

Motherwell, C.A.: Nephew of Motherwell.

McNish: Probably Robert, 1802–1837. Physician, philosopher, poet, and miscellaneous writer who may have contributed to the *Courier.*

Neilson, John, Jr.: Succeeded father, also a printer. Premises during Motherwell's life were at Causeyside (1817–19) and 15 St. Mirren (1820–25, 1830–36)

Street or Court (1832). Gathered important literary figures around him. Involved in publication of *Harp of Renfrewshire, Paisley Magazine* (three shares), *Certain Curious Poems.* Began and served as printer for *Paisley Advertiser.* Toyed with lithography; did the portrait of Dougal Graham in the last issue of the *Paisley Magazine.* In 1830 joined by Robert Hay. Printed Robertson's *Whistle-Binkie.* Involved in eclectic publications of diverse quality. Belonged to Philosophical Institution.

Paterson, A: Held one share of *Paisley Magazine;* may be Andrew, who wrote a memorial.

Peacock, Robert: Corresponded with Motherwell; member of Hadgis Club.

Ramsay, Alexander "Sandie": Present at signing of joking testament; possibly an Edinburgh bookseller.

Ramsay, Philip A.: Editor and writer of biography of Tannahill, having taken over from Motherwell; held two shares in the *Paisley Magazine;* contributor to the *Day;* corresponded with Motherwell; member of Hadgis Club, Paisley Philosophical Institution, Literary Institution, Maitland Club; writer to the Signet Library.

Robertson, David: 1795–1854. Bookseller, publisher, Trongate, Glasgow; bibliophile; had Tannahill materials from Motherwell, who had gotten them from R.A. Smith, who had known Tannahill; ended up with Motherwell's manuscripts. Business a place of rendezvous; printer of Henderson's *Scottish Proverbs* in Glasgow, (Oliver and Boyd in Edinburgh, Longman and Company in London). From Easter Garden Farm. Apprenticed at fifteen, in 1810, to William Turnbull, Trongate bookseller. After Turnbull's death, he took over, first with another (probably Thomas Atkinson) and then he bought him out. Said to have had the storytelling gift and much tact. Became publisher, bookseller, book manuscript collector, and the center of like-minded persons who generated such publications as *Laird of Logan* and *Whistle-Binkie.* Published Motherwell's *Poems.*

Rodger, Alexander: 1784–1846. Farmer's son from Mid-Calder, Midlothian; became handloom weaver, inspector of cloths, music teacher. Was politically involved; assisted in editing the *Liberator,* a Radical weekly, and was later on the staff of the *Loyal Reformer's Gazette,* edited by Peter MacKenzie. Belonged to Robertson's circle and the Sun Tavern group. Participated in the *Whistle-Binkie* project.

Scott, Sir Walter: Connected to Motherwell through correspondence and shared interest in ballads and songs; both were members of the Maitland Club. Author of the Waverley novels, and so on—perhaps *the* Scottish author of the generation; had published anonymously for fear his Tory politics would hurt sales; sometimes passed his work off as that of others; excelled in recording his reconstructions of a vanishing/vanished way of life. Trained in the law, interest in German literature, military enthusiasm.

Sharpe, C.K.: *Minstrelsy* dedicated to him; corresponded with Motherwell over their shared interest in ballads and songs. Recognized antiquary and artist (known especially for caricatures). Looked to people's frailties. Had originally thought to take Episcopal orders and had gone to Christ Church, Oxford. Became a collector of Scottish curios and antiques, interested in genealogy. Member of Bannatyne Club; edited and provided notes and contributed to numerous works.

Sim, John: Became poet and physician; may have been first editor of *Harp of Renfrewshire;* belonged to Literary Institution.

Smith, R.A.: 1780–1829. Robert Archibald was born in Reading, though his father was from Lanarkshire. Father a silk weaver, and R.A. was apprenticed to be a muslin weaver in Paisley. Left to follow his musical inclination; became teacher of music, composer, church choir director, and finally music director of St. George's, Edinburgh. Set songs for church and for poets. Known as editor of *The Scottish Minstrel.* Friend of Tannahill, who may have encouraged his shift from weaving to music; in turn he set Tannahill's songs to music. Contributor to *Paisley Magazine;* corresponded with Motherwell; signer of joking testament; involved in *Harp of Renfrewshire.*

Stevenson, John: Corresponded with Motherwell; Edinburgh bookseller and stationer in 87 Princess Street; signer of joking testament.

Stevenson, Robert: Grocer.

Strang, John: 1795–1863. Editor of the *Day;* contributor to *Paisley Magazine;* member of the Maitland Club and Robertson's circle. Later city chamberlain in Glasgow. Historian of Glasgow clubs.

Synburn: Said to have been Dux at Paisley Grammar School with Blair and Motherwell.

Tait, Alexander: Member of Brock's Club. Was tailor in Castle Street, Paisley, though he lived in Tarbolton. Published edition of poems in 1790. Had known Burns.

Taylor, James: Tailor.

Tennant, Alex: Member of Hadgis Club.

Thomson, George: 1757–1851. Corresponded with Motherwell over new texts for "national airs." Collector of Scottish music; amateur musician; commissioned musical settings by composers of the day.

Walkinshaw, Robert: Sheriff clerk, former sheriff clerk depute under whom Motherwell probably was apprenticed and who subsequently hired Motherwell as sheriff clerk depute.

Watson, James: Glasgow bank; present at social event.

Wilson, Alexander: 1766–1811. Author of "Watty and Meg." Born in Paisley; his father was a weaver and thus he was so apprenticed. Composed and published poems by subscription; subsequently a poem was judged too personal a satire and led him to leave for America. There he wove, peddled, taught school, and after meeting William Bartram, took up drawing and engraving, leading to his successful depiction of birds and the project on American ornithology.

Wylie, Dr. G: Two shares of *Paisley Magazine,* member of Burns Club.

Wylie, John: Publisher in Glasgow who published *Minstrelsy;* belonged to Maitland Club.

Notes

CHAPTER 4

1. McCarthy suggests that Scott's response set Motherwell on the right track editorially. See "William Motherwell as Field Collector," 304.

2. A lot of ink has been spilt over the question of Peter Buchan and his trustworthiness. Motherwell valued Buchan's work enormously, writing his friend R.A. Smith that Buchan "has done more than anyone I know to collect the ancient traditionary ballads of Scotland" (Robertson 3/1222: 60). He does admit that Peter is feckless, but adds that "still it is to be remembered that but for him Scotland might have lost a very large body of authentic revelation in her song" (Robertson 9/1207: 3). Francis James Child's views were virtually the opposite; in the preface to the 1857 edition of *English and Scottish Ballads*, he says that "some resolution has been exercised, and much disgust suppressed, in relating certain pieces from Buchan's collections, so strong is the suspicion that, after having been procured from very inferior sources, they were tampered with by the editor." Svend Grundtvig, on the other hand, valued Buchan's work and tells Child that he has evidence "through a comparison with undoubtedly genuine Scandinavian ballads" (Hustvedt 1916, 244) that will prove the authenticity of Buchan's work. See also David Buchan's defense of Peter Buchan in *Ballad and the Folk*, chap. 16.

3. Much of Crawfurd's ballad and song materials, collected between 1826 and 1828, has been edited by Emily Lyle (see Lyle's *Andrew Crawfurd's Collection*). Crawfurd, a disabled doctor, occupied himself with collecting ballads, songs, and other local materials, producing a forty-six-volume manuscript titled "The Cairn of Lochunyoch Matters." In volume 1, Lyle reproduces the repertoires of two men and two women. Volume 2 is more diverse but includes especially those materials collected by Thomas Macqueen, who, incidentally, was ardently supportive of the Reform Bill of 1832; immigrated to Canada in 1842; subsequently edited the *Huron Signal,* a pro-reform newspaper; and wrote a memorial poem to Motherwell, who had paid him to collect. Crawfurd's material was useful to Motherwell in preparing the introduction and the appendices.

4. McCarthy, "William Motherwell as Field Collector," offers a critical analysis of the notebook and the manuscript, especially the changes in focuses therein. This study is somewhat limited, however, because it is not derived from an analysis of the full range of Motherwell's writing and does not recognize the chronological sequence of the *Minstrelsy* texts, the notebook, the manuscript,

and the introduction.

5. In "William Motherwell as Field Collector," McCarthy suggests that the movement from the miscellaneous to the textual to the individual represents a shift in focus on the part of Motherwell the collector. There is certainly some merit to this suggestion, but the shift is not as dramatic or complete as McCarthy suggests.

6. McCarthy, *Ballad Matrix,* provides a book-length analysis of Agnes Lyle's repertoire.

7. For further discussion of commonplaces and their range of connotations, see Anderson, *Commonplace and Creativity.*

8. Motherwell refers here to Child no. 155, "Sir Hugh, or, the Jew's Daughter," which puts the Jew's Daughter in the villain's role: she supposedly entices Hugh into her garden and kills him to use his blood for ritual purposes. His mother searches for him and miraculously is informed to look for him at the bottom of a well.

CHAPTER 7

1. Susan Stewart calls the production of such artifacts "crimes of writing." Such a position, as cogent as it is, speaks to the general and abstract rather than the specific and concrete. Literary, social, and cultural contexts shed a different light—as I suggest throughout this chapter—on the production and/or fabrication of literature. See Stewart, *Crimes of Writing,* chaps. 1, 3, and 4, in particular.

APPENDIX 1

1. McCarthy (*Ballad Matrix,* 40) suggests "there are some problems identifying the ballads of Agnes Lyle. Child, on the basis of the Manuscript evidence, accurately identified 15. Kenneth Thigpen, the only scholar to publish a figure based on Child, finally settled on a count of 17 (1972). The actual figure seems to be 21 complete ballads, 1 nearly complete ballad, 7 fragments, and 3 titles."

2. Motherwell writes that "the only person I have heard recite this is a Malcolm Whyte change keeper in Moss-raw of Paisley—He states that what he sings is the only genuine edition of it and verbatim as he got it from Old Bailie Fyfe—Before beginning to sing he dresses himself in a woman's cap and petticoat and takes anything that may come to hand to represent a tow rock and spindle—He then begins" (Robertson 12/1217).

Bibliography

MANUSCRIPTS AND PUBLIC RECORDS

University of Glasgow Library, Department of Special Collections

1207—MS Robertson 9/1–79
1208—MS Robertson 10/1-18
1209/1—MS Robertson 27/1
1210—MS Robertson 28
1212—MS Robertson 15/1–36
1213—MS Robertson 29
1214—MS Robertson 13
1216—MS Robertson 2
1217—MS Robertson 12/1–21
1218—MS Robertson 16
1219—MS Robertson 11
1221—MS Robertson 5
1222—MS Robertson 3/1–69
1223—MS Robertson 6/1–13
1224—MS Robertson 25
1662—MS Robertson 4
4361—MS Gen 539/20
Murray 501 [Motherwell's ballad manuscript]

Harvard University, Houghton Library

25241.20
25241.56f
25242.16 [copy of Motherwell's notebook, original missing from Pollok House]
25263.19.6f
FMS Eng 862

Mitchell Library, Glasgow

898978–SR205 [1817 or 1818]
98559—2ALS, 1834, 1835
ALS, 1831 MS. 40 (314514)
M1.308887—SR 243

MS Gen 452
MS Gen 501 4196

National Library of Scotland, Edinburgh

2969 Ry II d 17
LC 2897–2900
MS 20.5.4
8399. Letters to Gavin Lang, Town Clerk of Paisley. 1831.

Paisley Central Library, Paisley, Scotland

B/Moth, OIS, PK 3216
PC862, Ref no. 395
Motherwell, William. Paisley Pamphlets, 1818. Vol. 21, 815–62.
———. "Poetic Underwoods." Manuscript collection of poems, 1830. R631.
Paisley Literary Institution Minutes, 1812–18. 651.77, Ren 1P, PC 2579.

Parliament

United Kingdom. House of Commons. *Bills, Public.* Vol. 2, 1830–31 Session,
26 Oct. 1830–22 Apr. 1831.
———. *Bills, Public.* Vol. 3, 1832 Session, 1 July 1831.
———. *Bills, Public.* Vol. 3, Parliamentary Representation Session, 6 Dec.–16
Aug. 1832.
United Kingdom. House of Lords. *XVII 1835 Reports/Committees 605: Report
of The Select Committee appointed to inquire into the Origin, Nature,
Extent, and Tendency of Orange Institutions in Great Britain and the
Colonies; and to report the Evidence taken before them, and their Opin-
ion, to the House.* Record Office.

Pollok House, Glasgow

Motherwell, William. Introduction to "Scottish Minstrelsy." Manuscript.
———. "Scottish Minstrelsy." Manuscript.
———. "Minstrelsy: Ancient and Modern." Bound fascicles. 1st frontispiece
1824, then 1827.

Public Record Office, Scottish Records, London

HO 102/44

Scottish Record Office, Edinburgh

SC58: Documents pertaining to the Paisley Sheriff Court. L.229–92

Strathclyde Regional Archive

Renfrew Index of Names of Persons to Abridgments of the Registers of Seisins
&c 1781–1820.

Renfrew Index of Names of Persons to Abridgments of the Registers of Seisins &c 1821–1830.

Sasines, Renfrew 1781–1807.

BOOKS AND ARTICLES

Abrams, M.H. *The Mirror and the Lamp: Romantic Theory and the Critical Tradition.* Oxford: Oxford University Press, 1953.

Addison, W. Innes. *The Matriculation Albums of the University of Glasgow from 1728–1858.* Glasgow: James MacLehose and Sons, 1913.

————. *Prize Lists of the University of Glasgow from Session 1777–78 to Session 1832–3.* Glasgow: Carter & Pratt, 1902.

Aird, Andrew. *Reminiscences of Editors, Reporters, and Printers During the Last Sixty Years.* Glasgow: Aird & Coghill, 1890.

Alexander, J.H., ed. *The Tavern Sages: Selections from the Noctes Ambrosinae.* Aberdeen: Association for Scottish Literary Studies, 1992.

Alison, Robert. *The Anecdotage of Glasgow.* Glasgow: Thomas D. Morison, 1892.

Anderson, Benedict. *Imagined Communities: Reflections on the Origin and Spread of Nationalism.* London: Verso, 1993.

Anderson, Flemming G. *Commonplace and Creativity: The Role of Formulaic Diction in Anglo-Scottish Traditional Balladry.* Odense: Odense University Press, 1985.

Attali, Jacques. *Noise: The Political Economy of Music.* Minneapolis: University of Minnesota Press, 1985.

Aubin, Robert Arnold. *Topographical Poetry in XVIII-Century England.* New York: Kraus Reprint, 1980.

Bateson, F.W., ed. *The Cambridge Bibliography of English Literature.* Vol. 3. New York: Macmillan, 1941.

Bendix, Regina. *In Search of Authenticity: The Formation of Folklore Studies.* Madison: University of Wisconsin Press, 1997.

Black, Jimmy. *The Glasgow Graveyard Guide.* Edinburgh: Saint Andrew Press, 1992.

Boehm, Alan. "The Poetics of Literary Commerce: Popular and Patrician Bookselling and the Rise of Publishing, 1700–1825." Ph.D. diss., Indiana University, 1991.

Bourdieu, Pierre. *Distinction: A Social Critique of the Judgement of Taste.* Cambridge: Harvard University Press, 1984.

————. *In Other Words: Essays Towards a Reflexive Sociology.* Cambridge: Polity Press, 1990.

————. *Outline of a Theory of Practice.* Cambridge: Cambridge University Press, 1977.

————. *The Rules of Art: Genesis and Structure of the Literary Field.* Stanford, Calif.: Stanford University Press, 1996.

Bourdieu, Pierre, with Loic J.D. Wacquant. *Reponses: Pour une anthropologie reflexive*. Paris: Seuil, 1992. (*An Invitation to Reflective Sociology*. Cambridge: Polity Press, 1992.)

Brown, Iain Gordon. *The Hobby-Horsical Antiquary: A Scottish Character, 1640–1830*. Edinburgh: National Library of Scotland, 1980.

Brown, Mary Ellen. "Mr. Child's Scottish Mentor." In *Ballads into Books: The Legacy of F.J. Child,* edited by Tom Cheesman and Sigrid Rieuwerts, 29–39. Berne: Peter Lang, 1997.

———. "Old Singing Women and the Canons of Scottish Balladry and Song." In *A History of Scottish Women's Writing,* edited by Dorothy McMillan and Douglas Gifford, 44–57. Edinburgh: University of Edinburgh Press, 1997.

———. "The Study of Folk Tradition." In Gifford, *History of Scottish Literature,* 397–409. Aberdeen: Aberdeen University Press, 1988.

Brown, Robert. *The History of the Paisley Grammar School*. Paisley, Scotland: Alex Gardner, 1875.

———. *Paisley Poets*. 2 vols. Paisley, Scotland: J & J Cook, [1889?].

Brown, Stewart J. *Thomas Chalmers and the Godly Commonwealth in Scotland*. Oxford: Oxford University Press, 1982.

Buchan, David. *The Ballad and the Folk*. London: Routledge & Kegan Paul, 1972.

Buchan, Peter. *Gleanings of Scotch, English, and Irish Scarce Old Ballads, Chiefly Tragical and Historical, &c, with Explanatory Notes*. Peterhead, England, 1825.

Carncross, A.K., ed. *The Scottish Economy*. Cambridge: University Press, 1954. Especially chap. 11, "Wages," by D.J. Robertson.

Carrick, John Donald. *The Laird of Logan, or Wit of the West being a Collection of Anecdotes, Jests and Comic Tales*. Glasgow, 1835.

Chambers, Robert. *A Biographical Dictionary of Eminent Scotsmen*. Glasgow: Blaikie & Son, 1835.

Chambers, W. of Glenormiston, F.R.S.E., F.G.S. "Historical Sketch of Popular Literature and Its Influence on Society." Paper read before the Royal Society of Edinburgh, 2 Feb. 1863. National Library of Scotland, 3/2682, Pamphlets.

Chartier, Roger. *Cultural History: Between Practice and Representation*. Ithaca, N.Y.: Cornell, 1988.

Child, Francis James. *The English and Scottish Ballads*. Boston: Little, Brown, 1857–59.

———. *The English and Scottish Popular Ballads*. 5 Vols. Boston: Houghton and Mifflin, 1882–98.

Chitnis, Anand C. *The Scottish Enlightenment*. London: Croom Helm, 1976.

Clark, Sylvia. *Paisley: A History*. Edinburgh: Mainstream Publishing, 1988.

Cleland, James. *Enumeration of the Inhabitants of the City of Glasgow and County of Lanark*. Glasgow, 1831.

Clifford, James. *The Predicament of Culture: Twentieth-Century Ethnography, Literature, and Art.* Cambridge: Harvard University Press, 1988.

Cohen, Anthony, ed. *Belonging.* Manchester: Manchester University Press, 1982.

Colley, Linda. *Britons: Forging the Nation, 1707–1837.* New Haven, Conn.: Yale University Press, 1992.

Cowan, R.M.W. *The Newspaper in Scotland: A Study of Its First Expansion, 1815–1860.* Glasgow: George Outram, 1946.

Crawford, Robert. *Devolving English Literature.* Oxford: Clarendon Press, 1992.

Crawford, Ronald Lyndsay. "Literary Activity in Paisley in the Early Nineteenth Century." Bachelor of letters thesis, University of Glasgow, 1965.

Crawford, Thomas. *Society and the Lyric.* Edinburgh: Scottish Academic Press, 1979.

Cromek, R.H. *Remains of Nithsdale and Galloway Song.* London: T. Cadell & W. Davies, 1810.

Daiches, David. *Glasgow.* London: Andre Deutsch, 1977.

Davie, George E. *The Democratic Intellect: Scotland and Her Universities in the Nineteenth Century.* Edinburgh: Edinburgh University Press, 1961.

———. *The Social Significance of the Scottish Philosophy of Common Sense.* Dow Lecture, University of Dundee, 1973.

Davis, Leith. *Acts of Union: Scotland and the Literary Negotiation of the British Nation, 1707–1830.* Stanford, Calif.: Stanford University Press, 1998.

Debord, Guy. *Society of the Spectacle.* Detroit: Black & Red, 1983.

de Certeau, Michel. *The Practice of Everyday Life.* University of California Press, 1984.

Devine, T.M., and Gordon Jackson, eds. *Glasgow: Beginnings to 1880.* Manchester: Manchester University Press, 1995.

Devine, T.M., and Rosalind Mitchison, eds. *People and Society in Scotland, 1760–1830.* Edinburgh: John Donald, 1988.

Donaldson, William. *Popular Literature in Victorian Scotland.* Aberdeen: Aberdeen University Press, 1986.

Donnachie, Ian, and George Hewitt. *Companion to Scottish History.* London: Batsford, 1989.

Douglas, George. *James Hogg: Famous Scots Series.* Edinburgh: Oliphant Anderson & Ferrier, 1899.

———. *Scottish Minor Poets.* In *The Canterbury Poets Series.* Edited by William Sharp. London: Walter Scott, n.d.

Ewald, William Bragg. *The Newsmen of Queen Anne.* Oxford: Basil Blackwell, 1956.

Ewing, A. McL. *A History of the Glasgow Herald, 1783–1948.* Printed for Private Circulation, n.d.

Eyre-Todd, George, ed. *The Glasgow Poets: Their Lives and Poems.* Glasgow: Wm. Hodge, 1903.

Frazer, Hamish W., and Irene Maver, eds. *Glasgow: 1830 to 1912.* Manchester: Manchester University Press, 1996.

Friedman, Albert B. "The Formulaic Improvisation Theory of Ballad Tradition—A Counter Statement." *Journal of American Folklore* 74 (1961): 113–15.

Fry, Michael. *Patronage and Principle: A Political History of Modern Scotland.* Aberdeen: Aberdeen University Press, 1987.

Galt, John. *Annals of the Parish & The Ayrshire Legatees.* With an introduction by Ian Campbell. Edinburgh: Mercat Press, 1994.

———. *The Ayrshire Legatees and The Gathering in the West.* Edinburgh: William Blackwood, 1823.

———. *The Member.* 1823. Reprint, edited by Ian A. Gordon, Edinburgh: Scottish Academic Press, 1975.

———. *The Provost and Other Tales.* London: Maclaren and Company, [1822?].

———. *Ringan Gilhaize.* 1823. Reprint, edited and with an introduction by Patricia Wilson, Edinburgh: Canongate Classics, 1995.

Garden, Mrs., ed. *Memorials of James Hogg The Ettrick Shepherd.* 2d ed. Paisley, Scotland: Alexander Gardner, 1887.

Geertz, Clifford. *The Interpretation of Cultures.* New York: Basic Books, 1973.

Gifford, Douglas, ed. *The History of Scottish Literature: Nineteenth Century.* Vol. 3. Aberdeen: Aberdeen University Press, 1988.

Glasgow Electors: List of the Names and Designations of the Persons Who Voted in the First Election of Two Members to Serve in Parliament for the City of Glasgow under the Scotch Reform Bill, 18th & 19th Dec 1832. Glasgow: Muir, Gowans, 1832.

Glasgow Illustrated in a Series of Picturesque Views Drawn and Engraved by J. Scott with Historical and Descriptive Illustrations by John Cullen Esq. Glasgow: J. Scott Engraver, 1834.

Graham, Michael. *The Early Glasgow Press.* Glasgow: Robt. Anderson, 1906.

Grant, James. *The Newspaper Press: Its Origin, Progress, and Present Position.* 2 vols. London: Tinsley Brothers, 1871.

Hall, Catherine. "The Sweet Delights of Home." In *A History of Private Life: From the Fires of the Revolution to the Great War,* edited by Michelle Perrot, 47–93. Cambridge: Harvard University Press, Belknap Press, 1990.

Hamilton, Henry. *The Industrial Revolution in Scotland.* Oxford: Clarendon, 1932.

Hamilton, Thomas. *The Youth and Manhood of Cyril Thornton.* 1827. Reprint (edited by Maurice Lindsay), Aberdeen: Association for Scottish Literary Studies, 1990.

Handley, James Edmund. *The Irish in Scotland, 1798–1845.* Cork, Ireland: Cork University Press, 1945.

Harker, Dave. *Fakesong: The Manufacture of British "Folksong" 1700 to the Present Day.* Milton Keynes, England: Open University Press, 1985.

The Harp of Renfrewshire: A Collection of Songs and Other Poetical Pieces. Glasgow: William Turnbull, 1820.

Hart, Francis Russell. *The Scottish Novel: From Smollett to Spark.* Cambridge:

Harvard University Press, 1978.

Harvie, Christopher. *Scotland and Nationalism: Scottish Society and Politics, 1707–1977*. London: George Allen & Unwin, 1977; 2d ed. London: Routledge, 1994.

Havens, Raymond Dexter. *The Influence of Milton on English Poetry*. Cambridge: Harvard University Press, 1922.

Henderson, Andrew. *Scottish Proverbs*. Edinburgh: Oliver & Boyd, 1832.

Herford, C.H. *The Age of Wordsworth*. London: G. Bell & Sons, 1922.

Hobsbawn, Eric, and Terrence Ranger, eds. *The Invention of Tradition*. Cambridge: Cambridge University Press, 1983.

Hogg, James [The Ettrick Shepherd], and William Motherwell. *The Works of Robert Burns*. 5 vols. Glasgow: Archibald Fullarton, 1834–36.

Hook, Andrew, ed. *The History of Scottish Literature, 1660–1800*. Vol. 2. Aberdeen: Aberdeen University Press, 1987.

Houston, R.A. *Scottish Literature and the Scottish Identity*. Cambridge: Cambridge University Press, 1985.

Hustvedt, Sigurd Bernhard. *Ballad Criticism in Scandinavia and Great Britain During the Eighteenth Century*. New York: The American-Scandinavian Foundation, 1916.

Hutchison, I.G.C. *A Political History of Scotland, 1832–1924: Parties, Elections and Issues*. Edinburgh: John Donald, 1986.

Jackson, J.R. de J. *Annals of English Verse, 1770–1824*. New York: Garland, 1985.

Jameson, Frederic. *Postmodernism, or, The Cultural Logic of Late Capitalism*. Durham, N.C.: Duke University Press, 1991.

Johnson, C.R. *Provincial Poetry 1789–1839: British Verse Printed in the Provinces*. London: Jed Press, 1992.

Jones, James H. "Commonplace and Memorization in the Oral Tradition of the English and Scottish Popular Ballads." *Journal of American Folklore* 74 (1961): 97–112.

Jousse, Marcel. *The Oral Style*. Edited and translated by E. Sienaert and R. Whitaker. New York: Garland, 1990.

Kaplan, Alice and Kristin Ross, eds. *Everyday Life*. Yale French Series 73. New Haven, Conn.: Yale University Press, 1987.

Kenner, Hugh. *The Mechanic Muse*. Oxford: Oxford University Press, 1987.

Kilpatrick, James A. *Literary Landmarks of Glasgow*. Glasgow: Saint Mungo, 1893.

Kinsley, James, ed. *The Poems and Songs of Robert Burns*. Vol. 1. Oxford: Clarendon Press, 1968.

"The Legendary Cabinet, or a Collection of British National Ballads, Ancient and Modern, from the best Authorities, with Notes and Illustrations. By the Rev. J.D. Parry, M.A., of St. Peter's College, Cambridge. 8vo. London: Joy. 1829. 2. Minstrelsy, Antient [sic] and Modern, with an Introduction and Notes. By William Motherwell. Glasgow: Wylie. 1829." *Monthly*

Review 11 (1829): 260–74. Art. viii.-1.

Lenman, Bruce P. *Integration and Enlightenment: Scotland, 1746–1832.* 1981. Reprint, Edinburgh: Edinburgh University Press, 1992.

Leonard, Tom, ed. *Radical Renfrew: Poetry from the French Revolution to the First World War.* Edinburgh: Polygon, 1990.

Lindsay, Maurice. *Glasgow.* Bury St. Edmonds: St Edmundsbury Press, 1972.

Lyle, Emily B. "Child's Scottish Harvest." *Harvard Library Bulletin* 25 (1977): 125–54.

———, ed. *Andrew Crawfurd's Collection of Ballads and Songs.* 2 vols. Edinburgh: Scottish Text Society, 1975, 1996.

Lythe, S.G.E., and J. Butt. *An Economic History of Scotland, 1100–1939.* Glasgow: Blackie, 1975.

MacGregor, George. *The History of Glasgow.* Glasgow: Thomas D. Morison, 1881.

Mackenzie, Peter. *Old Reminiscences of Glasgow and the West of Scotland.* 3 vols. Glasgow: James P. Forrester, 1890.

MacLaren, A. Allan, ed. *Social Class in Scotland: Past and Present.* Edinburgh: John Donald, [1976?].

Macqueen, John. *The Enlightenment and Scottish Literature: Progress and Poetry.* Vol. 1. Edinburgh: Scottish Academic Press, 1982.

———. *The Enlightenment and Scottish Literature: The Rise of the Historical Novel.* Vol. 2. Edinburgh: Scottish Academic Press, 1989.

MacQueen, Thomas. *The Exile.* Glasgow, 1836.

Maitland Club. *Catalogue of the Works printed for the Maitland Club, instituted March MDCCCXXVIII with Lists of the Members and Rules of the Club.* [Glasgow?], 1836.

———. *Descriptions of the Sheriffdoms of Lanark and Renfrew, Compiled about 1710 by William Hamilton of Wishaw.* Glasgow, 1831.

———. *Rob Stene's Dream: A Poem.* Glasgow, 1836.

Mason, Thomas. *Public and Private Libraries of Glasgow.* Glasgow: Thomas D. Morison, 1884.

Matheson, Ann. "Scottish Newspapers." *Library Review* 36 (1987): 179–85.

McCarthy, William Bernard. *The Ballad Matrix.* Bloomington: Indiana University Press, 1990.

———. "William Motherwell as Field Collector." *Folk Music Journal* 5 (1987): 295–316.

McFarland, E.W. *Protestants First: Orangeism in Nineteenth Century Scotland.* Edinburgh: Edinburgh University Press, 1990.

McKay, Ian. *The Quest of the Folk: Antimodernism and Cultural Selection in Twentieth-Century Nova Scotia.* Montreal: McGill-Queen's University Press, 1994.

Metcalfe, W.M. *A History of Paisley, 600–1908.* Paisley, Scotland: Alexander Gardner, 1989.

Miles, Alfred H., ed. *The Poets and Poetry of the Nineteenth Century.* London:

George Routledge, 1905.

Mitchison, Rosalind. *Life in Scotland.* London: Batsford, 1978.

Montgomerie, William. "William Motherwell and Robert A. Smith." *Review of English Studies* 9 (1958): 152–59.

Montrose, Louis. "Renaissance Literary Studies and the Subject of History." *English Literary Renaissance* 16 (1986): 5–12.

Motherwell Centenary, 1797–1897. Paisley, Scotland: Published by John Kent, 1897.

Motherwell, William [Ephriam Mucklewrath]. *An Answer to Hints of Matthew Bramble on the Winter Assemblies.* Paisley, Scotland: John Neilson, 1818.

———— [James M'Alpie]. *Certain Curious Poems Written at the Closse of the XVIIth and beginning of the xviith Century, on a variety of subjects, local and Political, Principally from the Pen of Mr. James M'Alpie, Sheriff-Substitute of Renfrewshire, Anno MDCXCIV, with a Few Pieces by Other Ingenious Hands.* Paisley, Scotland: Printed by J. Neilson, 1828.

————. *Minstrelsy: Ancient and Modern.* Glasgow: John Wylie, 1827.

————. *Poems, Narrative and Lyrical.* Glasgow: David Robertson, 1832.

————. *The Poetical Works of William Motherwell with a Memoir by James McConechy Esq.* 3d ed. Glasgow: Robert Forrester, 1865.

————. *The Poetical Works of William Motherwell with a Memoir of His Life Containing his Posthumous Writings.* Boston: Ticknor, Reed, and Fields, 1853.

————. *Posthumous Poems.* Boston: Ticknor, Reed, and Fields, 1851.

———— [Isaac Brown]. *Renfrewshire Characters and Scenery.* Paisley, Scotland: J. Neilson, [1825?].

"Motherwell's Poems." *Blackwood's Edinburgh Magazine* 33 (1833): 668–81.

Muirhead, Ian. "Catholic Emancipation: Scottish Reactions in 1829." *Innes Review: Scottish Catholic Historical Studies* 24 (1973): 26–42.

Nairn, Tom. *The Break-Up of Britain: Crisis and Neo-Nationalism.* London: NLB, 1977.

"Nestor." *Rambling Recollections of Old Glasgow.* Glasgow: John Tweed, 1880.

New Statistical Account of Scotland. Vol. 7 Renfrew, Argyle. Edinburgh: William Blackwood and Sons, 1845.

North, John S., ed. *The Waterloo Directory of Scottish Newspapers and Periodicals, 1800–1900.* Waterloo, Ontario: N. Waterloo Academic Press, 1989.

Parker, W.M. "William Motherwell: His Correspondence with Sir Walter Scott." *Scots Magazine* 24 (1935): 144–50.

Pentikainen, Juha. *Oral Repertoire and World View: Anthropological Study of Marina Takalo's Life History.* Helsinki: Suomalainen Tiedeakatemia, 1978.

Perrot, Michelle, ed. *A History of Private Life: From the Fires of Revolution to the Grand War.* Cambridge: Harvard University Press, Belknap Press, 1990.

Phillips, Alastair. *Glasgow's Herald: Two Hundred Years of a Newspaper, 1783–1983.* Glasgow: Richard Drew, 1982.

Phillipson, N.T. "Nationalism and Ideology." In *Government and Nationalism in Scotland,* edited by J.N. Wolfe, 167–88.. Edinburgh: Edinburgh University Press, 1969.

Phillipson, N.T., and Rosalind Mitchison. *Scotland in the Age of Improvement: Essays in Scottish History in the Eighteenth Century.* Edinburgh: Edinburgh University Press, 1970.

Poe, Edgar Allen. "The Poetic Principle." In *Essays and Reviews,* 71–94. New York: Library of America, 1984.

Polsgrove, Carol. "Short Country Tales in Great Britain 1820–40." Ph.D. diss., University of Louisville, 1973.

Post-Office Annual Directory, 1830–1, 1832, 1834, 1835. Containing an Alphabetical List of the Merchants, Traders, Manufacturers and Principal Inhabitants in Glasgow: With a Street Directory and an Appendix, Containing Many Useful Lists. 3d ed. Glasgow: Printed for the Letter-Carriers of the Post-office by John Graham, Melville Place, 1830, 1832, 1834, 1835.

Robbins, Derek. *The Work of Pierre Bourdieu.* Boulder, Colo.: Westview Press, 1991.

Scotland, James. *The History of Scottish Education.* Vol. 1. London: University of London Press, 1969.

Scott, Sir Walter. *Minstrelsy of the Scottish Border.* 4 vols. Edited by T.F. Henderson. Edinburgh: William Blackwood and Sons, 1902.

———. *Old Mortality.* 1816. Reprint, edited and with an introduction by Angus Calder, London: Penguin Books, 1975.

Selden, Raman, Peter Widdowson, and Peter Brooker. *A Reader's Guide to Contemporary Literary Theory.* 4th ed. London: Prentice Hall/Harvester Wheatsheaf, 1997.

Semple, David, ed. *The Poems and Songs of Robert Tannahill.* Paisley, Scotland: Alex. Gardner, 1876.

Sharp, William, ed. *The Canterbury Poets.* London: Walter Scott, 1891.

Smelser, Neil J. *Social Change in the Industrial Revolution: An Application of Theory to the Lancashire Cotton Industry.* London: Routledge & Kegan Paul, 1959.

Smith, R.A. *The Scottish Minstrel.* 6 vols. Edinburgh: Robt Purdie, n.d.

Smollett, Tobias. *Humphry Clinker.* 1771. Reprint, edited and with an introduction by Angus Ross. London: Penguin Books, 1985.

Stephen, Leslie, and Signey Lee, eds. *The Dictionary of National Biography.* London: Oxford University Press, 1921–22.

Steven, William. *The History of the High School of Edinburgh.* Edinburgh: Maclachlan & Stewart, 1849.

Stewart, Susan. *Crimes of Writing: Problems in the Containment of Representation.* Durham, N.C.: Duke University Press, 1994.

Strang, John. *Glasgow and Its Clubs.* London: Richard Griffin, 1856.

Thigpen, Kenneth A. "An Index to the Known Sources of the Child Ballads." *Folklore Forum* 5 (1972): 55–69.

Thompson, E.P. *The Making of the English Working Class.* London: Gollancz, 1963.

Thompson, Stith. *The Motif-Index of Folk-Literature.* 6 vols. Bloomington: Indiana University Press, 1955–58.

Thomson, George. *The Melodies of Scotland. New Edition. With Many Improvements.* 6 vols. London: Coventry & Hollier, 1838.

———. *The Select Melodies of Scotland* (Interspersed with those of Ireland and Wales United to the Songs of Robt Burns. Sir Walter Scott Bart. and other distinguished Poets: with Symphonies & Accompaniments for the Piano Forte By Pleyel. Kozeluch. Haydn & Beethoven). Vol. 4 of 5. London: Printed/sold by Preston, Hurst, Robinson & Co., G. Thomson, Edinburgh, 1823.

Tierney, James H. *Early Glasgow Newspapers, Periodicals and Directories.* Glasgow, [1934?].

———. *Scottish Newspapers and Extras: Revelations of The Good Old Days?* Helensburgh: Mecneur & Bryden, 1961.

Trumpener, Katie. *Bardic Nationalism: The Romantic Novel and the British Empire.* Princeton, N.J.: Princeton University Press, 1997.

Walker, David M. *The Oxford Companion to Law.* Oxford: Clarendon, 1980.

Ward, William S. *British Periodicals & Newspapers, 1789–1832: A Bibliography of Secondary Sources.* Lexington: University Press of Kentucky, 1972.

Watt, Robert. *Bibliotheca Britannica; or A General Index to British and Foreign Literature.* Edinburgh: Archibald Constable, 1824.

Weir, William, ed. *The Scottish Annual.* Glasgow: John Reid, 1836.

Whetstone, Ann E. *Scottish County Government in the Eighteenth and Nineteenth Centuries.* Edinburgh: John Donald, 1981.

Whisnant, David E. *All That Is Native and Fine: The Politics of Culture in an American Region.* Chapel Hill: University of North Carolina Press, 1983.

Whistle-Binkie: A Collection of Songs for the Social Circle. Glasgow: David Robertson, 1853.

Wilson, John. *Sentimental Scenes Selected from Celebrated Plays; and Calculated to Promote Morality, the Knowledge of Mankind, Facility in Articulate Reading, and Gracefulness in Public Speaking.* 2d ed. Edinburgh: James Muirhead, 1809.

Withers, Charles W.J. "Kirk, Club and Culture Change: Gaelic Chapels, Highland Societies and the Urban Gaelic Subculture in Eighteenth-Century Scotland." *Social History* 10 (1985): 171–92.

NEWSPAPERS AND PERIODICALS

Blackwood's Edinburgh Magazine. Edinburgh: William Blackwood, 1817–1905.

The Day: A Journal of Literature, Fine Arts, Fashions, &c. Glasgow, 2 Jan. 1832—30 June 1832.

Enquirer. Glasgow. 1820–21.

Glasgow Courier. Glasgow: Wm. Reid, 1791–1866. Especially 2 Feb. 1830–Nov. 1835.

Loyal Reformer's Gazette. Glasgow. Vols. 1 (1831), 2 (1831–2), 4 (1833–4), 5 (1834–5), and 6 (1835–6).

Paisley Advertiser. Paisley: Robert Hay, 1824–44.

Paisley Magazine. Paisley: D. Dick, 1828.

Renfrewshire Advertiser. Paisley: John Neilson, 1844–50. Especially 22 July 1849.

Scots Times. Glasgow: R. Malcolm, 1825–41.

Tait's Edinburgh Magazine. Edinburgh: W. Tait, 1832–61. Especially 1832.

Visitor, or Literary Miscellany. 2 Vols. Greenock, Scotland: Printed for John Turnet, 1818.

Index

Page numbers followed by (illus) refer to illustrations.